Medical and Dental Guidance Notes

A good practice guide on all aspects of ionising radiation protection in the clinical environment

prepared by
Institute of Physics and Engineering in Medicine

with the support of
National Radiological Protection Board
Health and Safety Executive
The Health Departments
The Environment Agencies

© Institute of Physics and Engineering in Medicine 2002
Fairmount House, 230 Tadcaster Road
York YO24 1ES
ISBN 1 903613 09 4

Published by the Institute of Physics and Engineering in Medicine
Fairmount House, 230 Tadcaster Road, York YO24 1ES

Legal Notice

Preface

This document replaces the *Guidance Notes for the Protection of Persons against Ionising Radiations Arising from Medical and Dental Use* published in 1988 by the National Radiological Protection Board (NRPB) on behalf of the Health Departments of the United Kingdom and the Health and Safety Executive (HSE).

The Institute of Physics and Engineering in Medicine (IPEM), with the aid of volunteers working in healthcare, produced a first draft as a consultative document in April 2000. After wide consultation with professional and specialist bodies (see Appendix 16), the NRPB, the Health Departments of the United Kingdom, the Environment Agencies (EA) and the HSE, the final version has been published by the IPEM. It takes into account the latest recommendations of the International Commission on Radiological Protection (ICRP), the relevant Directives of the European Council, the Ionising Radiations Regulations 1999, the Ionising Radiation (Medical Exposure) Regulations 2000, the Radioactive Substances Act 1993 and the very many helpful comments received during the consultation process.

These notes provide general guidance on good practice: they are not an attempt to repeat or interpret the legal requirements and advice contained in the legislation. Following the guidance is not compulsory but should suffice operationally to comply with the law; other actions may be equally valid. Individuals who carry responsibilities under the legislation are advised to acquaint themselves appropriately with the legal requirements.

Contents

Acknowledgements

This document could not have been prepared for the consultation process by the Institute of Physics and Engineering in Medicine (IPEM) Working Group without the massive input received from numerous sources. In particular the Working Group would like to thank: John Croft and his colleagues at the National Radiological Protection Board (NRPB) for the electronic version of the 1988 *Guidance Notes* which gave us a head start, and for comments throughout the drafting process; John Gill (Health and Saftey Executive; HSE) for providing much needed statutory information and for trying to keep us from going too far astray from the requirements of the regulations; Steve Ebdon-Jackson (Department of Health; DoH) for his patience as we struggled to get to grips with the medical exposures regulations; Joe McHugh and Martin Murray (Environment Agency; EA) and Sharan Packer (Leeds, now with the HSE) for reviewing and supplementing Chapter 18; Anne Walker (Manchester) for liaising with the dental practitioners to ensure the guidance on the use of X-rays in dental radiology is in line with their guidance; Alan McKenzie (Bristol), Tony Flynn and John Tuohy (Leeds) for input to the radiotherapy chapters; Andy Bradley (Manchester), Don Hancock (Swansea), Sandra Woods (Manchester, now at Belfast), Julian MacDonald (Rhyl), Michael Waller (York, now at Leeds), Sharan Packer and Stephen Evans (London) who provided first drafts of the chapters concerned with radioactivity; Cliff Double, Gordon Clarke and Walt O'Dowd (Medical Devices Agency; MDA) for equipment standards input; Stephen Evans for his major contributions to Appendices 10 and 11; all who volunteered their services in the drafting process, and all our colleagues, particularly those on the IPEM Special Interest Groups who have been badgered endlessly for information or comments during the process.

Since the consultation draft was published comments have been received from over 20 national organisations and government departments, over 15 medical physics departments and very many individuals. All the comments have been reviewed and incorporated taking possible conflicts into account. Reaching agreement on the practical implementation of the medical exposures regulations in hospital departments throughout the United Kingdom was only possible through the close co-operation of the Royal College of Radiologists (through Roger Buchanan) and the College of Radiographers (through Ann Cattell), to whom sincere thanks are extended as indeed they are to the DoH team through Steve Ebdon-Jackson.

Finally, our sincere thanks go to Margaret Erskine (NRPB) and Wendy Bines (HSE), for their editorial suggestions, and to Chris Gibson, Chairman of the IPEM Publications Committee, for his constant support and almost infinite patience.

IPEM Working Group
Andy Brennan
Hamish Porter
Marge Rose
Adam Workman
Penny Allisy-Roberts (Chairman)

Introduction

These medical and dental guidance notes (MDGN) have been prepared for those who use ionising radiation in medical and dental practice and in allied research involving human subjects. They apply wherever humans are irradiated for diagnostic, therapeutic, research or other medical or dental purposes, and where *in vitro* medical tests are conducted. This includes all private and National Health Service (NHS) practice in hospitals, medical schools, clinics, mobile units, laboratories, surgeries and consulting rooms, including medical departments in industry and prisons. They apply also to ancillary activities such as the maintenance, testing and calibration of equipment and the storage and disposal of radioactive substances where these are carried out in the above premises. The guidance given is for the protection of employed and self-employed persons, apprentices and students, patients and their friends and relatives who are acting as comforters and carers, volunteers in research projects and members of the public.

These guidance notes are a guide to good radiation protection practice on the use of ionising radiation in medicine and dentistry. They include additional information and practical advice related to some, but not all, of the requirements of the Ionising Radiations Regulations 1999 (IRR99) [1] and its Approved Code of Practice (ACoP) and non-statutory guidance (L121) [2] and to the requirements of the Ionising Radiation (Medical Exposure) Regulations 2000 (IR(ME)R) and supporting guidance [3, 4]. It is essential, therefore, that employers and those who advise them are fully aware of these requirements and those of other relevant acts and regulations, in particular the Medicines (Administration of Radioactive Substances) Regulations 1978 and subsequent amendment [5, 6], the Radioactive Substances Act 1993 [7] and any equivalent legislation applicable in their part of the United Kingdom.

Throughout these notes, the words 'must', 'required', 'should', 'advised' and 'recommended' are used. This is intended to provide general guidance on good practice and is not an interpretation of the legal requirements. When in doubt, the appropriate regulations should be consulted.

All persons (e.g. employers, scientific and technical staff, medical and dental staff) whose work directly concerns the use of ionising radiation in medical or dental practice should consult the relevant sections of these guidance notes for practical advice on radiation protection.

Chapters 1 and 2 lay the foundations of the regulations [1, 3] which are developed in the later chapters for specific applications.

Chapters 3 and 4 relate to good practice in the use of diagnostic X-rays for medical exposures and interventional radiology and the associated equipment requirements.

Chapters 5 and 6 relate to good practice in hospital and university dental departments and the associated equipment. They have been produced in collaboration with the British Dental Association and the NRPB and are consistent with the *Guidance Notes for Dental Practitioners on the Safe Use of X-ray Equipment* available from the DoH [8].

Chapters 7, 8 and 9 relate to good practice in the use of medical exposures for radiotherapy using external beam techniques and brachytherapy.

Chapters 10 and 11 cover good practice in the use of unsealed radioactive materials for diagnosis.

Chapter 12 covers good practice in the use of unsealed radioactive materials for radionuclide therapy.

Chapter 13 relates to good practice in laboratories using small amounts of unsealed radioactive materials or devices to irradiate clinical samples. For those working in research and teaching establishments, the Association of University Radiation Protection Officers (AURPO) has produced *AURPO Guidance Notes on Working with Ionising Radiations in Research and Teaching* [9].

Chapter 14 covers the use of small sealed sources.

Chapters 15 and 16 provide guidance when patients who have been administered with radioactive substances are no longer under the direct supervision of the IR(ME)R practitioner.

Chapters 17 and 18 cover the aspects including storage and disposal of radioactive waste products that relate to the use of unsealed radioactive materials.

Chapter 19 relates to contingency planning and emergency procedures.

The Appendices provide detailed information that is referred to in the text. The references in the text are listed, together with any usual acronym, in Appendix 21. A separate list of acronyms used in the MDGN is given in Appendix 19.

Advice should be sought from the relevant Health Department or the HSE with regard to any future developments in usage of ionising radiations that are not covered by these medical and dental guidance notes.

1   General measures for radiation protection

Scope

1.1   This chapter contains guidance on the organisational arrangements and general measures for radiation protection for staff, members of the public and comforters and carers within a hospital or healthcare environment. It also contains some measures for radiation protection of patients, but this is covered in more depth in Chapter 2. The guidance in this and the following chapters should be read in conjunction with *Work with Ionising Radiation* (L121) [2], non-statutory guidance (e.g. HSE Information Sheets) and professional advice. In some situations, the good practice guidance makes recommendations that are beyond that required in L121 [2]. In other situations, more comprehensive guidance is referenced to avoid repetition.

The employer

1.2   The responsibility for providing protective measures lies with the radiation employer, who may be a company, an NHS Health Authority Board or Trust, a visiting contractor, or a self-employed person such as a partner in a group practice. The role of the employer using radiation is clearly identified in IRR99 [1] (as are the different duties of the employer separately defined under IR(ME)R [3]). The employer may delegate tasks and allocate functions required by regulations to suitably trained individuals, but cannot delegate responsibility. The employer's responsibilities are summarised in Appendix 1.

1.3   The range of employers covered by this document is very wide, from a self-employed person to a large NHS Trust, and each will have a different management structure pertinent to the management of radiation protection. To avoid undue repetition, the core of the text assumes a structure typical of a large hospital. In some instances, guidance specific to the smaller user is given. However, where reference is made to posts that may not exist in their organisation, such as head of department or line manager, readers are encouraged to look at the functions and responsibilities assigned to that post and pose the question: 'Is it relevant to our work with radiation, and who should undertake that role?'

1.4   The employer should demonstrate a clear commitment to optimisation through a structured approach to operational management of radiation protection. This should include:

(a) radiation risk assessment
(b) restriction of exposure
(c) designation of areas (controlled and supervised)
(d) appropriate information and training in radiation protection for all staff
(e) radiation monitoring and record keeping, and
(f) review of procedures as appropriate.

Responsibilities

1.5   The commitment of senior management to restrict exposure to ionising radiation should be clearly demonstrated in a written radiation safety policy for both occupational and medical exposures. The safety policy should identify clearly those with responsibility, and the scope of their responsibility (see Appendix 2). The responsibilities of the employer and the roles of the radiation protection supervisor (RPS), radiation protection adviser (RPA) and qualified person (QP) are clearly identified and documented in IRR99 [1](Appendices 3 and 4).

1.6   Heads of departments and line managers should be involved in the implementation of radiation protection requirements, in respect of staff, comforters and carers, patients and members of the public (see also Chapter 2).

Communication

1.7   There should be co-operation and appropriate exchange of information between employers when employees of one employer work on the premises of another employer, particularly with respect to controlled areas and arrangements for persons working therein. The precise allocation of responsibility should be agreed between employers and communicated in writing to the employees. This should ensure that protection is optimised and exposures are restricted to a level as low as reasonably practicable (ALARP). For example, such agreements are required when premises are visited by maintenance contractors, physics staff, X-ray installation and service engineers, when agency staff are used or when medical consultants work for more than one health authority. A teaching hospital or medical school often has both academic and hospital staff working together. These responsibilities and agreements should be documented and reviewed as appropriate.

1.8   The employer must establish adequate arrangements for communication regarding staff safety, supervision and radiation monitoring results for classified workers and outside workers. The adequacy of these arrangements should be reviewed on an annual basis.

1.9   The employer must establish adequate communication and supervisory arrangements for:

(a) nuclear medicine patients being discharged into the care of another employer

(b) comforters and carers

(c) monitoring and training arrangements for radiation work performed on the employer's premises by employees of another employer or by their own employees on the premises of another employer

(d) the critical examination and commissioning of new installations and the installation and testing of new or modified equipment, particularly where the site is new-build and has not as yet been handed over to the Trust, or where employees of another employer (e.g. building contractor or sub-contractors) are involved or working in adjacent areas, and

(e) maintenance and quality assurance (QA) for equipment used for medical exposure on both their own premises and those of other employers, specifically with respect to the guidance in HSG226 *Radiation Equipment Used for Medical Exposure* [10] which is the revision for the guidance previously known as PM77.

1.10   The radiation employer should establish an effective system of internal communication on radiation protection issues, including arrangements to ensure that pregnant and breastfeeding employees are aware of and subject to the appropriate restrictions on exposure as described in *Guidelines for Expectant or Breastfeeding Mothers* [11]. The HSE provides guidance on the establishment of effective systems of internal communication within a health and safety framework in *Successful Health and Safety Management* [12].

Radiation protection committee

1.11   Employers are recommended to establish a radiation protection committee as part of the framework for the management of radiation protection. This will assist in reviewing the implementation of advice and should have good liaison with the health and safety committee [13, 14]. An additional function of the radiation protection committee might be to oversee medical exposures, as explained in paragraphs 2.45 and 2.46.

1.12   The composition and function of the radiation protection committee will be a local matter but should include senior management representatives, the medical director, clinical directors who use radiation, the health and safety manager, RPSs, RPA(s) and staff, trade union and safety representatives. In very large establishments, there could be separate radiation protection committees for:

- X-ray work (e.g. for radiology, cardiology, accident and emergency (A&E) and orthopaedic departments)

- radionuclides (e.g. for laboratories, Nuclear Medicine department, radionuclide dispensary), and

- radiotherapy (external beam, brachytherapy and other sealed sources), with appropriate communication arrangements at the managerial and operational levels.

Radiation protection adviser

1.13   Almost all radiation employers who use ionising radiation will need to consult and appoint a suitable RPA with recognised certification, appropriate knowledge and experience relevant to the scope of advice required (see Appendix 4). More than one RPA, or an RPA body, may need to be appointed if advice is likely to be needed on a wide range of subjects. The employer must consult their RPA about certain issues and about observance of IRR99 [1]. Appendix 4 identifies the matters needing RPA advice and indicates other matters where the advice of the RPA will be helpful for the employer.

1.14   RPAs should visit the departments to which their advice relates and should identify and review the protective measures in consultation with the RPSs and line managers, as appropriate. The frequency of the reviews should be determined by the employer in consultation with the RPA, taking into account the extent of the hazards involved, any change in practices and professional guidance, and should be identified in the contractual arrangement with the RPA. The frequency should ensure that all aspects of radiation protection are reviewed at least 3-yearly by the employer.

1.15   The HSE guidance on criteria for competence for RPAs is clearly defined. If the RPA is unable to fulfil an advisory function through a lack of competence or through a lack of information or facilities, professional codes of conduct require that this is brought to the attention of the employer.

Prior risk assessment

1.16   Employers who intend to undertake a new activity involving work with ionising radiation must make and record a realistic assessment of the associated radiation risk, prior to commencement of the work. This should be based on the advice of the RPA to restrict exposures both during routine operations and in the event of foreseeable radiation accidents. An example of a pro-forma approach to risk assessment is given in Appendix 6. An alternative approach, such as HSG163 *5 Steps to Risk Assessment* [15] or the general approach outlined in L121 [2] (paragraphs 36 to 58), may be used.

1.17   *5 Steps to Risk Assessment* [15] involves the following stages:

(a) identifying the hazards
(b) deciding who might be harmed and how
(c) evaluating the risks and deciding whether the existing precautions are adequate or need to be improved
(d) recording the findings, and
(e) reviewing the assessment and revising if necessary.

1.18   A prior risk assessment should be made for each installation or area. A documented risk assessment would be expected to be in place for all existing activities. Written details will facilitate the review of the risk, the associated control measures and actions required and their communication with the relevant staff. A summary may be included in the local rules to inform staff.

1.19   The risk assessments completed under the Management of Health and Safety at Work Regulations (MHSWR) [16] for existing procedures should be reviewed and expanded where necessary to meet the specific requirements of IRR99 with respect to dose limitation for pregnant or breastfeeding staff, and young or inexperienced staff.

1.20   The employer should establish a mechanism for the timely review of implementation of recommendations made regarding risk assessment. Risk assessments must be reviewed and updated by the employer when practices change or at least 3-yearly.

Prior authorisation

1.21   Prior authorisation is required under IRR99 [1] for the following practices:

(a) the use of X-ray units for research (research does not include exposures where there is a diagnostic or therapeutic benefit to the patient)

(b) the use of X-ray units for the exposure of persons for medical treatment

(c) the use of accelerators (other than electron microscopes) and also

(d) the use of electric equipment intended to produce X-rays for industrial radiography, and

(e) the use of X-ray units for processing of products.

In summary, the employer must comply with the conditions in a generic authorisation (see 1.23 and Appendix 18) before carrying out a practice which involves a medical accelerator, medical treatment using X-ray units or any X-ray equipment for research purposes unless there is a diagnostic or therapeutic benefit to the patient being exposed. Exceptionally, if compliance is not possible, the employer must obtain individual prior authorisation (written permission) from the HSE.

1.22   The following practices which involve the use of accelerators or X-rays units do not need authorisation under IRR99 [1]:

(a) the use of electron microscopes
(b) diagnostic use of X-ray units in medical and dental practice
(c) use of X-ray units for routine analytical diagnostic or investigation purposes
(d) use of X-ray units in baggage, postal or food screening
(e) use of X-ray gauging and detection systems in measurement processes, and
(f) diagnostic or therapeutic use of X-rays units for veterinary purposes.

1.23   HSE has developed two certificates of generic authorisation that together cover all the practices that should need authorisation under IRR99 [1]. Each certificate contains conditions which, if the employer meets them, will exempt them from the need to obtain written prior authorisation (see Appendix 18). For example, the use of medical accelerators for radiotherapy comes under a generic authorisation and the RPA can give advice on compliance. Similarly there is a certificate of generic authorisation which covers the use of X-rays in research, with specified conditions which must be met. The specified conditions are to ensure that radiation exposures are adequately restricted but are not sufficient to ensure full compliance with the whole of IRR99. It is recommended that the assessment of compliance with a generic authorisation is documented for reference during any future inspection.

1.24   It is expected that almost all hospitals will be able to meet the criteria for generic authorisation. However, if the conditions of a generic authorisation cannot be met for some reason, the employer together with the RPA may discuss the matter with the local HSE inspector who will provide guidance on applying for an individual authorisation. It is not envisaged that this will be necessary for normal medical radiological practice.

1.25   Most practices involving the keeping, use or disposal of radioactive substances will need to be registered and authorised to accumulate and dispose of radioactive waste under the Radioactive Substances Act (RSA93) [7] unless an Exemption Order applies [17]. Registrations and authorisations under RSA93 are granted by the Environment Agency (EA) in England and Wales, the Scottish Environment Protection Agency (SEPA) in Scotland, and the Environment and Heritage Service of Northern Ireland (EHSNI) in Northern Ireland. The practice of nuclear medicine regarding the administration of radioactive materials is covered under the Medicines Act [18] with authorisations required under the Medicines (Administration of Radioactive Substances) Regulations (MARS78 and MARS95) [5, 6].

Notification

1.26   Notification to the HSE of work with ionising radiation remains a requirement under IRR99 [1]. This needs to be made at least 28 days in advance of starting the work unless notification has already been made under previous statutory requirements, i.e. the revoked Ionising Radiations Regulations 1985 (L121 [2] paragraph 35). However, there is separate provision for nuclear medicine patients being discharged at short notice to a nursing home, or to the care of community nurses in the home. In such circumstances, notification can be by fax to the local HSE office as soon as the patient's situation becomes apparent and as soon as practicable before care of the patient commences.

1.27   Self-employed persons, for example in a radiology clinic or dental practice, also need to notify the HSE, but it is not necessary to repeat a notification made prior to January 2000 (L121 [2] paragraph 35).

1.28   It should be noted that a new or significant change in practice at a new or existing site will continue to require notification to the HSE, even though operation may be under a generic authorisation, e.g. use of a new procedure that may have different radiation protection implications, such as use of sealed or unsealed sources when only X-rays have been used previously. Schedule 2 of IRR99 [1] sets out the notification requirements in general terms. The details specified in Schedule 3 only need to be provided if requested by the HSE (see IRR99 regulation 6(3) [1]).

1.29   A change of name of the employer or change of site should also be notified to the HSE. In addition, if a site where radiation work has been notified is vacated, the cessation of that work needs to be notified to the HSE.

Critical examination and testing

1.30   A critical examination of any article or equipment (installed or erected) which has implications for radiation protection must be undertaken, usually by the installer who is responsible for the erection or installation. The purpose of the critical examination is to demonstrate to the purchaser that the designed safety features and warning devices operate correctly, that there is sufficient protection for persons from exposure to ionising radiation and that the equipment is safe to use in normal circumstances.

1.31   There should be prior co-operation, exchange of information and a written agreement between employers regarding the arrangements for the critical examination. The employer who will use the article or equipment should also consult his RPA who will advise on the adequacy of the test results with regard to safety features and whether the level of protection is sufficient.

1.32   When part of an article is dismantled for modification or repair, e.g. replacement of X-ray tube insert, repair to light-beam diaphragm (LBD) or automatic exposure control (AEC), replacement of sources in Selectron or intravascular radiotherapy unit, and where incorrect reassembly could have radiation protection implications, then a critical examination of the reinstalled part must be performed, prior to the equipment being used clinically. Appropriate routine performance tests should be performed by the employer's representative and checked against the baseline values of the commissioning tests prior to clinical use.

1.33   A critical examination is not required for a mobile X-ray unit or specimen cabinet, as these are usually delivered fully assembled and have not been installed or erected. The required critical examination should have been undertaken at the factory or wherever the assembly of the equipment took place. Similarly, a mobile dental X-ray unit does not require a critical examination, but a wall-mounted dental X-ray unit does. However, the replacement of an X-ray tube insert in any mobile X-ray unit does require a critical examination. It should be noted that in these cases, where a local critical examination is not a requirement, the functioning of safety features should still be checked prior to first use and acceptance testing and commissioning may still be required.

1.34   The employer must not allow any equipment to be used for medical exposures (including ancillary equipment that can control or influence the extent of medical exposures) unless and until the results of the critical examination are satisfactory, and the equipment has been accepted and commissioned to specification, as a check of the initial integrity of the equipment (see IRR99 regulation 32(1) [1]).

1.35 In some situations, the installer may retain the services of the local RPA to perform the critical examination. In all situations, it is the responsibility of the installer to ensure that the critical examination is performed to specification.

1.36 Critical examinations should be carried out on articles containing radioactive substances and on X-ray generating equipment, and include associated components intended to restrict exposure. Other devices and features (e.g. walls, shields, warning lights and signals) which are not components of the article itself should be included in the examination by the appropriate installer, if these devices are intended to restrict exposure. For example, if a supplier installs equipment and connects it to the door interlocks and warning signals that are already in place, the supplier would have to check that the interlocks and warning signals operated correctly as part of the critical examination. On the other hand, if a hospital installs interlocks and warning signals in a room that already contains installed equipment, the hospital must include the checks as part of its critical examination. The examination should include the protection provided for persons undergoing medical exposures, as well as the adequacy of protection for staff and members of the public.

1.37 Table 1.1 indicates radiation safety features and warning devices that should be included for consideration in a critical examination. It is the duty of the installer of the particular feature or device to undertake a critical examination. (Note that the listing is not exhaustive.)

1.38 IPEM Report No. 79 (1998) *The Critical Examination of X-ray Generating Equipment in Diagnostic Radiology* [19] provides useful advice and information on the critical examination of X-ray equipment in diagnostic radiology. Although written as professional guidance under earlier regulations, the structure and analysis in the report are still useful for IRR99 [1].

1.39 The critical examination should not be confused with the recommended standards for acceptance testing, commissioning tests or routine performance tests, e.g. see IPEM77 *Recommended Standards for the Routine Performance Testing of Diagnostic X-ray Imaging Systems* [20], some of which may be undertaken at the same time as the critical examination following an installation.

Table 1.1 A selection of items that need a critical examination

Interlocks	Warning systems	Safety design features	Barriers
Door interlocks	Warning signals	Exposure termination	Entrance doors/maze design
Emergency off buttons/ switches	Entry warning signs	Tube/head leakage	Primary and secondary barriers (position and adequacy for adjacent areas)
Beam off/disable buttons	Beam on indications	Beam filtration and collimators	Protective cubicle and mobile screens
Microswitch interlocks	Tube/beam selection indications (e.g. energy, HDR*, tube)	Protection of exposure switch against accidental activation	Heating, ventilation, air-conditioning and cable penetrations
Alignment and filter interlocks	Unambiguous labelling	Fluoroscopy (termination, maximum skin dose rate limitation)	Provision/adequacy of personal protection (drapes, aprons, shields)
Last man out systems		AEC (dose rate termination, back-up timer, chamber/mode selection)	

* high dose rate

1.40   For the *critical examination*, it is the responsibility of the installer to ensure that the safety features and warning devices operate correctly, and that there is sufficient protection from radiation exposure. Documentation and adequate demonstration of the radiation safety features must be provided.

1.41   In *acceptance testing*, the onus is on the installer to demonstrate to the purchaser's representative that all the equipment specified in the purchase contract has been supplied and that it meets the specification laid down in that contract. Acceptance testing is not required by IRR99 [1] but is a condition of the purchase contract and is covered by Health Department's guidance.

1.42   *Commissioning tests* are carried out by the purchaser's representative to ensure that the equipment is ready for clinical use and to establish baseline values against which the results of subsequent routine performance tests can be compared. Commissioning tests are a component part of optimisation and as such, the relevant medical physics expert (MPE) will normally be involved. In diagnostic radiology, these tests are usually performed jointly by both the installer and the purchaser's representative, as this facilitates corrective action and optimisation of the system. In radiotherapy, commissioning tests are performed by radiotherapy physics staff over an extended period, and may include the commissioning and integrity of the equipment data transferred to treatment planning systems.

1.43   *Routine performance tests* are undertaken at the frequency specified in the QA programme or after maintenance or repair to establish that the equipment continues to perform satisfactorily.

1.44   Commissioning tests and routine performance tests are legal requirements for equipment used for medical exposure (IRR99 regulation 32 (3, 4) [1]), and the employer must establish and maintain appropriate arrangements for their performance, and ensure that there are adequate resources to undertake the tests.

1.45   Although many of these tests may be combined in a single (acceptance) survey at installation which tests the initial integrity of the equipment, their purpose should remain distinct and their components should be clearly identified (preferably documented in protocols), as should the identity and role of the installer, purchaser and RPA.

1.46   The installation of software is not subject to the requirement for a critical examination, as software is not 'an article for use at work' as defined in the Health and Safety at Work etc. Act (HSWA) [21]. Software controlled devices, however (e.g. safety features, warning devices, exposure controls, AECs, etc.), require critical examination.

1.47   The associated risk assessment should be reviewed and updated following the critical examination. This should include consideration of occupancy and supervision of adjacent areas and planned changes in intended workload.

1.48   New or second-hand equipment used for medical exposures (including equipment on loan or being demonstrated, for which see 1.113) should be safe and appropriate for use and should be accompanied by the relevant operating instructions, original source activity calibration certificate (if applicable) and safety information. It should be critically examined for its radiation protection implications for the patient as well as for staff and members of the public (IRR99 regulation 32(1) and L121, paragraph 527 [1, 2]) and commissioned prior to being put into clinical use and included in a QA programme under HSG226 [10]. In addition, equipment must not be used clinically until the appropriate arrangements for training have been implemented and the training documented. Any employer who disposes of second-hand equipment for future use by another person, assumes the responsibility and liability as a supplier. Disposal to a dealer may not necessarily negate this responsibility. The MDA Device Bulletin 9801, Supplement 2, October 2001, contains useful guidance on the sale, transfer of ownership and disposal of medical devices [22].

Equipment use, maintenance and quality assurance

1.49   The employer must consider the restriction of exposure when purchasing equipment and should establish and implement an appropriate equipment replacement policy. Additionally, arrangements should be in place to ensure that the most appropriate equipment is selected for each medical exposure and that equipment is not used for procedures for which it is not suitable.

1.50   All equipment must be maintained, preferably to the specification and at the frequency recommended by the manufacturer. The employer should consult their RPA and RPS (and MPE and QP, as appropriate) on the specification of the maintenance contract, the adequacy of the maintenance arrangements, on the information supplied at each service and the information required by the employer, on the hand-over arrangements, and on the procedures for the acceptance of equipment back into clinical use following maintenance and repair. These equipment maintenance arrangements should be reviewed on at least a 3-yearly basis or when the equipment or maintenance contract is changed.

1.51   The employer must ensure the provision of a QA programme for equipment for medical exposure which is consistent with national and professional standards (e.g. HSG226 [10], IPEM77 [20]), and this should include the provision of appropriate test equipment and its calibration and maintenance. It should also include procedures for recording equipment faults and actions to be taken, including the need to obtain advice from the RPA when necessary. For equipment used in medical diagnosis, the QA programme should include a patient dosimetry programme to the appropriate national protocol, e.g. *National Protocol for Patient Dose Measurements in Diagnostic Radiology* [23].

Controlled areas

1.52   Radiopharmacies, radiation areas containing sealed sources used for radiotherapy, and wards, side-wards or rooms used for patients undergoing radionuclide therapy or brachytherapy, should all be designated as controlled areas. Radiation areas containing fixed X-ray generating equipment should usually be designated as controlled areas. Areas where there is a significant risk of radionuclide contamination outside the working area will also need to be designated as controlled. Other radiation areas, in which the likely exposures are much lower than in the controlled areas, may need to be designated as supervised areas.

1.53   There should be a documented risk assessment for each controlled area, clearly identifying the control measures and actions required to restrict exposure. These may be summarised in the local rules.

1.54   Radiation areas are designated as controlled to ensure that exposures from radiation sources are properly restricted. Consequently, the structural shielding around a designated area should limit the extent of exposures outside that area. It follows that only in special circumstances, where it is not otherwise practicable, should adjacent areas, not themselves containing a radiation source, also need to be designated as controlled. Outside a controlled area, the exposures should not exceed those permitted for a supervised area and, where the employer cannot exercise supervision, the radiation levels should be even lower so that radiation area designation is not required. In this case, access is freely available to members of the public and consequently the non-designated area can be deemed to be a public area, e.g. outside the external boundaries to a room or department, hospital corridors, public and patient waiting areas, the visitors' coffee bar.

1.55   Structural radiation shielding will be adequate when adjacent areas are protected, preferably so that no area designation is needed or, where that is not practicable, as supervised radiation areas. The determination of what is adequate structural shielding should be clearly documented by the employer in conjunction with the RPA and include consideration of present and future workload, beam quality, use, occupancy and appropriate time-averaging. Dose limitation and the ALARP principle both apply.

1.56   The adequacy or otherwise of the shielding should be verified by area monitoring. Results of monitoring including the measured IDR[1] and calculated TADR[2] at commissioning should be documented. When a particular group of people is likely to be exposed, the TADR2000[3] may also be calculated or determined from the results of appropriate environmental monitoring, with due consideration for occupancy of the group or particular individuals. The appropriate dose rates to aid in the designation process are given in Table 1.2. Appendix 11 presents flow diagrams and further detailed guidance on designation.

Table 1.2 Guideline dose rates in microsievert per hour (μSv h^{-1}) used to designate areas

	Controlled areas	Supervised areas	Unsupervised public areas
IDR	>2000	>7.5	<7.5
TADR	>7.5	>2.5	<0.5
TADR2000	> 3	>0.5	<0.15*

* 0.15 μSv h^{-1} is 3/10 of 0.5 μSv h^{-1} or 300 μSv year^{-1} – this is an appropriate dose constraint for an office worker, assuming an occupancy of 2000 h year^{-1}.

1.57   Additional guidance for designation on the basis of radionuclides dispersed in a human body is dealt with in paragraphs 9.46 and 10.32 (also see L121 paragraphs 248, 249 and 261 [2]). Whatever the designation of a radiation area, the employer and RPA should know, and have documented in a risk assessment, the IDR, TADR and TADR2000 at the boundaries of the radiation area where staff and members of the public have access. The employer should review the evaluation of the risk assessment at least 3-yearly.

1.58   The entrance to a controlled area should be marked with a warning notice that should state that the area is controlled. It should incorporate a radiation warning sign. It should also include other precise information, such as the reason why the area is controlled, e.g. 'X-radiation' or 'unsealed sources', and whether or not entry is permitted together with any conditions. Signs should give sufficient information to alert employees to the possible risks arising from the source (e.g. external γ, cloud β, inhalation or ingestion) and to enable employees to take appropriate action before entering the area (e.g. to wear appropriate personal protective equipment (PPE)). An illuminated warning light (preferably at eye level) may accompany the warning notice to indicate when access is strictly forbidden, e.g. during radiotherapy when the beam is 'on' and during diagnostic X-ray exposures if entry is directly into an unprotected area of the room. The light should be at the room entrance at a visible height and would normally incorporate appropriate wording depending on the conditions. (Appendix 12 gives examples.)

1.59   Systems of work (including written arrangements in local rules for non-classified staff) must be provided (IRR99 regulation 8(2) [1] and L121 paragraph 104 [2]) to restrict exposures for any persons working in the controlled area. If an X-ray generator has been effectively isolated from the electrical supply, or if all radioactive sources have been removed (e.g. to a store) and residual contamination is negligible (see later chapters for guidance), the designation can be temporarily withdrawn provided the warning notices reflect the correct designation. It may be more convenient for designation to be permanent and to allow entry under a written arrangement.

1.60   The designation of each radiation area should be confirmed periodically by undertaking monitoring, and reviewing the working conditions. This should be performed initially at commissioning and preferably annually or at least 3-yearly thereafter, or when the situation or practices change significantly (L121 paragraph 52 [2]). It is insufficient to rely on the records of assessed doses of individuals.

---

1   IDR is the instantaneous dose rate, averaged over 1 min.
2   TADR is the time-averaged dose rate, estimated over 8 h taking into account use and workload for the typical worst day case scenario (an occupancy factor of one is assumed).
3   TADR2000 is the time-averaged dose rate estimated over 2000 h taking into account occupancy in addition to use and workload.

1.61   Measurements must be made within each controlled area using personal monitoring or other suitable measurements such as area monitoring. These should demonstrate that any written arrangements in local rules are effective in ensuring that doses received by workers in the controlled area are ALARP and do not exceed 6 millisievert (mSv) per year or 3/10 of any dose limit for non-classified staff. Records of any such monitoring must be kept for at least 2 years to confirm appropriate designation and satisfactory working arrangements.

Dose constraints

1.62   Dose constraints should be used at the planning or design stage of radiation protection as an aid to restrict exposures. They should be used in risk assessments in the optimisation of radiation protection and procedures, for comforters and carers and for the protection of members of the public for new work activities or facilities. The NRPB has recommended that the dose constraint on optimisation for a single new source should not exceed 0.3 mSv year^{-1} for a critical group likely to receive the highest average dose from the work. It should be noted that dose constraints are neither investigation levels nor necessarily a routinely acceptable exposure level. The ALARP principle must always be followed for individual exposures.

Qualified person

1.63   A QP should be responsible for the examination, testing, calibration and maintenance of all equipment used for monitoring radiation in and around designated areas, in accordance with the requirements of measurement good practice guides, e.g. NPL Guide 14 *The examination, Testing and Calibration of Portable Radiation Protection Instruments* [24]. The QP may be an employee either of the radiation employer or of a manufacturer, supplier or specialist test house. A QP does not need to be appointed in writing by the radiation employer but it is important that the QP is fully aware of the type of radiation to be measured and the type of designated area. The QP should possess the necessary expertise in instrumentation, theory and practice to calibrate and maintain the type of instrument being tested, or supervise others to undertake the tasks. QPs should ensure that all dose, dose rate and contamination monitoring equipment has a current, appropriate and traceable calibration, and, if not, bring this to the attention of the employer, RPS and RPA. When in-house staff are acting as QPs, they should be identified in the local rules and a record of their training should be maintained in the QA documentation.

1.64   QPs should have an inventory of all the radiation monitoring equipment for which they are responsible, and a record of the results of the annual test on each monitor that should be kept for at least 2 years.

Local rules

1.65   Written local rules are required for controlled areas to restrict exposure to ionising radiation and to control exposures in the event of a radiation accident (IRR99 regulations 12 and 17, and L121 paragraph 272 [1, 2]). If arrangements are needed in supervised areas to restrict exposures or to prevent accidents, e.g. where unsealed sources are being used in a pathology laboratory, local rules are also likely to be appropriate. A summary of the contents of local rules is given in Table 1.3.

1.66   Local rules do not need to contain detailed protocols of working practices, to which reference should be made, but should contain at least the information listed in L121 paragraph 278 (essential contents) [2], a brief summary or reference to the general arrangements listed in L121 paragraph 280 (optional contents) [2] and information on aspects of the health and safety management system of L121 paragraph 281 (general health and safety items) [2]. A diagram or a clear description of the designated areas should be provided.

Table 1.3 Summary of the contents of local rules

Essential contents	Optional contents	General health and safety items
Identification/description of designated areas	Management /supervision responsibilities for radiation protection	Significant findings of the risk assessment
Names of RPSs	Testing/maintenance of engineering controls and safety features	Programme to review whether doses are ALARP
Arrangements for restricting access	Radiation/contamination monitoring	Programme to review local rules
Dose investigation level e.g. 2 mSv to 6 mSv	Testing of monitoring equipment	Procedures for initiating investigations
Summary of working instructions including written arrangements for non-classified persons	Personal dosimetry arrangements	Procedures for ensuring staff have information, instruction and training
Contingency arrangements	Arrangements for pregnant and breastfeeding staff	Procedures for contact and consultation with the RPAs

1.67   The local rules should be relevant, kept up to date and reviewed preferably annually but at least 3-yearly. Employees should read the local rules for their work area, and should sign an undertaking to that effect, at induction and after any amendments have been made to the local rules.

Radiation protection supervisor

1.68   An RPS should be appointed to help ensure compliance with the IRR99 [1] in any area subject to local rules. The RPS should preferably be a full-time employee of the department and be in a sufficiently senior/supervisory position to supervise the arrangements made by the employer to secure compliance with the requirements of the local rules and the IRR99. It should be noted that there are no legal duties on the RPS, and although the employer may allocate certain tasks and functions to the designated RPS, the legal responsibility still lies with the employer.

1.69   The RPA and head of department should be consulted about the appointment of the RPS. The RPS should be appointed formally in writing by the radiation employer, clearly specifying the area of his or her responsibility and the allocated functions (see Appendix 3). The names of the RPSs should be displayed in the areas for which they are appointed. An RPS experiencing difficulties in supervising the arrangements to secure compliance should report immediately to the head of department, who, in consultation if necessary with the RPA, should decide what action is to be taken and should implement appropriate arrangements.

1.70   It may be helpful if the RPS provides an annual report to the radiation protection committee demonstrating compliance with local rules and any recommendations for improvements or other changes.

1.71   It should be noted that, under the MHSWR [16], ensuring adequate and appropriate supervision at work, as part of establishing control of preventive and protective measures, is a general safety requirement and not just applicable for ionising radiation risks.

Comforters and carers

1.72   'Comforters and carers' are individuals who (other than as part of their occupation) knowingly and willingly incur exposures to ionising radiation resulting from the support and comfort of another person who is undergoing a medical exposure. Comforters and carers are normally adult[4] (as children cannot usually give their consent), often relatives or friends of the patient, acting in this supporting role. They must be informed of the risks involved in incurring exposures while supporting and comforting the patient, the special procedures to follow to restrict their exposure, and they must be willing to incur the exposure that they will receive. In rare circumstances it might be acceptable for an under-age person to act as a comforter and carer as long as it is clear that the person was competent to understand and act of his or her own free will.

1.73   The exposure of comforters and carers should be sensitively controlled to be ALARP. They are not subject to dose limits, and a dose constraint of 5 mSv for such an episode has been recommended by NRPB. Normally, it should be possible to design procedures such that doses actually received are well below this level.

1.74   In general, pregnant women should not be comforters and carers but should be subject to procedures to ensure that the dose to the fetus does not exceed 1 mSv. It is recognised that situations might occur which make strict adherence to this recommendation extremely difficult and such personal situations should be handled sensitively. A level of control should be maintained and the dose accrued during the period should be actively reviewed; use of an electronic personal dosemeter (EPD) could assist in this process.

Classified workers

1.75   Persons who are likely to receive an effective dose in excess of 3/10 of any relevant dose limit must be classified. The results of the prior risk assessment should be used to identify those persons. Those engaged in the following types of work should be considered for classification on the basis of potential extremity doses:

   (a) therapeutic interventional radiology and cardiology procedures
   (b) endoscopy procedures using X-rays
   (c) radiopharmaceutical or radionuclide preparation
   (d) diagnostic and therapeutic radiopharmaceutical administrations
   (e) source preparation, insertion or removal in brachytherapy procedures, or
   (f) intravascular and intraoperative radiotherapy procedures.

1.76   Risk assessments and appropriate monitoring should be performed to aid the decision process on classification. However, no one may be designated as classified unless an appointed doctor has certified in the health record that the person is fit for the work with ionising radiation. Subsequent health reviews should be made at least annually and the health records kept as appropriate (see Appendix 9).

1.77   Procedures for classified persons working in the controlled area should include the optimisation of their radiation protection to ensure that doses of all workers are ALARP.

1.78   Regulation 21 of IRR99 [1] requires that employers of classified persons arrange dosimetry for those persons from an approved dosimetry service (ADS). This includes the issue and return of dosemeters for assessing doses from external radiation and the making and maintaining of dose records. If there is good reason to believe that a dose actually received is much greater or much less than the recorded dose, an investigation should be made and the report submitted to the ADS. The employer should keep a copy of the report. The ADS should provide summaries of dose records and the employer should keep these

---

4   For this purpose, an adult is normally a person over the age of 18 years. They must also have the mental capacity to understand and accept the risks associated with the exposure.

for at least 2 years. The type of dosemeter(s) worn should be suitable to assess all doses that are likely to be significant (see L121 paragraphs 385 and 386 [2]). If necessary, committed doses from internal radiation would also be assessed by appropriate means.

1.79   When entering the controlled area of another employer (but still acting in the employ of the original employer), the classified person will be an outside worker. The employer in control of the area must make an estimate of the radiation dose received by that person whilst in the controlled area and enter the estimate in the worker's radiation passbook (regulation 18(4) IRR99 [1]).

1.80   When the classified person has more than one employer or works as self-employed on occasion, each employer has responsibilities under regulation 21 IRR99 [1]. This means that each employer should make separate arrangements for dosimetry with an appropriate ADS, although in practice the same ADS may be used. In addition, each employer will need to try and establish the total dose received by the employee (to demonstrate that a dose limit has not been exceeded or whether an investigation level has been reached). L121 paragraphs 243 and 405 [2] provide further guidance.

Outside workers

1.81   An outside worker is a classified person who carries out services in the controlled area of an employer other than that of his or her own employer. Some NHS establishments may have their own outside workers, e.g. classified interventional radiologists or cardiologists, who work with radiation in the controlled area of other employers, or the establishment may have outside workers who carry out services in their controlled areas, e.g. service engineers for radiotherapy equipment, or HSE inspectors. There should be arrangements for the exchange of information between employers, regarding entry into the controlled area and for identifying any training required for the outside workers.

1.82   The employer of the outside worker must arrange for the appropriate dosimetry assessments to be provided for the outside worker from an ADS. In the case of any radiation passbooks issued prior to 31 December 1999, the employer of the outside worker must maintain the record of issue, and of subsequent return, for at least 5 years from the date the passbook ceases to be used. The outside worker must wear the personal monitoring equipment provided by their employer at all times. The employer in control of the controlled area in which the outside worker is working must have facilities for estimating the radiation dose accrued by the worker while in the controlled area, and for ensuring that the estimate is entered in the HSE approved radiation passbook issued by the ADS. Any additional dose monitoring equipment provided for this purpose by the employer of the controlled area should also be used for the duration of the work in that area. It is not necessary that this additional dose monitoring equipment be provided by an ADS. It should, however, be appropriate for its intended use, have a traceable calibration and come under the supervisory control of the RPS and QP.

Non-classified workers

1.83   If a worker is unlikely to receive an effective dose in excess of 3/10 of any relevant dose limit, there is usually no need for him or her to be classified. This will apply to many persons working in controlled areas and all those not working in controlled areas. Non-classified workers may be subject to dosimetry if required under written arrangements in local rules and this should be carried out by an ADS or by a service that conforms to the same standards in order that their employer can demonstrate compliance with regulation 8(1) and/or regulation 18(3) IRR99 [1].

1.84   In the NHS, it is common for some workers to work with ionising radiation in the premises of several different employers although employed by one employer. Co-operation is required between the employers to obtain an estimate of the worker's collated dose to ensure that the correct decision concerning classification is made. The advice of the RPA will be pertinent.

1.85   Non-classified employees who receive the majority of their radiation dose from duties with one main employer, with only a small proportion of the total dose coming from other (e.g. private) work, should be instructed to use personal monitoring dosemeters from the main employer, at all times that they work with radiation. However, if the employee is likely to receive a significant proportion of their total dose (1/10 of any relevant dose limit) from work carried out for other organisations, a separate and additional estimate of the dose received for work with each employer should be made by each employer. A system for collating dose should be instituted, with each employer having access to the collated data. This will ensure that exposures are restricted according to ALARP but, if investigations levels are reached, the appropriate action is initiated (see paragraph1.97).

1.86   Sometimes such employees have more than one employer or act as self-employed on occasion. In these circumstances, the employers should co-operate to ensure that exposures to ionising radiation are restricted to a level which is ALARP and that, if investigation levels are reached, the appropriate action is initiated.

1.87   Each employer should consider the need to issue one or more dosemeters as part of his or her risk assessment. Factors to consider should include the practicability of issue, wearing and return of multiple dosemeters, variations in type or magnitude of radiation hazards, and differences in the systems of work operated, at the different workplaces.

Personal monitoring for external radiation

1.88   Where exposure is from external sources (other than low-energy beta emitters with no significant bremsstrahlung emission), personal monitoring could be by means of one or more dosemeters worn on an appropriate part or parts of the body. A direct-reading device, such as an electronic dosemeter or a pocket ionisation chamber, may also be worn if an immediate indication of the dose received is necessary, and if the person is not classified, a reliable direct-reading electronic dosemeter may be worn instead of passive devices. Area monitoring, including contamination monitoring, should be carried out at appropriate intervals to check the dose, dose rate and surface or airborne contamination levels to which persons are exposed and to detect inadequacies in procedures or practices.

1.89   The length of time for which a dosemeter will be allocated will depend on the doses likely to be received during the period, and the probability of an accidental exposure. Each dosemeter should be returned promptly after use for a valid dose assessment, and be replaced with a new one. Most staff that are monitored will be monitored monthly. However, periods ranging from 2 weeks to 3 months can be appropriate in certain circumstances, e.g. 2 weeks could be appropriate in a high risk area with high dose rates and 3 months in a dental clinic where the probability of receiving a recordable dose within 1 month is low.

1.90   Where there is a likelihood of an accidental exposure, a direct-reading dosemeter should be worn by classified staff in addition to their normal personal monitoring, so that there is an early indication of the accidental exposure and appropriate measures can be taken to ensure ALARP. Such situations might include source replacement, a stuck source, source insertion or removal, nursing brachytherapy patients, mIBG therapy administrations and contingency arrnagements previously identified in risk assessments. For non-classified staff involved in such situations, a direct-reading dosemeter may be worn instead of a passive device. Records of accidental exposures exceeding 3/10 of any dose limit must be kept (Appendix 9).

1.91   Pregnant classified (and occasionally non-classified) workers could also wear a direct-reading dosemeter in addition to the normal personal monitor. This will enable them to monitor their body dose on a daily and monthly basis to identify those procedures that result in higher doses. Appropriate measures should then be taken to ensure ALARP and that the dose to the fetus is unlikely to exceed 1 mSv for the remaining term of pregnancy. A risk assessment should help identify those non-classified workers for which these arrangements are appropriate [11].

1.92   Persons who are issued with a dosemeter should wear it as instructed all the time they are at work. Care should be taken to prevent the dosemeter, while not being worn, from being exposed inadvertently to ionising radiation or subject to other conditions, e.g. heat, which could affect the assessment of doses. A dosemeter should normally be worn on the trunk at chest or waist height: it may then be interpreted as monitoring the dose to the whole body. However, more than one dosemeter may be needed if there is any reason to suspect that doses to other parts of the body may exceed 1/10 of the appropriate dose limit.

1.93   A trial programme of monitoring should be undertaken to determine the likely levels of dose for other parts of the body. Routine monitoring of extremity doses is advisable if doses to the hands or other extremities are likely to exceed 1/10 of the appropriate dose limit. Similar considerations apply also to the eyes. In the hospital environment, extremity and eye monitoring may be appropriate in those cases indicated in paragraph 1.75.

1.94   In a routine situation, e.g. where the hands are being monitored for external radiation from X-ray, it is not critical to identify that area of skin on the hands which receives the highest dose. Limiting the average dose to the hands by using a dosemeter worn on a finger or wrist will adequately assess the dose to the hands. Situations for which the 1 cm^2 averaging of skin dose is important are those where a localised part of the skin has the potential to receive a much higher dose than the rest. In this case, the skin dose should be assessed at the position of maximum likely dose, to ensure compliance with the dose limits as averaged over 1 cm^2. However, the dose may be recorded at an adjacent area, if the position of maximum likely dose is known, and a dosemeter worn at this position would adversely affect the efficacy of the procedure and the optimisation of protection. An example is in radiopharmaceutical preparation where the position of maximum likely dose may be the fingertip but wearing a dosemeter on the fingertip could adversely affect tactile function and procedures. In this case a thermoluminescent dosemeter (TLD) ring may be worn on that finger, if an appropriate conversion factor to the fingertip dose has been identified and recorded together with the actual dose measured.

1.95   If a person is wearing a protective apron, then, in addition to the primary dosemeter worn on the trunk under the apron, one or more dosemeters may need to be worn on the unprotected parts of the body if there are likely to be significant contributions to the effective dose from the exposure of unprotected organs. In all cases, additional protective clothing or devices (e.g. thyroid shield or ceiling suspended shield) should be used where practicable to restrict exposure, consistent with the ALARP principle.

Personal monitoring for internal radiation

1.96   When using unsealed radioactive materials, consideration should be given to monitoring for internal contamination, if the likelihood of internal exposure is identified in the risk assessment. If measurable levels of surface contamination are consistently recorded for radionuclides which could produce significant internal radiation doses, monitoring by means of bioassay, or whole or part body counting techniques, may be necessary. This is likely to be the case when working with radioiodine. The use of personal air sampling methods is unlikely to be justified. Further guidance can be obtained from the HSE Contract Research Report of 1998 on *Guidance on Monitoring and Dose Assessment for Internal Exposure of Workers* [25]. This latter type of monitoring is particularly important when using ^{14}C or other low-energy beta emitters, which are not detectable on film-badges.

Dosimetry investigation

1.97   The employer must carry out a formal investigation in consultation with the RPA if a member of staff exceeds an effective dose of 15 mSv in a calendar year. However, it is recommended that an investigation level is set at a lower effective dose, between 2 mSv and 6 mSv, and the level should be identified in the local rules. The report of the investigation should be kept for at least 2 years.

1.98   It is advisable to investigate the reason if any member of staff receives a dose in any monitoring period in excess of a normal value for that group of staff (pro-rata for part-time staff). It is recommended that the cause of an exposure in excess of 1/20 of any annual dose limit in a month should be investigated and appropriate measures identified to restrict future exposures. There should be established communication arrangements between the ADS, the employer and the RPS to flag these doses and to investigate them in a timely manner.

1.99   Any suspected overexposure, i.e. an exposure in excess of any dose limit, must be investigated immediately and, if confirmed or not ruled out, must be notified as soon as practicable to the HSE, the employer of the individual concerned, the appointed doctor and the individual concerned. Reports of such investigations must be kept for 2 years and, if the overexposure is confirmed, the report must be kept for at least 50 years or until the person is aged 75 years. This requirement for investigation and reporting includes suspected overexposures for all employees and for members of the public who are exposed in excess of the public dose limit. It does not include medical exposures, nor a fetal exposure during a medical exposure nor exposures of comforters and carers as dose limits do not apply.

Radiation incidents

1.100   The radiation employer should establish a radiation incident reporting procedure providing for compliance with the legal duties to report incidents of specified kinds to the HSE, to the relevant EA or to the relevant Health Department or to more than one of those as appropriate. The reporting procedure should provide for the separate reporting of adverse incidents, where equipment faults may have health and safety implications for patients or staff. Such incidents should be reported to the Adverse Incident Centre at the MDA (for England), to the Scottish Healthcare Supplies (for Scotland), to the Welsh National Assembly (for Wales) or to the Department of Health, Social Services and Public Safety (for Northern Ireland) (see Appendix 16).

1.101   The incident reporting procedure should follow relevant guidance such as HSG226 [10] and make clear the respective roles of the RPS, RPA and management in investigating incidents and reporting them to the statutory authorities. An example of a basic template is given in Appendix 7 and a more general example is available on the web site of the Scottish Healthcare Supplies at http://www.show.scot.nhs.uk/ shs/hazards_safety/advrep1.pdf. The senior management representative on the radiation protection committee should take responsibility for notifying the relevant statutory authorities of any suspected overexposure, usually on the advice of the RPA (Appendix 1 (points 21 and 41)).

1.102   Radiation incidents that are medical exposures significantly greater than intended, resulting from a malfunction or defect in radiation equipment which is within the guidance criteria of HSG226 [10], must be reported to the HSE.

1.103   Incidents where a radiotherapy or brachytherapy patient is underexposed can also have serious consequences. Whilst these are not notifiable under IRR99 [1] or IR(ME)R [3], a full investigation should be undertaken and documented by the employer, involving the RPS, RPA, practitioner, MPE responsible for equipment quality control (QC) and any other operators or external service staff involved in the incident. Such incidents may arise from a failure to comply with the employer's written procedures either under IR(ME)R or IRR99 regulation 32 (3 and 4) [3, 1].

1.104   It should be noted that IRR99 regulations 7, 8, 11, 16, 17, 18, 23, 25, 31(1) and 34(1) [1] do not apply in relation to persons undergoing medical exposures. An unintended exposure of a fetus during a medical exposure is not notifiable to HSE under IRR99, as a fetus is not a person independent of the mother. An accidental exposure of a fetus during a medical exposure is notifiable as part of the mother's exposure if it results from an equipment malfunction or defect (IRR99 regulation 32(6)) and falls within the guidance criteria of HSG226 [10].

1.105   The unintended exposure of a breastfeeding child during a medical exposure of the mother (or wet-nurse) may be notifiable if it exceeds the dose limit in IRR99 schedule 4 paragraph 7 (5 mSv in 5 years) [1]. The child is a person (not undergoing a medical exposure) and therefore IRR99 regulations 11 and 25 [1] apply.

1.106   Notification of a medical exposure that is significantly greater than intended is covered in paragraph 2.59.

1.107   Although certain regulations (see paragraph 1.104) do not apply in relation to persons undergoing medical exposures, ALARP still applies. For example, in a two-bedded Selectron suite with two patients being treated with medical exposures contemporaneously, one patient may receive some radiation exposure from the other patient's medical exposure. IRR99 regulation 11 (dose limitation) does not apply, but ALARP does. It would be advisable to perform an assessment of the radiation exposure of one patient from the medical exposure of the other. The control measures used and procedures implemented should be documented and be consistent with ALARP, e.g. the use of appropriate shielding or removing one patient when he or she is no longer undergoing a medical exposure.

1.108   Similarly, in a patient waiting area designated for radionuclide patients only, ALARP also applies. Either persons not undergoing medical exposure should be excluded, or there should be procedures and arrangements in place such that no person can exceed 5 mSv in 5 years and ALARP is actively applied. There should be adequate space or shielding to minimise exposure, proper segregation of higher activity patients, dedicated toilet facilities for radionuclide patients only, and appropriate monitoring and supervision arrangements.

Ionising Radiation Incident Database

1.109   The radiation employer may wish to arrange for incidents (including near misses) that involve occupational exposure to be reported to the Ionising Radiation Incident Database (IRID) (see Appendix 8). The database is operated by NRPB (Appendix 16) on behalf of an NRPB/HSE/EA partnership. IRID was established to provide a mechanism to capture the lessons learned from accidents and incidents and to provide a feedback mechanism, details of which are given in *Specifications for the Ionising Radiations Incident Database* [26]. The data on IRID are anonymous and the regulators have given an undertaking not to try and use these data to prompt an investigation of an incident that has not been reported to them by a different means. Descriptions of incidents and the lessons learned are published periodically, e.g. *First Review of Cases Reported and Operation of the Database* [27] and are available through the IRID website http://www.nrpb.org/publications/misc_publications/irid.htm.

Notification of accidental releases and spillages

1.110   The employer must notify the HSE and EA/SEPA/EHSNI of any accidental releases and spillages of radioactive substances that occur internally within the building or in the external atmosphere. Activities notifiable to the HSE for releases and spills are as specified in IRR99 schedule 8, column 4 [1], unless the release occurs in an enclosure or localised facility designed to prevent the release going beyond that facility.

Radiation emergencies

1.111   In addition to the requirements of IRR99 for contingency planning (see Chapter 19), the Radiation (Emergency Preparedness and Public Information) Regulations 2001 (REPPIR) [28] complement these requirements for emergency preparedness. They apply to premises and rail transport. There are exemptions for non-dispersible sources (e.g. iridium wire) and sealed sources (for premises only, not for transport) and radioactive substances in live bodies or human corpses. REPPIR [28]are likely to apply where there are centralised radiopharmacies holding activities in excess of 2 TBq of ^{99}Mo or 90 GBq of ^{131}I, for example, or the equivalent quantity ratio. REPPIR are unlikely to apply to the transportation of radioactive materials between hospitals, or to any other similar transport operations, because of the exemptions provided and because they are almost exclusively carried by road. However, any contingency plan prepared under the IRR99 [1] (see Chapter 19) will also be valid under REPPIR [28] although other actions will also be necessary. EA and SEPA are statutory consultees on the emergency plans. Other than as already identified, the impact of REPPIR on non-nuclear sites is expected to be minimal. Actions concerning other transport modes do not come within REPPIR and will be implemented and enforced by the Radioactive Materials Transport Division of the Department for Transport, Local Government and the Regions (DTLR) for road, the Civil Aviation Authority for air and the Maritime and Coastguard Agency for sea and inland waterways.

Records

1.112   Appendix 9 refers to statutory and some non-statutory requirements that relate to record keeping.

Equipment on loan

1.113   The use of equipment on loan for medical exposures is subject to the general requirements of IRR99 [1] and IR(ME)R [3]. The arrangements outlined, in paragraphs 1.114 for the employer and 1.115 for the supplier, must be in place before the equipment may be used clinically. An appropriate medical equipment loan or indemnity agreement should be signed unless the supplier is another NHS organisation that performs medical exposures: in which case an indemnity agreement may not be required.

1.114   For equipment which will be used clinically in connection with medical exposures, the employer must:

(a) consult their RPA, relevant RPS, relevant MPE and device manager prior to accepting the loan of medical equipment

(b) agree an appropriate medical equipment loan or indemnity agreement with the supplier as necessary

(c) perform appropriate risk assessments (including where appropriate an assessment of the location of the equipment)

(d) ensure that the hand-over documentation includes
   (i) operating instructions
   (ii) critical examination and other safety information
   (iii) relevant safety information (e.g. electrical, mechanical, laser, Control of Substances Hazardous to Health (COSHH))
   (iv) source activity calibration (when relevant), and
   (v) an agreed protocol for clinical use

(e) confirm that appropriate arrangements are in place for the preventative maintenance and inspection of the equipment as specified in any medical equipment loan or indemnity agreement

(f) confirm that commissioning tests have been performed and that the equipment has been included in a QA programme

(g) make appropriate arrangements, usually with the supplier, for training which is activity and equipment specific, of the employees who will use the equipment (operators), prior to the equipment being put into clinical use, clearly identifying the individuals involved and the scope of this training under IR(ME)R [3] (see also 7.14)

(h) document the appropriate IR(ME)R training records (see 2.34), and

(i) cease using the equipment at the end of the agreed loan term.

1.115   The supplier of equipment on loan must:

(a) agree and comply with the terms of the medical equipment loan or indemnity agreement

(b) provide hand-over documentation as specified in paragraph 1.114

(c) conduct a critical examination

(d) confirm that the equipment is performing to specification

(e) provide preventative maintenance and inspection as specified in the medical equipment loan or indemnity agreement

(f) specify and agree the scope of the training needed to operate the equipment under IR(ME)R [3]

(g) provide appropriate training as agreed (activity and equipment specific) under IR(ME)R to the identified employees

(h) supervise an agreed number of clinical cases, and

(i) remove the equipment at the end of the agreed term and reinstate the premises where appropriate.

2 Radiation protection of persons undergoing medical exposures

Scope

2.1 This chapter gives guidance on the roles and responsibilities of all duty holders under IR(ME)R [3]. It includes other professional and general guidance on the radiation protection framework for justification and optimisation of all medical exposures, to ensure the adequate protection of patients or other individuals receiving medical exposure. The guidance should be read in conjunction with the DoH notes on good practice for IR(ME)R [3], which are available from their web site http://www.doh.gov.uk/irmer.htm [4], and other associated professional advice.

General principles of patient protection

2.2 All diagnostic and therapeutic procedures involving exposure to ionising radiation for medical purposes may carry some personal risk to the patient.[1] Irradiation during pregnancy may also involve a risk to the fetus, and administration of radioactive medicinal products to a breastfeeding patient may also involve a risk to her infant. It is important, therefore, that only those medical exposures that are justified are undertaken. Alternative methods to obtain the required diagnostic information with less risk to the patient, a fetus or infant should be considered, e.g. by using non-ionising radiation.

2.3 All types of practice involving medical exposure must be justified before first being adopted, following DoH guidance. In addition, IR(ME)R [3] require all procedures involving medical exposure to be justified, taking into account the clinical objectives of the exposure for the individual concerned. This involves ensuring that the potential benefit of the exposure to the patient and his or her family (or society) outweighs the radiation detriment that the exposure may cause. Additionally, for a particular medical exposure to be justified, the net benefit should be greater than that for any alternative procedure that is readily available locally that would produce the required diagnosis or therapeutic effect. (Note that it is possible for a type of practice that is not generically justified nevertheless to be clinically justified for an individual patient, e.g. some Administration of Radioactive Substances Advisory Committee (ARSAC) research certificates for new or unestablished procedures.)

2.4 All doses arising from diagnostic medical exposures must be kept ALARP, consistent with the intended purpose. This involves selecting equipment and methods that will optimise the exposure and ensuring that a procedure exists for assessing the consequent patient dose.

2.5 All therapeutic medical exposures must be individually planned, ensuring that doses of non-target organs are ALARP, consistent with the intended therapeutic purpose of the exposure.

The employer

2.6 The primary responsibility for providing a framework for radiation protection of the patient lies with the employer through the provision of employer's written procedures (see Appendix 1). The duties of the employer are clearly identified in IR(ME)R [3]and are consistent with clinical governance. The employer must make provision for clinical audit consistent with national and professional guidance. The employer's written procedures must clearly identify those individuals who are entitled to act as referrers, IR(ME)R practitioners, operators and MPE, and should also identify the range of practices for

---

1 For the purpose of this guidance, patient is used to indicate any person receiving a medical exposure.

which individuals take on the various roles. The employer must have up-to-date records of the training of IR(ME)R practitioners and operators.

2.7 Decisions on who is entitled to act as a referrer, IR(ME)R practitioner or operator should be taken by the employer following agreement at local level with the healthcare professionals involved in medical exposures.

2.8 Referrers who are registered medical or dental practitioners need not necessarily be identified as individuals in the employer's procedures, but may be identified as a professional group (e.g. orthopaedic surgeons, urology registrars, general practitioner (GP) practices). However, any person entitled to act as a referrer in accordance with the employer's procedures and who is not a registered medical or dental practitioner should be clearly identified by name in the employer's written procedures.

2.9 The employer should establish referral criteria for medical exposures and make these available to the referrers. In most cases these will be based on national and professional guidance and be agreed with those health professionals involved in medical exposures. For diagnostic radiology referrals, the Royal College of Radiologists (RCR) has published a booklet, *Making Best Use of a Department of Clinical Radiology,* that is a useful source document [29].

2.10 The employer should make adequate provision for the continuing education and training of all practitioners and operators identified under IR(ME)R [3]

2.11 The employer's written procedures should be sufficiently robust to ensure adequate co-operation and agreement between such persons as may be separately responsible for the justification (IR(ME)R practitioner) and optimisation (operator) of medical exposures. There should also be adequate co-operation and agreement between the referrer and the IR(ME)R practitioner.

2.12 When IR(ME)R practitioners and operators from different employers are involved in a medical exposure, their employers must provide evidence of adequate training to each other (and to the radiation employer if different). If duty holders believe that the employer's written procedures are inadequate they have a professional responsibility to bring this to the attention of the employer, preferably in writing.

2.13 The employer must have QA programmes for all standard operational procedures, e.g. patient identity, referral criteria conformance, training records, etc., in addition to those required for equipment performance under IRR99 [1] (see paragraphs 1.43 and 1.51).

2.14 Even in those types of practices where the employer is actually the IR(ME)R practitioner, and indeed perhaps also functions as the operator, e.g. a general dental practitioner, the appropriate written procedures must be established (see Appendix 1, point 40) and followed.

The referrer

2.15 The referrer must be '... a registered medical practitioner, dental practitioner or other health professional who is entitled ... to refer individuals for medical exposure to a practitioner ...' [3] under the employer's written procedures. Any patient group and range of diagnostic radiological examinations that may be referred by another health professional group must be clearly identified.

2.16 The referrer requesting the examination or treatment does so under a protocol that conforms to the employer's procedures and referral criteria. The request should be clear and legible and the following information must be supplied by the referrer:

(a) unique patient identification

(b) sufficient details of the clinical problem to allow the IR(ME)R practitioner to justify the medical exposure or an operator to authorise the exposure against justification guidelines produced by the IR(ME)R practitioner

(c) if applicable, information on the patient's menstrual status (possible pregnancy) and, if a nuclear medicine procedure is envisaged, whether the patient is breastfeeding, and

     (d) a signature uniquely identifying the referrer (which may be electronic if a radiology information system (RIS) is used).

     In addition, the referrer may indicate the examination that is thought to be appropriate.

2.17   Blank request cards, pre-signed by a referrer, are a breach of the employer's procedures with respect to referrals and should be identified by audit. Any entries on the request card made by others (e.g. patient identity, clinical details) should be checked and initialled by the referrer prior to signing the card.

The IR(ME)R practitioner

2.18   The IR(ME)R practitioner is defined as 'a registered medical practitioner, dental practitioner or other health professional who is entitled in accordance with the employer's procedures to take responsibility for an individual medical exposure' [3]. The primary responsibility of the IR(ME)R practitioner is to ensure the requested medical exposure is justified in accordance with the employer's written procedures. This practitioner may also provide the appropriate medical diagnosis or treatment prescription, although this is not an IR(ME)R practitioner function. IR(ME)R practitioners must be appropriately trained (see paragraph 2.73) and possess the necessary understanding and knowledge to interpret and apply:

     (a) the clinical information supplied by the referrer

     (b) the specific objectives of the requested procedure and its relevance to the individual involved

     (c) the potential benefit and detriment associated with the requested procedure, and

     (d) the efficacy, benefits and risks of suitable available alternative techniques involving less medical exposure.

2.19   The legal responsibility for justification always remains with the IR(ME)R practitioner. However, authorising that the exposure has been justified is a separate function, the responsibility for which can rest with the IR(ME)R practitioner or a suitably qualified operator who may authorise defined medical exposures against justification guidelines produced by the IR(ME)R practitioner.

2.20   It should be noted that the person responsible for authorisation (either the person who justified the exposure or an operator authorising against justification guidelines) may be someone other than the operator who subsequently carries out the exposure. For example, a senior radiographer may authorise but another radiographer may take the radiographs; in nuclear medicine, a physicist may authorise but a medical technologist may administer the radionuclide.

Radiotherapy

2.21   Treatment exposures are inextricably linked to the medical management of the patient. Justification of treatment exposures for an individual patient should be undertaken with due regard to a local site-specific treatment protocol. Normally there will be only one IR(ME)R practitioner for all the treatment exposures in any course of radiotherapy, and this is currently the clinical oncologist. However, in the future, as therapy radiographers develop competencies and experience within specific areas, they may be designated as IR(ME)R practitioners; these developments will need to be evidence-based.

2.22   In addition to treatment exposures, there are likely to be concomitant exposures and these too must be justified. Concomitant exposures are defined as all exposures within the course of radiotherapy other than the treatment exposures. These will include simulation, check simulation, computed tomography (CT) localisation and portal localisation and verification images (when these are additional to the treatment exposure). Concomitant exposures irradiate normal tissue outside the target volume or the intended path of the primary treatment beam and therefore contribute to the potential detriment to the patient.

2.23   The IR(ME)R practitioner responsible for the treatment exposures can justify the concomitant exposures at the outset or during the radiotherapy course, but in doing so must be aware of the likely exposures and the resulting dose so that the benefit and detriment can be assessed. This can be achieved by including likely concomitant exposures within site-specific protocols with a total effective dose agreed (e.g. 200 mSv). Where it is not practicable for the practitioner to authorise such exposures, IR(ME)R [3] allows for authorisation for individual patients against justification guidelines. This could be carried out by radiographers or other health professionals in accordance with local employer procedures.

2.24   Alternatively, concomitant exposures could be justified by another IR(ME)R practitioner, such as an experienced and appropriately trained radiographer or other health professional entitled by the employer to act as an IR(ME)R practitioner for these exposures and identified on the departmental list of IR(ME)R practitioners. This approach may provide additional flexibility, particularly where a patient's condition or response changes in an unanticipated manner and concomitant exposures that were not included in the site-specific protocol become necessary.

2.25   Whichever approach is adopted, it is important that departmentally agreed estimates of dose from all concomitant exposures are recorded in the relevant patient record; this is particularly important for children and young adults. The IR(ME)R practitioner for the treatment exposures may need to review the procedures, or the medical management of the patient, if the dose from concomitant exposures significantly exceeds that expected when the original justification was undertaken.

Clinical radiology

2.26   The IR(ME)R practitioner for diagnostic X-ray procedures is, in most cases, a clinical radiologist, but for specifically identified procedures may be an appropriately trained and experienced radiographer, orthopaedic surgeon, cardiologist, A&E consultant or other health professional, as identified in the employer's written procedures and agreed with the other health professionals involved in medical exposures. Some guidance is given by the RCR, *A Guide to Justification for Clinical Radiologists* [30].

2.27   The IR(ME)R practitioner justifies, and usually authorises, the medical exposure. The authorisation confirms that justification has taken place on the basis of the information included in the request and on the IR(ME)R practitioner's own knowledge, in accordance with the employer's written procedures. The method of authorisation (to demonstrate that justification has taken place) should be clearly specified by the employer in the employer's written procedures. An electronic signature is sufficient to authorise the procedure if this is stated in the employer's procedures.

2.28   For many standard diagnostic X-ray examinations, a suitably qualified operator may be identified as responsible for authorisations and will apply the pre-arranged procedures for justification provided by the IR(ME)R practitioner against the medical data included in the referral for an individual patient. The diagnostic examinations and the particular protocols to be followed should be agreed locally between the health professionals involved, to ensure a consistent approach, and then included in the employer's procedures.

Nuclear medicine

2.29   For radionuclide procedures, the ARSAC certificate holder is the practitioner, with responsibility for the administration of the radioactive medicinal product under MARS78 [5], MARS95 [6] as well as IR(ME)R [3]. For example, for radioiodine treatment of thyrotoxicosis, the ARSAC certificate holder (and therefore IR(ME)R practitioner) may be a nuclear medicine consultant, an oncologist, or perhaps an endocrinologist. To be an IR(ME)R practitioner for a particular radionuclide procedure at a specific site, the ARSAC certificate holder must have a current site-specific ARSAC certificate for that procedure. Although the IR(ME)R practitioner for radionuclide procedures is always the ARSAC certificate holder, it is possible for authorisation of routine diagnostic exposures to be carried out by a named health professional, such as a physicist, radiographer or medical technical officer, following pre-arranged procedures for authorisation as justified by the IR(ME)R practitioner.

The operator

2.30   The operator is any person who carries out any practical aspect of the medical exposure. The primary responsibility of the operator is to optimise those practical aspects of the exposure for which they are responsible, in accordance with the employer's written procedures.

2.31   The term 'practical aspect' covers a range of functions, each of which will have a direct influence on the medical exposure and can be separately identified. Therefore it is not only performing the medical exposure, but also undertaking any supporting aspects in the optimisation process. Some practical aspects are undertaken in the presence of the patient and are patient specific (e.g. administration of a radiopharmaceutical, performing the exposure, handling and use of radiological equipment), whilst other practical aspects are undertaken by other staff who are removed from the patient. These latter aspects are likely to be more equipment specific (e.g. calibration of equipment, preparation of radiopharmaceuticals, development of films).

2.32   All operators must be identified as specified in the employer's written procedures. For certain procedures, e.g. some fluoroscopic studies, interventional radiology and some nuclear medicine procedures, the person identified as an IR(ME)R practitioner may also be identified as an operator.

2.33   An operator must ensure that the patient is correctly identified, that the exposure has been authorised according to pre-arranged procedures and that, for female patients, their status regarding possible pregnancy is the same as that recorded on the request card. When the examination is completed (possibly by another operator), it should be signed off by the operator (this is not a legal requirement, but may avoid unnecessarily repeated examinations). Any additional information required to facilitate a retrospective estimation of the effective dose to the patient should be recorded. This should not normally be required where standard examination protocols have been followed.

2.34   In radiotherapy, nuclear medicine and diagnostic radiology, the many different operator tasks must be clearly identified, as must those persons qualified to undertake such tasks. To undertake new techniques, and use new equipment (including equipment on loan, paragraph 1.113), the employer must ensure that the operators are appropriately trained and the training should be supervised and documented.

2.35   In fluoroscopy, at least two different operators may be involved in undertaking the medical exposure – the radiologist who depresses the footswitch and the radiographer who changes the factors and adjusts the collimation are both performing operator functions. Operators must use their professional judgement to optimise the exposure for each patient, taking the appropriate radiographic views with the appropriate exposure factors.

2.36   In nuclear medicine, operator tasks which may be carried out by different professional groups include radiopharmaceutical preparation, administering radionuclides to the patient, imaging, image processing and analysis, and equipment QC.

2.37   An operator who administers a radiopharmaceutical acts under the written directions of the ARSAC certificate holder (see MARS95 [6]) and will need to be clearly identified in the employer's procedures under IR(ME)R [3].

2.38   In some circumstances, e.g. dental surgery, the employer, referrer, IR(ME)R practitioner and operator may be the same person. In this case, the dental practitioner must comply with all the duties placed on these duty holders.

2.39   Where significant changes to equipment have been made by a service engineer that may affect performance or dose, the outcome or effect of these changes should be checked where practicable by an operator before the equipment is brought into clinical use. This is both part of the normal equipment QA programme (routine performance tests) and part of the optimisation process (see also paragraph 1.51).

2.40   Service engineers are not normally considered to be operators, except where they have a contractual arrangement with the employer to perform additional commissioning tests post-servicing to demonstrate and confirm the acceptance of the equipment for clinical purposes to the employer. The employer should establish that the scope of the tests is suitable, that the service engineer is adequately trained for performing the tests, and that there are adequate communication arrangements with the other duty holders.

Medical physics expert

2.41   The MPE is defined as a state-registered clinical scientist with corporate membership of the IPEM (MIPEM) or equivalent and 6 years of appropriate experience in the clinical specialty.

2.42   There is a legal requirement on the employer that an MPE shall be:

(a) full-time contracted to the radiation employer and available at all times in radiotherapy practices

(b) available and contactable in nuclear medicine practices and clearly involved in certain circumstances (see Chapters 10 and 12), and

(c) available under contract and involved as appropriate in radiological practices, each as specified in the employer's written procedures.

2.43   In diagnostic radiology, the involvement of the MPE will be especially warranted in the following circumstances:

(a) where doses are known to be high, e.g. CT and interventional radiology
(b) for optimisation of doses for high risk groups such as infants
(c) for dose constraints in health screening
(d) for risk assessment in research proposals
(e) when new techniques are introduced or changes to practices or equipment are made, and
(f) when new or revised national or professional standards are introduced.

2.44   The role of the MPE is described in Appendix 5. This role includes some tasks additional to those duties required by IR(ME)R [3]. The MPE may also perform some operator duties. It should be noted that the RPA and QP (appointed under IRR99 [1]) may undertake some MPE duties, provided that they are competent to do so. This should be described and documented (see Appendices 4 and 5 for guidance).

Medical exposures committee

2.45   In large hospitals, as medical exposures involve many different professional groups and departments, it may be helpful if the employer establishes a Medical Exposures Committee (MEC) to review the employer's written procedures, particularly regarding justification and optimisation. Once the framework is established, these written procedures should be reviewed annually and documented accordingly.

2.46   However, the responsibility for establishing procedures remains with the employer. To reinforce this, the MEC should be part of the Clinical Governance management arrangements with a reporting route to the Chief Executive or Medical Director. In smaller hospitals, this committee may be part of the radiation protection committee, with relevant representation. The MEC can undertake other useful roles. For example, it could liaise closely with the Local Research Ethics Committee (LREC) for research proposals that include medical exposures, and review diagnostic reference levels.

Diagnostic reference levels

2.47   Diagnostic reference levels (DRLs) consistent with the appropriate diagnostic image quality should be established by the employer for standard sized patients undergoing:

(a) standard radiological investigations
(b) routinely undertaken interventional procedures, and
(c) nuclear medicine investigations.

2.48   DRLs should be expressed in easily recordable quantities which have a direct relevance to patient dose (screening time, milli ampere second (mAs), dose–area product (DAP), radionuclide activity, etc.) and should be set locally with due regard to regional, national (e.g. ARSAC for nuclear medicine) or European data. The level should be reviewed annually or when changes are made to equipment or procedures. While the concept of DRLs was not originally developed to be applied to individual patients, they can be an aid to optimisation for individual exposures. A particular example is fluoroscopic exposures in theatres, where knowledge of the DRL for the procedure can help to inform the surgeon undertaking the operation. If the DRL is exceeded during a given procedure, the operator should record the dose quantity and any contributing clinical factors (e.g. patient size, compliance, etc.).This will help to identify if DRLs are being consistently exceeded.

2.49   If DRLs are consistently exceeded for standard-sized patients there should be an investigation, followed by corrective action. If DRLs are never exceeded, they should still be reviewed and possibly revised downwards. If locally set DRLs are not relevant to local practice they will have little value as an optimisation tool.

2.50   The MPE in conjunction with the MEC should review DRLs on a yearly rolling programme. Patient dosimetry, imaging performance and QC measurements should be examined to identify the potential for dose and performance optimisation and a report made for the practitioners. This should be a component part of the dose reduction strategy and the imaging equipment replacement policy.

2.51   For periodic assessments of patient doses in diagnostic radiology as part of the QA programme (see IRR99 regulation 32(4)c [1]) it should be noted that the recommended frequency is at least once every 3 years.

Equipment

2.52   The IR(ME)R [3] require the employer to keep an equipment inventory which should list equipment that delivers ionising radiation to patients undergoing medical exposures and also equipment which directly controls, or which influences, the extent of the exposure. In nuclear medicine, the inventory should include imaging equipment and dose calibrators and, in diagnostic radiology and radiotherapy (see paragraph 8.5), all auxiliary equipment which can influence the exposure. This inventory should be distinct from the mandatory medical devices inventory but all radiation equipment should also be on the latter. Where practicable, the MDA structures and recommendations should be followed to avoid duplication and confusion. The MDA Device Bulletin 9801, section 7, lists a table of inventory fields [22].

2.53   For example, for general radiographic and fluoroscopic installations in diagnostic radiology, an inventory should identify the following components:

•   generator
•   tube stand
•   table
•   vertical bucky/chest stand
•   film processor, and
•   film-screen combination;

according to:

(a) type of equipment
(b) name of manufacturer
(c) model number
(d) serial number or other unique identifier
(e) year of manufacture
(f) year of installation
(g) location, and
(h) service agent.

It is recommended that complete, integral installations (e.g. dental/orthopantography (OPT), dual energy X-ray absorptiometry (DEXA) (see Appendix 19) and mobile units) be listed as a single component. For multi-component systems (e.g. a catheterisation laboratory) it is recommended that associated equipment and their reference codes be uniquely identified and listed as above [22].

2.54 All equipment involved in medical exposures must be subject to a QA programme. Any equipment faults should be recorded, as should the subsequent actions. In addition, the employer must establish and maintain appropriate checks and tests following maintenance and repair as advised in HSG226 [10] and Chapter 1.

Clinical evaluation report

2.55 There is a legal requirement that the outcome of the medical exposure (including factors relevant to the patient dose as appropriate) be recorded in accordance with the employer's procedures. This may be done electronically, with an electronic signature. It should be noted that the person who generates the diagnostic or therapeutic report is not defined in IR(ME)R [3], but should be identified in the employer's procedures. The DoH notes on good practice guidance for IR(ME)R state that 'if it is known prior to the exposure ... that no clinical evaluation will occur, then the exposure is not justified and should not take place' [4]. A system should be in place to ensure that clinical evaluations do occur.

2.56 An outcome of the examination must also be recorded for biopsy procedures and even for abandoned (discontinued) procedures.

Repeat exposures and repeat examinations

2.57 A repeat exposure due to patient movement or incorrect exposure factors should not normally need to be rejustified. However, repeated exposures should be recorded in both the QA programme (reject analysis) and the patient dose record and they should be reviewed and audited accordingly.

2.58 For repeat examinations where a complete examination has failed, whether due to human error or an equipment malfunction or defect, the incident should be recorded, investigated and reported to a senior member of staff, following departmental procedures (see Appendix 1). If the additional dose will contribute more than 10 mSv, the examination should be rejustified by an IR(ME)R practitioner.

Suspected radiation incident

2.59 The employer must establish and implement procedures for the investigation of radiation incidents caused by factors other than equipment failure, such as failure of procedures, failure to follow procedures or inappropriate professional judgement or human error. The employer must also establish and implement procedures for the notification of those radiation incidents where the radiation exposure was significantly greater than intended. The guidelines for incident notification under IR(ME)R [3] are set by the Health Departments but in most cases will be consistent with those for equipment malfunction or defect [10].

However, they will include advice on reporting of incidents involving radiation exposure when none was intended, as in the case of a mistaken identity. Procedures similar to those outlined in Chapter 1 (1.100 to 1.106) should be established and followed, with the involvement of the IR(ME)R practitioner and the operators concerned. Notifications should be made to the appropriate IR(ME)R inspectorate.

2.60   These procedures must include those radiation incidents that involve the unintended or accidental exposure of the fetus or a breastfed infant during a medical exposure. Such incidents are notifiable to the IR(ME)R Inspectorate if the exposure of the fetus or breastfed infant has not been included in the justification process and must be investigated under the employer's written procedures as part of normal audit and review. The fetus/infant has not undergone a medical exposure (the mother has), but has had an unintended or accidental exposure due to a failure in the employer's written procedures.

2.61   It is strongly advised that the procedures for the investigation of radiation incidents caused by human error should include medical exposures significantly lower than intended in radiotherapy, as these can also have serious consequences.

2.62   As a matter of good practice, the patient should be informed of any incident in accordance with the employer's procedures. It is normal practice to record any decision not to inform the patient (or his or her representative or guardian) in the patient's case notes.

Research

2.63   Guidance on the establishment, composition and functions of the LREC is provided by the Health Departments. Ideally, the LREC should have a radiation professional as a member or be able to co-opt such a person when dealing with submissions that involve medical exposure.

2.64   The primary legal responsibility lies with the employer to provide appropriate procedures for research that uses medical exposures. The IR(ME)R practitioner and operators are legally obliged to follow these procedures. All research programmes must be submitted to the LREC for approval before commencing, and the LREC should have appropriate guidance from the MEC for adherence to the employer's written procedures. ICRP62 *Radiological Protection in Biomedical Research* [31] provides valuable and authoritative advice on categories of risk and benefit for biomedical research projects (see also Appendix 10).

2.65   Where there is no direct medical benefit to the individual from the exposure, the employer must establish dose constraints that should not be exceeded. Where some benefit to the patient is expected from experimental diagnostic or therapeutic practices, individual target levels of doses are set by the IR(ME)R practitioner, such that the benefit outweighs the detriment and excessive doses are avoided.

2.66   Generic risk assessments can be performed to help inform the LREC about the risks of the exposure. As all individuals involved in research studies do so on a voluntary basis, the risks associated with the exposure must be communicated to the volunteers. This requirement should be included in the employer's procedures, but in practice this might be carried out by the referrer or research co-ordinator and confirmed by the operator.

2.67   If the IR(ME)R practitioner or operator suspects that the employer's procedures for research have not been strictly followed, they should not proceed with the medical exposure and should inform the MEC, LREC and the research co-ordinator. If appropriate, an investigation should be conducted, documented and reported accordingly by the MEC.

2.68   For research involving radionuclides or therapy procedures with sealed or unsealed sources, the IR(ME)R practitioner must have a current site-specific ARSAC research certificate for the specified procedure. This applies to all diagnostic procedures that are performed solely for the research protocol, even if this type of examination is performed routinely in other circumstances on other patients for diagnostic purposes.

2.69   The number of volunteers required for each project should be sufficient for statistical purposes and not exceed that number. Each volunteer should be examined medically prior to the project to determine suitability.

2.70   Pregnant women and children should not be accepted as volunteers unless the project concerns their condition specifically. In normal circumstances, adults who lack the capacity to consent should be excluded as volunteers. Healthy volunteers who have taken part in any other research projects involving medical exposure during the previous year may be included, if an annual dose constraint is not exceeded.

Information and instructions for nuclear medicine patients

2.71   Patients undergoing treatment or diagnosis with radioactive medicinal products must be appropriately informed about precautions to be taken to protect those around them. The IR(ME)R practitioner has the duty to identify the most appropriate person to whom information about the risks of ionising radiation should be given. In routine practice, this task is frequently delegated to the operator.

2.72   If written instructions are required, they should be given prior to the patient leaving the department, in accordance with the employer's procedures. Although the primary responsibility lies with the employer to ensure that this is performed, the task may be delegated to an operator as identified in the written procedures. Generic risk assessments, performed by the IR(ME)R practitioner in conjunction with the MPE and RPA as appropriate, should be documented and available to support this advice. Specific risk assessments will be needed in non-routine circumstances. Written instructions and information should be reviewed at least every 3 years (see Chapter 15).

Training

2.73   IR(ME)R practitioners and operators must be adequately trained health professionals and should not perform tasks, without appropriate supervision, for which they have not been adequately trained.

2.74   Training requirements (including practical experience) are agreed by the professional colleges and other health professional bodies. The IR(ME)R notes on good practice give some scope for employer-defined competency in identifying operators, but IR(ME)R practitioners and operators themselves should conform to the standards and requirements of the relevant professional bodies given in Appendix 16.

2.75   Current training records for all IR(ME)R practitioners and operators should be kept by the employer separately from general personal records, be available for inspection, and kept for periods consistent with Health Departments' guidance on retention of records (see Appendix 9). These records should be maintained, for example, by the personnel/human resources department. Training records should include continuing education records.

2.76   There should be adequate communication, of the training records required under IR(ME)R, between employers when staff of one employer work in the establishment of another employer.

3 Diagnostic (other than dental) and interventional radiology

Scope

3.1   This chapter contains guidance on radiation protection in diagnostic radiology, other than in dentistry, and in interventional radiology. It covers all applications of X-rays in radiography, fluoroscopy, CT and bone densitometry. For convenience, the subject of the X-ray examination is referred to as 'the patient' in this guidance, where this term also includes an individual undergoing medical exposure for health screening, a volunteer in a medical research project and an individual exposed for a medicolegal purpose. The guidance also applies when diagnostic X-ray equipment is used for the training of radiographers, in research including that for the optimisation of examination techniques, for examinations of corpses and pathological specimens, and when it is in fact used for purposes other than for diagnostic examinations, training or research, such as testing or measuring the radiation output in a clinical environment.

Principles of radiation protection

3.2   For medical exposures in diagnostic radiology, applying the radiation protection principles, as required by IR(ME)R [3], of justification, optimisation and dose limitation indicates, amongst other issues, that:

(a)   a radiological examination should be carried out only after the medical exposure has been justified, and

(b)   each exposure should be optimised so that all patient radiation doses during X-ray examinations are kept ALARP, consistent with the intended clinical objective.

Roles and responsibilities in radiology

3.3   Employers must develop referral criteria for all their normal X-ray investigations. The RCR booklet, *Making the Best Use of a Department of Clinical Radiology* [29], may help departments define their criteria and advice is available from other professional bodies (e.g. the Royal College of Physicians for bone mineral densitometry). Referrers should be informed of the criteria that apply to the investigations they may request, including information on radiation doses and associated risks, particularly for use in the case of child patients, or female patients who might be pregnant. The information should be given to referrers in writing but could also be disseminated through appropriate training and update sessions.

3.4   The referrer in the radiology process will usually be a medical practitioner or other health professional. The referrer should provide sufficient information about the patient, including past X-ray examinations, for the IR(ME)R practitioner to decide if radiology is the appropriate diagnostic (or interventional) method for the patient. Referrers should be identified in the employer's procedures.

3.5   IR(ME)R practitioners must take information supplied by the referrer into account when justifying examinations. Referrals should be clear and unambiguous and the IR(ME)R practitioner should consult the referrer if insufficient clinical information has been provided to enable them to justify the examination. Relevant clinical information may include previous diagnostic information, medical records, images from other investigations and, for a female patient, whether she is known to be or could possibly be pregnant. Employers should have adequate systems to provide practitioners with previous images. Referrers should discuss requests not covered by the normal referral criteria directly with the IR(ME)R practitioner.

3.6 Clinical radiologists will usually be IR(ME)R practitioners and have the responsibility to authorise medical exposures. For a defined scope, another health professional can undertake the duty of an IR(ME)R practitioner when so designated and identified under local arrangements. For example, some radiographers will be IR(ME)R practitioners.

3.7 The IR(ME)R practitioner should:

(a) assess the information provided by the referrer and if necessary ask for more information from the referrer

(b) decide if diagnostic or interventional radiology is an appropriate modality for the patient, and

(c) justify in writing (see paragraph 3.8) the medical exposures necessary for the diagnosis or intervention.

3.8 All examinations must be justified by an IR(ME)R practitioner and authorised either by the IR(ME)R practitioner or an operator who is delegated the task of authorising exposures under pre-arranged procedures and following prescribed justification guidelines produced by the IR(ME)R practitioner. Employer's procedures should be designed to assist IR(ME)R practitioners with justification, particularly:

(a) in the case of medicolegal exposures
(b) where the exposure is part of medical research, and
(c) where a female referred for abdominal or pelvic investigations may be pregnant.

3.9 Before an examination can proceed, it is necessary to record that it has been justified. This may be recorded by the IR(ME)R practitioner, e.g. by signing an appropriate box on the request form which then authorises the examination. Alternatively, when justification is made through a pre-arranged procedure, radiographers who are clinical practitioners are likely to have the responsibility as IR(ME)R operators to authorise many diagnostic exposures by recording that the request complies with that procedure. An employer's procedures may also require operators to record on the request form that other checks have been performed for individual patients, e.g. patient identification and whether female patients may be pregnant.

3.10 Clinical radiologists will often undertake medical exposures and other related practical aspects, and as such will be designated as IR(ME)R operators. Radiographers who are clinical practitioners will usually be IR(ME)R operators. Physicists and medical technologists will need to be designated as IR(ME)R operators if they undertake equipment-specific practical aspects which may affect the medical exposure, rather than the patient-specific aspects.

3.11 All staff involved in the practical aspects of medical exposures (operators) must be adequately trained (see paragraph 2.10) and competent to operate their equipment. They should be aware of all the safety features and warning devices that may affect the exposure to the patient (and staff), including emergency off-switches. They should also know how to use any particular features of a piece of equipment that enhance patient dose reduction and exposure optimisation, such as selection of additional beam filtration or using pulsed fluoroscopy.

3.12 Operators are directly responsible for the practical aspects of a medical exposure that they perform. In addition to following the employer's procedures and protocols, they should optimise the exposure by selecting the practical methods and, where possible, the equipment to ensure that the necessary diagnostic information is obtained for the lowest dose to the patient. They should clearly understand the extent of their own responsibilities in order to avoid accidental overexposure of the patient. A trainee operator must be supervised by one who is adequately trained in those practical aspects.

3.13 MPEs in radiology (see paragraphs 2.41 to 2.44) should be available to make measurements and provide advice on dosimetry and equipment performance as described in this and the following chapter (also see Appendix 5). They should be capable of providing advice on all aspects of patient dosimetry, including dosimetry assessments in a research proposal, on the optimisation and safety of diagnostic exposures, on the QA programme (including QC procedures) and on any other matters relating to the safety of the equipment or procedure. An MPE should also be consulted before complex interventional techniques are introduced, or specialised services such as paediatrics or a screening programme is proposed. MPEs may also be responsible for the acceptance testing of new or modified radiology equipment, its commissioning and its calibration. The MPE may be involved with the local RPA in the evaluation of the critical examination results (of the installation of new or modified equipment) supplied by the installer. A list of MPEs should be available in the radiology department or service.

3.14   The RPA for the radiology services should have appropriate experience in the application of radiation protection principles in radiology. The RPA should be consulted on all matters specified in IRR99 schedule 5 [1] relevant to the radiology department (see Appendix 4). Management should ensure that all controlled areas within the areas to be used for radiology, and, if appropriate, supervised areas, have local rules for the use of ionising radiation appropriate for the equipment and practices to be used. This should be ensured through regular audit, and review with the RPA. The RPA may be the same person as the MPE, though it should be recognised that their roles are separate and distinct.

3.15   A sufficient number of RPSs should be appointed to ensure that all staff members are aware of the local rules and that the local rules are observed. The RPSs can also provide a communication channel with the RPA (see Appendix 3).

Structural aspects of a radiology facility

3.16   In hospitals, all X-ray examinations should be carried out in a purpose-built facility whenever practicable (such as a diagnostic radiology department or dedicated facility for cardiac catheterisation, mammography or population screening). Sometimes, the condition of the patient may make it necessary for the examination to be carried out elsewhere, e.g. in a ward or in an operating theatre. Entrances to radiology departments and doors of X-ray rooms should be wide enough to allow beds to pass through (see paragraphs 3.94 to 3.98 regarding examinations carried out in wards using mobile or portable equipment).

3.17   All X-ray rooms should include features to avoid unnecessary exposure to the room occupants. In general, X-ray rooms should have a lead screen incorporating lead glass or acrylic viewing panels, to protect the operators whilst still enabling them to have a clear view of the patient whilst the exposure takes place. Where staff are not shielded by a fixed or mobile screen, they should be able to stand at a large enough distance from patient and equipment to minimise exposure, and adequate protective clothing should be provided. If necessary, the room design should allow easy access for ancillary equipment, e.g. a bed or anaesthetic trolley. IPEM79 [19] and *Radiation Shielding for Diagnostic X-rays* [32] give information on X-ray room shielding.

3.18   Protected areas should normally be provided for staff at all control panels such that the radiation dose received there by a person not wearing protective clothing is not significant (normally an annual dose of less than 1 mSv should be attainable). Protective aprons and screens, including any lead glass or acrylic, should be marked with the lead equivalent thickness at an appropriate kilovoltage (kV).

3.19   An X-ray room should not be used for more than one radiological procedure at a time unless the room has been designed and built with this possibility in mind. Examples include cardiology 'swing labs', resuscitation rooms and dedicated dual table intravenous pyelography (IVP) rooms. In this case, there should be some means (e.g. a protective panel separating parts of the room) to ensure that there is no significant additional exposure, either of one patient from radiography of another or of staff from examinations in which they themselves are not engaged.

3.20   If the structure of the X-ray room does not provide adequate shielding to persons in adjacent areas, the room configuration and working practices should be arranged so that:

(a)   the radiation beam is directed away from those areas (see paragraph 3.41), and

(b)   the residual beam and scattered radiation are absorbed close to the X-ray image receptor (e.g. film or image intensifier) and patient, or appropriate protective material is applied as necessary to the floor, ceiling, walls, windows and doors.

3.21   The room should not constitute a throughway from one place to another except in emergencies. Dark rooms and processing areas should have separate access. However, in small departments access from an X-ray room when radiography is not in progress may be acceptable, although not desirable.

3.22   Parts of the X-ray equipment, or mobile or ceiling-mounted protective screens, may be used to absorb scattered radiation and attenuate the residual beam close to the image receptor and patient.

3.23   The radiation warning symbol and recommended forms of words for the signs on an X-ray room door are shown in Appendix 12.

3.24   A warning notice and visible X-ray warning signal are required at all entrances to the X-ray room. The warning signal should be red, positioned to be clearly visible and illuminated during the warning period. The significance of the warning should be self-evident or be stated in a notice (e.g. 'Do not enter when the red light is on'; see Appendix 12). The signal should normally operate when the tube is in the preparation stage, which for the purposes of a room warning corresponds to the state of readiness, and should continue while radiation is emitted. Illuminated signs and lights should give an immediate indication of exposure status, by using filament bulbs rather than fluorescent tubes, for example.

3.25   The visible X-ray warning signal may be combined with an illuminated sign to indicate the temporary presence of a controlled area. These signals should be distinct and separately visible with the significance of each clearly stated in a notice (see paragraph 3.24 and Appendix 12).

3.26   Some types of equipment do not have a well-defined preparation stage, e.g. fluoroscopy and some CT and mammography sets. In these situations the room entrance warning signals should operate during the period of X-ray emission only.

3.27   A visible warning signal is advised when a mobile image intensifier is permanently used in one location, e.g. a cardiac pacing room, endoscopy suite, etc. Where it is not possible to wire the signal directly into the mobile unit, it should be connected into a mains socket dedicated to the mobile image intensifier. The warning signal is activated manually whenever the unit is connected to the mains or, if a current sensitive relay is installed, when the unit is emitting X-rays.

Equipment, installation, maintenance and quality assurance

3.28   Radiation protection aspects of X-ray equipment are covered in this section and, in addition, paragraph 1.113 applies to X-ray equipment that is on loan. Standards that are related to X-ray equipment design and European Community/Communitè Europèen (CE) marking requirements are referred to in paragraph 4.2.

3.29   New radiological installations require a critical examination to ensure that safety features and warning devices function correctly and that the radiation protection arrangements for the installation are satisfactory (see IPEM79 [19]). The critical examination is the responsibility of the installer and must be performed following consultation with an RPA. The installer and purchaser should identify who will perform the examination before the equipment is purchased. The components of the critical examination (see Table 1.1) and the results should be communicated to the purchaser, who should consult the RPA as to their adequacy. Before radiological equipment enters clinical use, it should undergo acceptance testing to ensure that it operates safely and performs to specification. Further commissioning tests should aim to provide baseline results for subsequent QA tests and should assess different patient dose and image quality options to inform users of the optimum settings [10].

3.30   All X-ray departments should undertake QA to ensure the continual production of optimum quality images with the minimum necessary dose to the patient. QA programmes should include checks and test measurements on all parts of the imaging system, at appropriate time intervals, with clear action levels for notification, corrective action and suspension. Representative measurements should be made of the doses administered to persons undergoing medical exposures. The RPA and MPE should be consulted about the form of a suitable programme. Guidance is provided in IPEM77 [20] and the *National Protocol for Patient Dose Measurements in Diagnostic Radiology* [23]. Departments should appoint a QA co-ordinator to supervise in-house QA and to co-ordinate this with service and maintenance work together with radiation surveys and performance testing. Routine equipment testing (QC) should involve a broad cross-section of department staff, rather than being the responsibility of a few individuals. The QA co-ordinator, with help from a QA group in larger departments, should monitor the effectiveness of the QA programme and make improvements as appropriate. (Other guidance on QA is given in IPEM32 *Measurement of the Performance Characteristics of Diagnostic X-Ray Systems* [33] and HSG226 [10]). The functioning of warning devices should also be checked regularly.

3.31   All equipment should be maintained to the specification and at the frequency recommended by the manufacturer. Regular maintenance and routine QC is particularly important on systems where dose is controlled automatically (e.g. image intensifiers and radiographic AEC), where image brightness or optical density is not dose limited (e.g. computed radiography), and on collimation and beam alignment systems.

3.32   A record of maintenance including QA should be kept for each item of X-ray equipment. This record should include information on any defects found by users (fault log), interim remedial action taken (e.g. changes to AEC sensitivity settings), subsequent repairs made and results of testing before equipment is reintroduced to clinical use [10]. For fluoroscopic and radiographic AEC systems, the record should include details of the set and measured levels of the air kerma (rate) at the image receptor associated with the various control settings.

3.33   A person who carries out modifications or maintenance which could affect the radiation dose to patients or staff, or affects image quality, should immediately inform the RPS or other delegated responsible person before the equipment is returned to clinical use. Where this is not possible, e.g. when the work is performed out-of-hours, a notice drawing attention to the modification or maintenance should be attached to the equipment. In all cases, a clear written report of the changes and current operational status should be given, including the name of the person concerned and the date, either in the maintenance log or in the form of a hand-over questionnaire. This should include details of any changes affecting dose or image quality that may require further measurements.

3.34   After work affecting equipment performance, as described in paragraph 3.33, the RPS (or other delegated responsible person) should seek advice from the MPE. The MPE will decide whether the changes are sufficient to require a survey of the performance and safety of the equipment, possibly after consulting the RPA. Any testing required by the in-house QA programme should be performed before the equipment is returned to clinical use.

3.35   As a result of these changes, the RPS (or other delegated responsible person) may need to alter operating procedures, equipment exposure protocols or local rules. The RPS should inform users of these changes. Revised assessments of representative patient doses may also be required (see paragraph 3.30).

3.36   All staff involved in maintaining and testing X-ray equipment should take care to avoid exposing themselves to the radiation beam or to scatter from test objects. In particular, they should avoid exposing their hands to the beam while performing beam alignment procedures or QA tests on image intensifiers. Whenever practicable, mobile equipment should be maintained and tested in adequately shielded X-ray rooms. If this is not practicable, a temporary controlled area should be designated, with suitable measures to restrict access to the area.

Protection of staff and members of the public

3.37   Only those persons whose presence is essential should remain in an X-ray room when radiation is being generated; they should stand well away from the radiation beam and preferably behind a protective screen.

3.38   Any person not behind protective screens should wear appropriate protective clothing unless the RPA has assessed that it is unnecessary. He or she should also stand away from the patient unless this requirement is not clinically practicable. These measures are particularly important in operating theatres and with cardiological and interventional procedures, where there may be several people in the room and where close proximity of protective devices might interfere with the procedure. Staff should not expose parts of their body, even if protected, to the unattenuated primary beam (see paragraph 3.117). Staff should also be aware of the sources and direction of scattered radiation, so that they can occupy areas of least exposure. In general, the greatest intensity of scattered radiation will be from the side of the patient directly exposed to radiation (backscatter) rather than from the side nearest to the image receptor.

3.39   Particular care is needed when performing examinations with multiple projections, such as with C-arm systems, and other systems where the extremities may be close to the incident X-ray beam or greater intensity of scattered radiation. In such cases, there is an obvious requirement for an appropriate and rigorous extremity monitoring programme, and the advice of the RPA must be sought.

3.40   The doors of X-ray rooms should be closed during examinations and equipment testing. It may be appropriate to lock certain X-ray room doors, to prevent unauthorised entry where the door is remote from the operator (e.g. CT) and outside their immediate field of view.

3.41   The radiation beam size should be kept to a minimum in order to limit patient dose and reduce scattered radiation. The beam should be directed away from adjacent occupied areas if they are not protected by adequate primary shielding. The unshielded primary beam should not be directed at protected areas of the control panel or mobile protective screens.

3.42   Children or weak or anaesthetised patients sometimes need to be supported for radiography. Wherever possible mechanical devices should be used to ensure immobilisation. If these devices cannot be used, care should be taken to ensure that the same member of staff is not used to support patients on every occasion. Any person supporting a patient should have adequate instruction and be informed of the level of risk involved. Employers must make suitable arrangements to provide this information. If appropriate, the person supporting the patient should wear protective clothing. A record should be kept of those holding patients and, where possible, a suitable dosemeter used to measure dose to the relevant part of the body. Alternatively, if such a device is not available, details of the examination, including the positioning of the person supporting, should be recorded to enable a retrospective dose to be calculated. Protection arrangements for hospital carers who regularly hold patients should be defined in the local rules. Particular attention should be given to the arrangements for staff from paediatric wards.

3.43   In the case of child patients, their parents or another comforter or carer (see paragraph 1.72) may hold them. Comforters and carers must be informed of the risks beforehand and must be properly protected. The protection arrangements for restricting or monitoring the exposure to carers should be based on a documented risk assessment for each type of procedure. These should be agreed in advance with the RPA.

3.44   Pregnant women should not be permitted to hold patients being X-rayed unless absolutely necessary and then only if based on a satisfactory risk assessment.

3.45   Patients and their carers, or any other persons, e.g. contractors, porters, cleaners, etc., should not be left unattended in an X-ray room, unless the equipment has been left in a 'safe' condition, where the single-step activation of hand or foot exposure switches will not produce X-rays.

Protection of the patient

3.46   The beam should not be directed towards parts of the body other than those to be examined, especially avoiding the gonads and female breast, unless this is essential to the conduct of the examination. This should be borne in mind in examination of the limbs, especially of the hands with the patient in the sitting position. In the latter case the use of lead sheeting or a lead apron on the tabletop is desirable.

3.47   For all children, and for persons of reproductive capacity, gonad shields should be used in examinations which are likely to give a significant gonad dose, unless these shields interfere with the proposed examination.

3.48   For women known or likely to be pregnant, where the examination has been justified on the basis of clinical urgency and involves irradiation of the abdomen, operators must optimise the technique to minimise irradiation of an actual or potential fetus. Radiography of areas remote from the fetus, e.g. the chest, skull or hand, may be carried out safely at any time during pregnancy as long as good beam collimation (see paragraph 3.49) and properly shielded equipment is used.

3.49   Strict limitation of field size (or of irradiated length in CT) to the area necessary for the particular examination should be routinely practised. It is important particularly with children that the field should be restricted to the essential area and should always be smaller than the detector size to confirm collimation (excepting at the chest wall in mammography). When the equipment incorporates cassette sensors to provide automatic collimation, operators should confirm and optimise collimation using a light beam, if available. All radiographic and fluoroscopic automatic sensing and collimation systems, particularly those with pre- and post-patient collimation, should be subject to routine QC and regular maintenance to ensure their correct operation (see paragraphs 3.31 and 3.32).

3.50   Poor collimation in both radiography and fluoroscopy as well as in CT (see paragraph 4.15) leads to unnecessary irradiation of the patient as well as to increased scattered radiation. Automatic collimation to the image receptor and limitation of the beam by adjustable collimators such as LBDs will largely eliminate one of the major sources of unnecessary radiation (see paragraphs 4.12 to 4.15). With fluoroscopy, laser positioning and 'virtual collimation' devices should be used if available, to enable 'radiation free' positioning and collimation.

3.51   The direction in which the radiation passes through the patient should be optimised, since it can greatly influence the distribution of absorbed dose to sensitive organs. For example, posteroanterior (PA) (rather than anteroposterior (AP)) projections of the chest and left (rather than right) lateral lumbar spine views (left side of patient nearest film) on adult patients can reduce the effective dose from these examinations by 30–40 per cent (Nicholson *et al.* [34]). Also the use of PA rather than AP projections of the skull will reduce dose to the lens of the eye.

3.52   Similarly, in CT, for scanners employing 'overscan' in standard axial mode, if this overscan occurs at constant angular position, the patient should be appropriately positioned to minimise dose to sensitive organs.

3.53   Human subjects must not be used for training in radiography and for optimising new examination techniques or imaging technology, such as digital radiography. Anthropomorphic phantoms and test objects should be used where appropriate.

Diagnostic reference levels

3.54   The employer must establish DRLs for normal X-ray examinations. These may be based on the representative patient doses measured within the QA programme (see paragraph 3.30), but should also take account of relevant national and European reference levels. The dose quantity used for the DRL should be appropriate to the type of equipment and examination. For example, entrance surface dose would be appropriate for simple radiographs and could be determined on the basis of exposure factors and standard procedures; whereas DAP could be more appropriate for more complex examinations. Fluoroscopic exposure duration might be a suitable DRL quantity for fluoroscopy examinations using equipment that has no other form of dose indication. Likewise, weighted computed tomography dose index ($CTDI_w$) and dose–length product (DLP) may be used in CT (see paragraph 4.40). An MPE should be asked to advise on the appropriate quantities and values for DRLs.

3.55   Where examinations using a particular X-ray unit or performed by an individual operator regularly exceed the appropriate DRL, this should be brought to the attention of the operator and IR(ME)R practitioner and the reason should be investigated. Consequent corrective action might involve improvements to equipment performance, additional operator training or reassessment of the DRL. Local DRLs should be reviewed regularly in the light of current practice and also be compared periodically with current national and European reference levels where these exist. A more extensive review of radiographic practice and technique is required if local DRLs exceed these guideline levels for an examination.

Female patients

3.56   Female patients aged between 12 and 55 years (see ARSAC *Notes for Guidance* [35], or within an age range defined in the employer's procedures) having an examination of the lower abdomen or pelvis should be asked if there is any possibility of pregnancy. The responsibility for this action should be defined within the employer's 'pregnancy enquiry' procedure, but would normally be that of the referrer or IR(ME)R practitioner and be confirmed by the operator. The action, response and the decision to proceed or otherwise should be recorded, as required by the employer's procedures. If pregnancy is suspected, the practitioner must consider this information specifically before authorising that the examination can proceed. This includes cases where justification has previously been made through a pre-arranged procedure. Notices (with translations into the common local languages) should also be displayed in X-ray departments to alert patients to the importance of informing radiographers if they may be pregnant.

3.57   The procedures for identifying possibly pregnant patients should include a policy covering examinations that may give a dose to the fetus in excess of some tens of milligray (mGy). Such situations may indicate deferment of the examination to within a period of 10 days following the onset of menstruation, when conception is unlikely to have occurred, often known as the 'Ten Day Rule'. Further guidance on managing examinations for patients who are or may be pregnant is given in *Advice on Exposure to Ionising Radiation During Pregnancy* [36].

Radiography

3.58   Exposure factors and the selection of receptor (e.g. table or bucky stand) should be checked by the operator on each occasion before an examination is performed. AEC devices should be used where possible as an aid to the achievement of consistent radiographs and the reduction of repeat exposures. Where AEC devices are used the operator should be aware of the typical ranges of post-exposure mAs values for the projections undertaken. Where anatomically programmed radiography is used, the operator should check that the programmed factors are suitable for the individual patient, and that appropriate guard mAs values are programmed for each examination, to minimise the likelihood of excessive exposure in the event of equipment malfunction.

3.59   Protocols for each type of radiographic examination carried out in an X-ray room should be displayed in the room. These should be specific to the particular room. If more than one X-ray tube may be used to carry out a particular X-ray examination in a room, separate protocols should be defined for each piece of equipment. The protocol should include information on film-focus distance, radiographic exposure factors, receptor speed and selection of equipment options, e.g. AEC, for each radiographic projection.

3.60   The X-ray exposure should be controlled from the control panel, and the exposure switch should be so situated that the operator cannot leave the protected area during the exposure. Protective lead glass or lead acrylic screens should be installed in front of the control panel such that they give adequate protection for the operators for all the examinations intended in that room. Where this cannot be done, the local rules should specify alternative protective arrangements that should be followed. In such cases, staff not behind protective panels should wear protective clothing.

3.61   The operator should always have a clear view of the patient and any entrance to the X-ray room.

3.62   The imaging system should be chosen to ensure that patient doses are kept ALARP, consistent with the production of the required diagnostic information. Doses to patients and staff should be reduced by using low attenuation materials such as carbon fibre in ancillary equipment, e.g. tables, grids and cassettes, and fast receptors (e.g. 400+ speed class film-screen systems) should be used wherever clinically acceptable.

3.63   The measured value of the patient dose quantity as identified in the employer's local procedures should be recorded for each radiograph. Where a standard exposure protocol has been followed, no further information need be recorded other than an indication that the protocol was followed. The incorporation of information relating to exposure factor selection for patients with non-standard body part thickness into the radiographic protocols (see paragraph 3.59) will facilitate the process of dose recording and aid in the identification of incidents of any exposure suspected of being significantly greater than intended (see paragraph 1.100).

3.64   In advance of the procedure taking place, where practicable, patients should be given adequate instructions as to what is expected of them for their part in the examination, in terms of positioning, breath holding, etc. This may be in the form of verbal advice or a written card with instructions in an appropriate language.

3.65   Optimum processing of the film is very important to produce good quality radiographs. This will improve interpretation and reduce the number of repeat examinations. The MPE should ensure that the processor performance is optimised with respect to speed and contrast indices at commissioning prior to being put into clinical use. Manufacturer's advice should be followed concerning developer temperature and replenishment rates, adjustment for type of film and workload, chemistry storage and disposal.

3.66   Attention should be paid to film viewing conditions. The use of low ambient light, masking of uncovered parts of the illuminator and the matching of fluorescent tubes in terms of light output and colour temperature are recommended.

3.67   Dedicated equipment should always be used for mammography. The total filtration should never be less than the equivalent of 0.5 mm aluminium (e.g. 0.03 mm molybdenum). As some modern equipment may incorporate systems that automatically change the factors (e.g. filter, anode material and kVp) during the patient exposure to optimise either the mean glandular tissue dose or the contrast rendition, the users should be aware of and understand these systems (if used clinically).

3.68   The focal spot to skin distance should never be less than 30 cm for any X-ray examination including oblique views in cardiology, and preferably not less then 45 cm when stationary equipment is used. For radiography of the chest, the distance should not be less than 60 cm.

3.69   Protection of the lens of the patient's eye by lead or lead-containing shields may sometimes be required in cerebral angiography. Lead eye shields should be specifically designed for that purpose and should be covered, e.g. plastic coated. The advice of the MPE should be sought.

Digital radiography

3.70   Digital radiographic equipment, in particular computed radiography (photostimulable phosphor radiography) and direct digital radiography, allows images to be produced over a very wide range of dose per image. Regular QA tests on this equipment should include measurements of dose per image for all commonly used sets of programmed exposure factors. Operators should be aware of the doses per image set and of the particular requirement to keep doses ALARP on this type of equipment, which is normally capable of operating at much higher doses per image than are necessary for the production of clinically acceptable images.

3.71   Exposure factors should be chosen according to local protocols, as the operator may have no indication from the image as to whether the exposure is 'correct' or not. Operators should be aware that exposure factors and techniques suitable for film/screen radiography may not translate well to digital or computed radiography; a full optimisation exercise should be carried out when establishing local protocols. The advice of an MPE should be sought at this stage.

Fluoroscopy

3.72   Fluoroscopy should be carried out only when indicated by the examination protocol, usually when radiography alone is not expected to provide the required information, e.g. in dynamic studies. Fluoroscopy should never be used as an aid to patient positioning for radiography.

3.73   Fluoroscopic equipment should be under the direct control of an adequately trained operator. The operator should communicate to others in the room in a clear and unambiguous manner when he or she is about to initiate an exposure and when it has terminated. This will enable the other persons to position themselves to ensure that their doses are ALARP.

3.74   Fluoroscopic examinations involving the use of directly viewed fluorescent screens are not justified and are therefore prohibited.

3.75   The use of fluoroscopic equipment not fitted with an automatic dose rate control system should be limited to specific justified circumstances only.

3.76   Fluoroscopy should be conducted for short periods rather than continuously if this is clinically and technically feasible. Total fluoroscopy dose can be reduced by effective use of last image hold and cineloop replay features, low dose rate and pulsed fluoroscopy options where these are available. Under no circumstance should the X-ray tube be energised when the person carrying out the examination is not looking at the display monitor as this could involve the irradiation of the patient without attaining any diagnostic information.

3.77   Full use should be made of DAP indication or some other appropriate dose indication (e.g. skin dose) and displayed exposure time to limit patient dose. Display of the DAP and time of operation on the television monitor can also help to reduce the patient exposure time. Operators should monitor these values during each procedure in relation to the diagnostic reference level for that examination. The accumulated DAP and/or exposure time should be recorded for each patient.

3.78   It is recommended that the absorbed dose rate at the skin of a standard patient (20 cm water) should not exceed 100 mGy min^{-1} for all available field sizes in any available fluoroscopy mode. Remedial action is required where the skin entrance dose rate exceeds 50 mGy min^{-1} for the largest available image intensifier field of view for a standard patient (20 cm water). Guidance on the skin entrance dose rates at which adequate image quality should be achievable for modern X-ray image intensifier systems is available [37].

3.79   As a guideline, the skin entrance dose rate for a standard patient (20 cm water) should not normally exceed the values tabulated in Table 3.1 (Martin *et al.* [37]). Measurement and consideration of the skin entrance dose/frame in digital angiography and/or digital cinecardiography, and the maximum obtainable skin entrance dose rates in fluoroscopy, should also be included in the commissioning and optimisation process.

Table 3.1 Guideline skin entrance dose rate limits

Image intensifier field size (cm)	Guideline skin entrance dose rate limit (mGy min^{-1})		
	Dose setting		
	Low	Normal	High
< 20		50	
20–30	< 0.5 × normal	35	< 1.5 × normal
> 30		25	

3.80   Where the automatic dose rate control system features user selectable kV versus mA curves, the optimum curve should be chosen for the examination, e.g. iodine or barium curves for examinations involving the use of contrast media. The operator should be aware of the relative dose rates provided by the available automatic settings and should employ the lowest dose rate consistent with the clinical objective. The values of the intensifier input and skin entrance dose rates should be recorded in the equipment maintenance and QA records (see paragraph 3.32). If manually controlled systems are employed, the dose rates corresponding to the manual fluoroscopic factors used should be determined and recorded in the equipment records.

3.81   Care should be taken to minimise the area of the X-ray field consistent with the requirements of the examination. Collimation should be used rather than magnification, since reducing the field of view by using intensifier magnification will usually increase the dose rate selected when using automatic dose rate control. It should be noted, however, that collimation to very small areas may also produce unexpected increases in automatic dose rate if the collimator overlaps the sensor area of the automatic control system. Disabling the automatic control system by locking the fluoroscopic exposure factors is therefore recommended prior to using tight collimation to small areas.

3.82   Where thin body parts are being examined, e.g. in paediatrics, removal of the anti-scatter grid may not significantly degrade the image and can result in a large dose saving.

3.83   The ambient light level in the examination room should be set to a comfortably low level for television monitors to give optimal image contrast and resolution when set to low-to-moderate brightness. Lighting and monitor positions should be chosen to avoid reflections obscuring the monitor screen, and direct glare to the observer. Where low light levels are not always achievable, or for mobile fluoroscopy systems that are moved to locations where the ambient light levels are variable, use of monitors with automatic adjustment of the display intensity is desirable. Image display monitors should be positioned so that the person carrying out the examination can fully appreciate the detail in the image.

3.84   Continuous cinefluorography should not be undertaken in view of the very high absorbed doses delivered to patients. Acceptable alternatives are pulsed cinefluorography, digital cinefluorography and video recording. Digital cine-acquisition should be used in preference to film-based systems whenever possible since the input dose rate required is lower.

3.85   The focal spot to skin distance should never be less than 30 cm, and when stationary equipment is used preferably not less than 45 cm.

3.86   During fluoroscopy with the patient in the erect position, the radiologist (or other clinician), operator and any other essential person(s) who are present should ensure that they are protected by the intensifier, its surround and, if provided, the protective aprons suspended from it.

3.87   During fluoroscopy with the subject in the horizontal position, use of an undercouch X-ray tube is recommended, with the image intensifier as close to the patient as possible. If the examination being undertaken specifically requires the use of an overcouch or C-arm tube, then particular care is necessary both to prevent inadvertent insertion of the operator's hands or head into the primary beam and to avoid exposure to scattered radiation. Where lateral beams are used, staff should work on the beam exit side of the patient. Whenever possible, examinations should be carried out from the remote control panel. When it is necessary for persons to be near the table, e.g. for specialised examinations involving catheterisation, they should make every reasonable effort to shield themselves from scattered radiation by use of lead aprons, eye and thyroid shields, mobile or ceiling-suspended shields as appropriate. Doses to the lower limbs can be significant, so extra shielding to protect them may be necessary. Wherever possible during examinations known to give high doses to patients or staff (e.g. cardiac, neuroradiological and interventional procedures), staff should stand away from the patient during image acquisition 'runs' (see paragraph 3.17). The likely eye doses of such staff should be established, e.g. by monitoring. If appropriate, the RPA may recommend that leaded glass spectacles be worn.

3.88   During fluoroscopy, palpation with the hand should be reduced to a minimum. It should only be undertaken on the image receptor side of the patient and therefore should not be carried out at all with an overcouch tube; in the latter case, automatic compression devices should be available. A protective glove with a lead equivalent thickness of at least 0.25 mm for up to 150 kV should always be worn during palpation. The need to wear a fingertip dosemeter should be considered (see paragraph 1.94). The presence of the glove used for palpation can cause a significant increase in absorbed dose rate when an automatic dose rate system is used. Care should be taken to minimise this effect by keeping the glove outside the sensing area of the automatic system (which is normally close to the centre of the field of view) and/or by locking the fluoroscopic factors before palpation begins.

3.89   During a fluoroscopic examination when radiography is to be undertaken, the use of image-intensifier based recording devices, such as a 100 mm rapid-sequence camera or digital fluorographic imaging system, may greatly reduce the radiation dose to the patient and to any staff in the room. On dose and efficiency grounds, their use is preferred over direct radiography using a large screen/film cassette. Operators should take care to obtain only those images necessary to fulfil the diagnostic requirements of the examination.

Interventional radiology

3.90   Complex interventional procedures involving long fluoroscopy times and the acquisition of numerous images can result in skin doses to the patient that exceed the threshold for radiation-induced skin injury (ICRP85 *Avoidance of Radiation Injuries from Interventional Procedures* [38]). Possible examples of such procedures are radiofrequency cardiac catheter ablations, percutaneous transluminal angioplasties, vascular embolisations (especially neuroradiological) and angiograms, stent and filter placements. For such examinations standard operating procedures and clinical protocols should be established to minimise the likelihood of this outcome. Particular attention should be paid to optimisation for interventional procedures. The advice of an MPE should be sought regarding those examinations for which high skin doses are likely.

3.91   Dose assessment should be carried out for any examinations likely to result in entrance surface (skin) doses exceeding 1 Gy. A system should be established for recording the measured or estimated skin dose in the patient's record so that the cumulative dose from multiple examinations can be evaluated and necessary medical care arranged. The patient should be counselled regarding potential symptoms and risks and appropriate consent gained.

3.92   For long and complex procedures, more than one projection should be used during the course of the procedure wherever possible to reduce the maximum localised radiation dose to the skin. Dose-reduction features, such as additional beam filtration (Nicholson *et al.* [39]), pulsed fluoroscopy, cineloop, fluorograb and virtual collimation, should be used if available.

3.93   The employer must establish appropriate extremity radiation monitoring arrangements for interventional radiology staff and review the effectiveness of the measures for their radiation protection.

Precautions with mobile equipment

3.94   The precautions recommended in paragraphs 3.2 to 3.15 and 3.28 to 3.53 also apply to mobile X-ray units. Portable X-ray units are included in the definition of mobile X-ray units.

3.95   When mobile X-ray units are used, operators should be particularly careful to ensure that no part of their body is exposed to the radiation beam and that all persons in the vicinity of the patient are afforded adequate protection from the primary beam and from scattered radiation. Operators should wear a protective apron of at least 0.25 mm lead equivalent thickness.

3.96   The focal spot to skin distance should never be less than 30 cm.

3.97   For radiography with mobile X-ray units on wards, in A&E departments, etc., the employer, in consultation with the RPA, should devise a procedure to ensure adequate protection of the patient, the operator and all those in the vicinity of the examination. This should normally be agreed with ward management and documented in the local rules. Particular care is necessary with regard to the direction and size of the radiation beam as partition walls may not provide sufficient X-ray attenuation; local shielding may be needed (e.g. a lead-plastic apron over the bed-head and use of lead-backed film cassettes). Use of horizontal beams should be avoided where possible. The immediate vicinity of the patient may be a controlled area; control of access may be exercised by the operator giving a verbal instruction and ensuring that staff and visitors leave the area. Portable free-standing radiation warning signs may also be used to avoid inadvertent access to the controlled area while the X-ray procedure is being performed.

3.98   Mobile equipment should not be capable of use by unauthorised persons and should be left in a 'safe' condition when it is left unattended (see paragraphs 3.45 and 4.30).

Precautions with computed tomography scanners

3.99   During 'warm up' and detector calibration procedures, persons should not be allowed to enter or remain in the scanner room. For mobile CT scanners with no separate control room, all persons should remain behind protective barriers during 'warm up' and detector calibration procedures.

3.100   Management should consult the RPA about protection for staff who need to remain in the examination room during clinical procedures. This is particularly important for CT fluoroscopy. Remote injection facilities and appropriate spacers should be available to enable staff to stand away from the patient and to keep the interventionalist's hands out of the beam.

3.101   An operator should be at the control panel of a CT scanner during the scanning sequence, since the equipment will not normally have an exposure switch that has to be pressed continuously. From this position, the operator should have a clear view of the patient and of all doors leading into the scanner room. Alternatively, the doors should be locked to prevent inadvertent entry by unauthorised persons.

3.102   In view of the potential for high patient doses, CT examinations should only be carried out after there has been proper clinical justification for the examination of each individual patient by an experienced IR(ME)R practitioner, which is consistent with local IR(ME)R procedures. Examinations on children require a different level of justification to that for adults, since such patients are at greater risk from radiation than are adults. CT examinations should not be performed on the abdomen or pelvis of pregnant patients without overriding clinical indications and particular attention to low dose techniques [40]. When clinically appropriate, the alternative use of safer non-ionising techniques (such as ultrasound and magnetic resonance imaging (MRI) where available) or of low dose X-ray techniques should be considered.

3.103   The relatively low dose technique of scan projection radiography over the region of interest should be used to aid scan selection and to limit the amount of subsequent cross-sectional scanning.

3.104   Operators should ensure that the minimum number of CT slices necessary to obtain the required diagnostic information are acquired [40]. This is particularly important when scanning contiguous volumes using pre-set scanning protocols.

3.105   The parameters of standard scanning protocols should be modified according to the size of the particular patient to deliver the lowest dose consistent with the required image quality [41].

3.106   Slice increment (axial scanning) or pitch (helical scanning) together with beam collimation should be chosen with regard to the z-axis sensitivity (imaged slice width) and low contrast detectability required, whilst maintaining the lowest practicable patient dose.

3.107   Care should be taken to minimise exposure to the eyes of the patient. Dose to the lens tissue can often be substantially reduced by angulation of the gantry to exclude the eyes from the primary beam during head examinations.

3.108   The necessity for the use of contrast agents should be assessed to reduce the number of regions that are rescanned with contrast.

3.109   The impact of post-patient collimation on patient dose should be considered when selecting CT scanners and optimising protocols. It may be appropriate to seek the advice of an MPE on these matters.

Computed tomography fluoroscopy

3.110   All the general principles of radiation protection apply, in addition to paragraphs 3.88 and 3.93.

3.111   The operator should be aware of the potential for high skin doses in CT fluoroscopy when scanning in the same place continuously. As entrance surface dose rates can range from 4 mGy s^{-1} to 9 mGy s^{-1}, they should be mindful of the fluoroscopy time taken to reach a specified dose (e.g. 1 Gy).

3.112   When operating a CT scanner at standard CT fluoroscopy parameters for the pre-set time limit, the time limit should be set such that the dose at the periphery position in a standard CTDI phantom should not exceed 500 mGy.

3.113   A maximum limit on the mA selectable for CT fluoroscopy should be set locally, if not physically restricted in the equipment design.

3.114   Under no circumstance should the X-ray tube be energised for CT fluoroscopy when the person carrying out the examination is not looking at the monitor.

3.115   For procedures where needle manipulation is performed whilst screening, holders should be used which allow the hands of the person carrying out the investigation to remain well outside the plane of the primary beam. The need to wear an extremity dosemeter should be considered.

Precautions with radiotherapy simulators

3.116   Examinations should be carried out only on patients who will be treated subsequently by radiotherapy. All the general radiation safety precautions that are applicable in diagnostic radiology should be applied to radiotherapy simulators (see paragraphs 8.87 to 8.89).

Protective clothing

3.117   Gloves, aprons and eye protectors are designed to protect the wearer only from primary radiation transmitted through the patient, and from scatter. They will not provide adequate protection from the unattenuated primary beam.

3.118   Gloves should be available with a protection equivalent throughout both front and back (including fingers and wrist) to not less than 0.25 mm lead for X-rays up to 150 kV. They should be labelled with a CE mark and an indication of their lead-equivalence. They may comply with BS EN 61331-3:1999 *Protective Devices Against Diagnostic Medical X-Radiation* [42].

3.119   Body aprons should be available with a protective equivalent of not less than 0.25 mm lead for use with X-rays up to 100 kV and not less than 0.35 mm lead for use with X-rays over 100 kV. They should be labelled with a CE mark and indication of their lead equivalence. They may comply with BS EN 61331-3:1999 [42]. Where extra protection is required, the addition of a thyroid shield is generally more useful to reduce effective dose than moving to thicker body aprons. Half body aprons should not be used except for specific applications for which the RPA has advised they will offer sufficient protection.

3.120   A range of PPE should be provided in all X-ray rooms and for use with mobile X-ray equipment. PPE should be used and stored properly, and employees should be aware of their duties relating to PPE (see L121 paragraph 163 [2]).

3.121   When not in use, lead aprons should be accommodated appropriately (IRR99 regulation 9(3) [1]). They should be supported in a suitable manner to prevent damage, e.g. by using dedicated hangers or rails of sufficiently large diameter to prevent creasing. Aprons should never be folded.

3.122   Gloves, thyroid shields, aprons and other protective clothing should be examined visually at frequent intervals. Any defects in protective clothing found by the wearer should be reported immediately and defective items should be taken out of use and replaced as soon as possible. Protective clothing should be thoroughly examined at least once a year to ensure that no cracks in the protective material have developed; radiographic or fluoroscopic examination will be required. The results of the inspection should be recorded, and the protective devices themselves should be identified (e.g. by serial number), given the likelihood that they may be moved from one location to another.

4 Diagnostic X-ray equipment excluding equipment for dental radiography

General recommendations

4.1 Diagnostic X-ray equipment should be designed, constructed and installed to comply with the relevant British and International Standards (e.g. BS EN 60601 *Medical Electrical Equipment. General Requirements for Safety* [43] together with the particular and associated collateral standards) or other recognised standards of construction that will enable the recommendations in this chapter to be met.

4.2 All medical devices placed on the European market since 1998 should also be CE-marked according to the requirements of the Medical Devices Directive [44] as in the Medical Devices Regulations 1994 [45]. Meeting the requirements of this Directive is a declaration that the device meets the essential requirements for device safety.

4.3 Readers should be mindful of the requirements of the Electricity at Work Regulations 1989 [46], and the Provision and Use of Work Equipment Regulations 1998 [47].

4.4 All newly installed or reinstalled fixed X-ray installations should comply with the current edition of the IEE Wiring Regulations [48] and the requirements of TRS89 *Technical Requirements for the Supply and Installation of Equipment for Diagnostic Imaging and Radiotherapy* [49], if the latter is specified in the equipment purchase specification or tender documentation. Prior to installation, the supplier should supply a pre-installation specification to the purchaser (to include mechanical and electrical safety and installation requirements) to facilitate the safe installation, use and maintenance of the equipment. The purchaser should identify who does the necessary pre-installation work, and confirm that it is done to specification as part of the acceptance process.

4.5 Equipment should be maintained in accordance with the recommendations of the manufacturer. It cannot be considered safe, from a radiation point of view, unless it is in good working order both mechanically and electrically.

X-ray source assembly

4.6 Every X-ray source assembly (comprising an X-ray tube, an X-ray tube housing and a beam limiting device) should be constructed so that, at every rating specified by the manufacturer for that X-ray source assembly, the air kerma from the leakage radiation at a distance from the focal spot of 1 m does not exceed 1 mGy in 1 h averaged over an area not exceeding 100 cm^2. Reference should be made to the leakage technique factors of the X-ray tube that describe the maximum continuous ratings for the X-ray tube, e.g. 125 kV and 3.6 mA for a 450 W tube.

4.7 Every X-ray source assembly should be marked to identify the nominal focal spot position as in BS EN 60601-2-28:1993 *Specification for X-ray Source Assemblies and X-ray Tube Assemblies for Medical Diagnosis* [50]. When an X-ray tube assembly is covered with additional protective or aesthetic covers, then the covers should also be marked with the nominal position of the focal spot. The exception to this case may be the gantry covers of a CT scanner.

Beam filtration

4.8 The permanent filtration of every X-ray tube assembly should be marked durably and clearly on the housing by the installer [50]. If the assembly is totally enclosed, e.g. within a CT gantry, a duplicate label should be placed on the exterior of the equipment.

4.9   Every added filter should be marked permanently and clearly in terms of its material composition (e.g. chemical symbol) and thickness (in mm). Materials other than aluminium, e.g. copper, molybdenum, rhodium and rare-earth materials, may be used as alternative materials for X-ray beam filtration. The aluminium equivalence may also be marked for filters of materials other than aluminium. However, the beam energy at which the Al equivalence is determined should also be stated. Where there is a means of adjusting the added filtration, either manually or motor driven, and such facilities are not used in the examination protocols in the room, the means of altering the filtration from the standard setting should be disabled. The Al equivalence of any permanently installed DAP meter should be marked.

4.10   The total beam filtration includes the permanent filtration, any added filtration and filtration afforded by attenuating material that always intercepts the beam, e.g. the mirror of a LBD or a DAP meter. For normal diagnostic work the total filtration of the beam should be equivalent to not less than 2.5 mm of aluminium of which 1.5 mm should be permanent (ICRP33 *Protection Against Ionizing Radiation from External Sources Used in Medicine* [51]). The total filtration (or its constituent parts plus, in the case of under-table tubes, the filtration of the tabletop) should be written down and be readily available. The total filtration should also be marked on the tube assembly.

4.11   Mammography is a technique that requires very soft radiation. The total permanent filtration should never be less than the equivalent of 0.03 mm molybdenum or 0.5 mm aluminium.

Beam size

4.12   Beam collimators should be designed to minimise extra-focal radiation. The maximum beam size should be permanently limited to that required in practice for each particular source assembly. The maximum cross-section should correspond to the largest dimension of the imaging device at the minimum focus to detector distance that would be used in clinical practice.

4.13   All radiographic X-ray equipment, including mobiles, should be provided with properly aligned adjustable LBD beam-limiting devices or, in special circumstances, e.g. skull units, cones to keep the radiation beam within the limits of the X-ray detector selected for each examination. Any cones should be marked with their coverage details, e.g. 15 cm diameter at 100 cm focus to film distance (FFD).

4.14   Equipment for fluoroscopy, except radiotherapy treatment simulators, should be provided with the means, preferably automatic, to confine the radiation beam within the image reception area. The collimation should automatically adjust for the focus to detector distance and the selected intensifier field of view. Preferably, it should also be optimised to match the shape of image, e.g. using multi-leaf iris diaphragms. Additional shaped and semi-transparent collimators may be provided to optimise the beam size, shape and profile. It should be possible for the operator to adjust the field size during examinations down to the equivalent of 5 cm × 5 cm at 1 m from the focal spot.

4.15   For CT scanners, the radiation beam profile width in the 'z-axis' should be as close as possible to the total imaged thickness. It is preferable that the slice width is solely controlled by pre-patient collimation for all slice widths. The scanner operating instructions should state the radiation beam width and the imaged slice thickness for all widths. Where the scanner is claimed to conform to BS EN 60601-2-44:1999 *Particular Requirements for the Safety of X-ray Equipment for Computed Tomography* [52], the geometric efficiency (paragraph 29.103.4) should be displayed on the console if less than 70 per cent. The impact of post-patient collimation on patient dose should be considered when selecting CT scanners and optimising protocols. It may be appropriate to seek the advice of an MPE on these matters.

Image receptors

4.16   An image intensifier television system or an equivalent suitable modern flat-plate dynamic image detector must be used in fluoroscopy. The use of non-intensified fluoroscopy is unacceptable and must be discontinued.

4.17   Appropriate dose reduction features should be provided on fluoroscopy systems. These include storage or memory devices such as 'last-image hold', cineloop, fluorograb, pulsed fluoroscopy at a range of frame rates, additional filtration, variable image receptor dose levels and a range of kV and mA operating characteristics to optimise patient dose for different applications.

4.18   The fastest image receptor in terms of radiological speed, that will give acceptable image quality, should be chosen (see paragraph 3.62). Where digital image receptors are adopted, care should be taken to optimise the sensitivity of the system, taking into account the speed of the film/screen combination being replaced. Digital radiography systems may have a wide operating dynamic range enabling them to produce acceptable images over a wide exposure range (see paragraphs 3.70 and 3.71). Such systems should have a means of indicating to the operator the extent of the exposure to the imaging system. This is particularly important where manual selection of radiographic factors is used. It may be appropriate to seek the advice of an MPE on these matters.

Selection of materials for ancillary equipment

4.19   The attenuation of the X-ray beam between the patient and the image receptor should be minimised by the use of suitable materials for the construction of the tabletop (in the case of over-table tubes), the front of the film cassette and anti-scatter grid.

4.20   The housing and supporting plates of an X-ray image intensifier, or the image receptor of a CT scanner or bone densitometer, should provide shielding equivalent to at least 2 mm lead for 100 kV or 2.5 mm lead for 150 kV. From 100 kV to 150 kV an additional lead equivalent of 0.01 mm kV^{-1} is required. The lead equivalence should be clearly labelled on the equipment by the installer.

Signals and marking

4.21   There should be a visible indicator on the control panel, preferably including an indicator light or illuminated display, to show that the mains is switched on. In the context of the control panel signal, 'mains on' indicates a state of readiness to emit radiation. Room warning signals are covered in paragraphs 3.23 to 3.27.

4.22   All X-ray radiographic and fluoroscopic equipment control panels should be fitted with a light giving a clear and visible indication to the operator that an exposure is taking place. The light should be triggered by conditions associated uniquely with the commencement and termination of the emission of radiation, but arranged to remain on long enough for the indication to be seen irrespective of the exposure duration. For equipment fitted with an audible warning, the warning should be triggered by the same conditions.

4.23   Where it is possible, from a single exposure switch location, to initiate the production of X-rays from more than one X-ray tube, each X-ray tube should be provided with means for automatically giving a warning signal whilst that X-ray tube is selected to emit X-rays. The tube-selection warning signal should be clearly visible in the vicinity of the X-ray tube and from the control panel. The electrical circuitry should be such that it is impossible to initiate an exposure if the warning system fails; however, the system should be designed to avoid the likelihood of a diagnostic examination being interrupted.

4.24   All exposure controls, including footswitches, should be marked clearly. All other controls, instruments and indicating devices should be marked permanently and clearly to indicate their functions and settings.

On any equipment where X-ray tube selection is possible, there should be a clear and unambiguous indication on the control panel as to which tube has been selected. Markings by symbols should be clear, preferably following international standard notation, and their meaning should be described in the operating instructions: where there is no suitable standard symbol, markings should be in plain English.

Exposure factors

4.25   Fluoroscopic equipment should normally have an automatic dose rate control facility. This should be capable of optimising the balance between image quality and patient dose (see paragraph 3.80) and should include a range of exposure control or dose-reduction features.

4.26   CT scanners should have a suitable range of tube current-time product (mAs) selections available for each tube voltage selection. This will be effective in allowing the optimisation of exposure factors for patients of different cross-sectional thickness, especially in paediatrics. Where available, dose-reduction packages should also be used, to further reduce the dose to the patient.

Exposure switches

4.27   Exposure switches on all X-ray diagnostic equipment should be arranged so that an exposure continues only while continuous pressure is maintained on the switch, and terminates if pressure is released (i.e. 'deadman') unless it is previously terminated by other means, e.g. at the end of the set exposure time. Exceptions are equipment that scan along the patient, e.g. bone mineral densitometers, some lithotriptors and CT scanners (other than in CT fluoroscopy mode).

4.28   Exposure switches relying on a remote control to initiate the exposure should contain all the safety features of conventional exposure switches with regard to exposure control and release, e.g. deadman. The position of the exposure switch should be as follows:

(a) for fixed equipment, at the control panel or at the positions intended to be occupied by the operators, and

(b) for mobile and portable equipment, such as to enable the operator to be outside the radiation beam and to be at least 2 m from both the tube housing and from the patient.

4.29   Exposure switches should be designed to prevent inadvertent production of X-rays. Detailed advice is given in BS EN 60601-1-3 [43] and in particular it should not be possible for fluids to enter the switch and cause a short circuit. Additionally, foot switches should be constructed so that exposure does not take place if they are accidentally overturned. Switches should be positioned so that they cannot be depressed accidentally during stowage. Ideally, a stowage bracket should be provided and used. If resetting is automatic, it should be ensured that pressure on the exposure switch has to be released completely before the next exposure can be made. Remote control devices should be designed so that exposures are not inadvertently triggered by other devices in the vicinity.

4.30   A key-operated switch (or equivalent) should normally be provided for mobile equipment to prevent the generation of radiation by unauthorised persons (see paragraph 3.98), but should always be provided:

(a) whenever radiation can be generated without connecting the equipment to the electrical mains supply, or

(b) when connected to the electrical mains supply, if the equipment requires such a connection to be made for battery charging.

Keys should be removed from the unit when not in use and returned to a secure location.

Control of exposure duration

4.31   For radiography, there should be a means for terminating the exposure automatically after a pre-set time, electrical charge (mAs) or quantity of radiation or after a tomographic scan has been completed (see paragraph 4.34). To guard against failure, an additional means of termination should be provided which is independent of the normal means. The release of an exposure switch (see paragraph 4.27) may be regarded as the additional means for manual systems. AEC systems should have an 'early termination device' that aborts unnecessary exposure if an inappropriate exposure is taking place (i.e. IDR too high or too low), or a back-up timer which is preferably one programmable by the user.

4.32   For fluoroscopy, the release of an exposure switch should be regarded as the normal means of termination. An additional means of termination should be provided which operates automatically. Older equipment should terminate exposure after 10 min accumulated fluoroscopy, with an audible warning at least 30 s before termination, to enable the operator to reset the device if the exposure needs to be prolonged. Modern generators meeting the requirements of BS EN 60601-2-7:1998 *Specification for High Voltage Generators of Diagnostic X-ray Generators* [53] should terminate exposure after 10 min of uninterrupted fluoroscopy. The equipment should have a separate timer that indicates the accumulated fluoroscopy exposure time for the patient, with a resolution of 0.1 min or better, with an independent resettable alarm that sounds after 5 min of accumulated fluoroscopy.

4.33   AEC devices should be provided for radiography and used where appropriate, as an aid to the achievement of consistent radiographs and the reduction of repeat exposures. To achieve consistent results it is important that AEC devices are correctly set-up and maintained. In case of failure of this device, a back-up mechanism should be provided to terminate the exposure (see paragraph 4.27).

4.34   Equipment for CT should have a device that terminates the exposure automatically as soon as the selected scan or scan sequence has been completed, or if scanning is interrupted before completion. There should be a means whereby the exposure may be terminated, if necessary, before the scanning sequence is completed (e.g. abort scan). For CT fluoroscopy, the release of an exposure switch should be regarded as the normal means of termination. Initiation of an exposure should not be possible if the scanning motor fails to start, unless 'warm up' conditions or a localisation exposure have been selected.

4.35   If a tube 'warm up' or detector calibration facility is provided on CT or other X-ray equipment, there should be a clear indication on the control panel when the mode has been selected and there should be a device which de-energises the X-ray tube on completion of this phase. There should be a means of terminating the exposure before completion of this phase (see paragraph 4.32).

4.36   When operating a CT scanner at standard CT fluoroscopy parameters for the pre-set time limit, the time limit should be set such that the dose at the periphery position in a standard CTDI phantom should not exceed 500 mGy.

Exposure measurement

4.37   A DAP meter should be fitted to all X-ray equipment whenever practicable. Ideally, the instruments should be permanently installed, but where this is not possible portable instruments should be used to make periodic dose checks. All equipment with the potential of delivering large doses to patients, such as those in the interventional environment, in cardiology and neuroradiology should be provided with instruments to measure and record DAP and preferably provide a continuous indication of DAP rate.

4.38   All diagnostic X-ray equipment first installed after 1 January 2000 should, where practicable, give an indication of the radiation produced during the examination, using either hardware (e.g. DAP meter) or software. All automatic exposure devices should have a post-exposure mAs display.

4.39   New equipment for interventional radiological procedures should give an indication of the cumulative dose to a patient's skin, in order to assist in the overall management of the patient and the avoidance of potential deterministic radiation injuries of the skin.

4.40   New CT scanners should give an indication of patient dose for a selected scan sequence, to increase operator awareness of dose levels and facilitate the comparison of scan protocols with European and national reference dose levels, with the advice and support of the MPE. Identification of patient dose, using, for example, $CTDI_w$ and DLP, then forms part of the optimisation process.

4.41 $CTDI_w$ and DLP should be measured locally for each new CT installation at commissioning, to check the validity of display console values. Checks should include measurements of $CTDI_w$ at a range of pitch settings in order to confirm that displayed values are automatically adjusted with pitch (BS EN 60601-2-44:1999, paragraph 29.103.3 [52]).

4.42   When choosing new X-ray equipment, consideration should be given to equipment capable of automatically recording information relevant to patient dose and ideally exporting these data to the electronic RIS.

Protection against scattered radiation for fixed fluoroscopy installations

4.43   All equipment used for fluoroscopy should be provided with adequate protection for staff against scattered radiation arising from the patient and from materials between the X-ray tube and the patient. Protective materials should be equivalent to not less than 0.5 mm lead at 100 kVp.

4.44   Over-table and C-arm tubes should be operated remotely where possible, with operators protected by a fixed lead glass screen installed between them and the X-ray equipment. When remote operation is not feasible, alternative screens and aprons should be provided for protection against scattered radiation. These may be:

(a) ceiling suspended screens to protect the operator's head and upper body

(b) attached to the sides of the table and configured to reduce back and side scatter from the patient

(c) suspended from the X-ray tube and extending down to the patient to provide local protection, or

(d) floor standing mobile screens to provide general protection.

4.45   Equipment with an enclosed under-table tube and over-table intensifier should provide adequate protection in the side of the table, including bucky slots and openings. Above the tabletop, the operator should be protected, normally by a lead rubber apron suspended from the intensifier support. The apron should be large enough to provide adequate shielding (not normally less than 45 cm wide and 40 cm long) and be adjustable in position so that the operator protection is maintained when the table is tilted. Special attention should be paid to the mechanical robustness of the drapes when switching between vertical and horizontal table positions.

5   Dental radiology

Scope

5.1   This chapter applies to the use of equipment specifically designed for radiography of the teeth or jaws including radiography using an intra-oral image receptor (or, with the same equipment, an extra-oral receptor), panoramic radiography with an extra-oral X-ray tube and cephalometric radiography. While primarily concerned with the use of the equipment for the examination of patients, the guidance is also relevant during equipment testing, measurement of the radiation produced, staff training, research into examination techniques, the examination of volunteers in approved research projects and other uses at the place where the equipment is normally used. Reference should be made to Chapter 3 if general purpose X-ray equipment is used.

5.2   The guidance in both Chapters 5 and 6 is intended primarily to cover the use of dental X-ray equipment within the hospital environment, whether the equipment is under the control of a radiology department or some other department, such as oral surgery and orthodontics. Users of dental X-ray equipment who do not have the support of a hospital administrative structure are referred to the *Guidance Notes for Dental Practitioners on the Safe Use of X-ray Equipment* [8]. It is likely that this latter guidance will also apply to many users of X-ray equipment within community dental services. Nevertheless, much of the content of these chapters is universal to all users of dental X-ray equipment and is very similar, if not identical, to that in chapters 3 and 4 of the dental practitioners' guidance notes [8].

Roles and responsibilities

5.3   The general advice given in Chapters 1 and 2 applies equally to users of dental X-ray equipment. In addition, the advice given at the beginning of Chapter 3 relating to roles and responsibilities (see paragraphs 3.3 to 3.15) is applicable, in particular where the equipment is under the control of a radiology department.

Radiation protection adviser

5.4   Most radiation employers will need to consult an RPA on matters as listed in Appendix 4 from time to time. There is no exemption from this requirement for dental X-ray equipment users and when advice is required an RPA must be formally appointed (paragraphs 1.13 to 1.15). The appointment of an RPA does not have to be a permanent arrangement. However, a formal ongoing appointment is recommended since it ensures that advice is always immediately available and it provides continuity of advice.

Referrer

5.5   For dental radiography the referrer will normally be a dental or medical practitioner. As at January 2001, it is not permissible for a profession complementary to dentistry (PCD) to act as a referrer. In departments outside radiology, it will be common for the referrer and IR(ME)R practitioner to be the same person, in which case the formal exchange of clinical information is unnecessary. Referral criteria must always be provided, even when the IR(ME)R practitioner and referrer are the same person. When establishing such criteria, the employer may wish to make use of the booklet published by the Faculty of General Dental Practitioners – Royal College of Surgeons (FGDP-RCS), *Selection Criteria for Dental Radiography* [54], or similar guidelines such as *Guidelines for the Use of Radiographs in Clinical Orthodontics* [55].

IR(ME)R practitioner

5.6　　The IR(ME)R practitioner for dental radiology will usually be a dental practitioner, oral surgeon, orthodontist or radiologist but may be another qualified healthcare professional designated for this role for specified examinations within the employer's procedures. The primary function of the IR(ME)R practitioner is to undertake the justification of individual exposures. All IR(ME)R practitioners must be adequately trained to undertake this function. Appendix 3 of the dental guidance notes [8] gives details.

Operators

5.7　　In dental radiology it will be common for the referrer and IR(ME)R practitioner to be the same person, who may also act as an operator, especially for dental equipment located outside radiology departments. However, many dental nurses or other PCDs will also perform some or all of the functions of an operator. All operators must be adequately trained to undertake these functions. Appendix 3 of the dental guidance notes [8] gives details.

Controlled area

5.8　　The advice of an RPA should be sought concerning the designation of the controlled area because of the work with dental X-ray equipment. The decision to designate an area either around the unit or encompassing the whole room is dependent on several factors, including the type of X-ray unit in use, its operating kilovoltage and the workload.

5.9　　For dental radiography it should be the intention to define the controlled area so that no additional protection is needed for anybody remaining outside it during exposure. One approach, valid for rooms containing a single intra-oral or panoramic unit with a low workload, is to designate the controlled area whilst X-rays are being generated as extending:

　　　　(a)　within the primary X-ray beam until it has been sufficiently attenuated by distance or shielding, and

　　　　(b)　within 1.5 m of the X-ray tube and the patient, in any other direction.

5.10　　The definition of the controlled area in paragraph 5.9 should be adequate for a weekly workload that does not exceed 100 intra-oral or 50 panoramic films, or a pro-rata combination of each type of examination. At this workload, it is unlikely that anyone's annual dose would exceed 1 mSv, so long as staff stay outside the controlled area during exposure. The designation of a 'Supervised Area' is then unnecessary.

5.11　　Since the beam is not always fully attenuated by the patient, it should be considered as extending beyond the patient until it has been intercepted by primary protective shielding, eg. a solid brick or block wall.

Location and installation

5.12　　Dental radiography should be carried out in a room (the X-ray room) from which all persons whose presence is unnecessary are excluded while X-rays are being produced. This room, which may be a dental surgery or a separate examination room, should not be used for other work or as a passageway whilst radiography is in progress.

5.13　　In consultation with an RPA, the X-ray room should be chosen and designed to provide safe accommodation for all persons. Either the room should be large enough to allow the operator to stand well outside the controlled area (ie. preferably 2 m or more from the X-ray tube and patient, and well out of the direction of the primary X-ray beam), or a protected area should be provided behind which the operator stands. The X-ray tube warning light and the patient should be visible to the operator throughout the radiography. It may be necessary to use mirrors or lead glass/perspex windows to achieve this.

5.14   The decision as to whether or not a protected area is provided for the operator should be reviewed by the RPA. Such a protected area should not normally be required if the total equipment workload does not exceed that stated in paragraph 5.10. Where a protected area is provided it should be sited out of the direction of the main X-ray beam and should incorporate protection of not less than the equivalent of 0.5 mm of lead.

5.15   Control panels (where possible), exposure switches, mains isolators and power switches should be positioned such that they are outside the controlled area. In particular, it should be possible to isolate the equipment from the mains supply without having to enter the controlled area.

5.16   If more than one X-ray unit is sited in any room (e.g. in open plan accommodation), arrangements should be made in consultation with an RPA to ensure that patients, staff and all other persons are adequately protected. In particular, it should not be possible for an operator to inadvertently energise the wrong X-ray unit nor to accidentally irradiate persons working independently in another part of the room. In particular, when it is possible from a single location to initiate the production of X-rays from more than one X-ray tube, each tube should be fitted with a warning signal that is arranged to operate automatically whilst that tube is selected to emit X-rays.

5.17   Persons in areas outside the X-ray room should be adequately protected, meaning that the controlled area should not normally extend beyond the X-ray room. It is only acceptable for adjacent areas outside the room to be designated as controlled or supervised if they are inaccessible during radiography (e.g. a locked storeroom). The X-ray room should be arranged so that use is made of the natural shielding of the walls, floor and ceiling of the room, where these are relatively thick or dense, e.g. of solid brick or concrete construction.

5.18   If the normal structural materials do not afford sufficient shielding (e.g. a light-weight partition wall) additional protective material such as lead or X-ray protective plaster may be needed depending on the use of the area beyond the partition. Intra-oral equipment should be installed and used so that the useful beam is directed away from any door and away from any window if the space immediately beyond the window is occupied. Panoramic and cephalometric equipment should be installed and used so that windows and doors are not within the controlled area.

Room warning signs and signals

5.19   When a controlled area extends to any entrance of the X-ray room, a warning notice, bearing the basic ionising radiation symbol (see Appendix 12), should be provided on the outside of the door. Additionally, an automatic warning light should normally be provided at the entrance to indicate when radiography is in progress. For low workload situations, this light should be illuminated whilst the mains supply to the X-ray unit is on, and the mains supply should be switched off when radiography is not imminent. For high workload situations, an automatic illuminated warning signal that indicates that radiation is being emitted should also be given, if practicable. The warning notice should explain the significance of the warning lights and should include words such as 'do not enter when light is on'. Such warning lights may be unnecessary if the operator is physically able to prevent access to the room whilst radiography is in progress.

Equipment

5.20   Dental X-ray equipment should conform to the requirements of Chapter 6. The recommendations in paragraph 1.113 should be followed for any dental X-ray equipment that is on loan.

Maintenance, testing and quality assurance

5.21   The radiation safety features of equipment must be properly maintained. It cannot be considered safe, from a radiation point of view, unless it is in good order both mechanically and electrically. Maintenance and associated checks should be in accordance with the advice of the manufacturer, the supplier and the RPA. Automatic processors should also be subject to a maintenance schedule.

5.22   Suppliers, erectors and installers of dental X-ray equipment are required, under IRR99 regulation 31(2)(c) [1] and under the Medical Devices Regulations 1994 [45] to provide the employer with adequate information about the proper use, testing and maintenance of that equipment. All dental X-ray equipment should be subject to the following tests:

(a) a 'critical examination' by the installer, immediately following installation unless the unit is intended for 'mobile' use

(b) an adequate test before the equipment is put into clinical use (the 'acceptance test')

(c) further adequate tests at appropriate intervals ('routine tests') and after any major maintenance procedure, and

(d) at suitable intervals, measurements to assess representative patient doses.

Guidance on the content of such tests, including necessary RPA and MPE involvement, is given in appendix 5 of the *Guidance Notes for Dental Practitioners* [8].

5.23   It is recommended that routine tests normally be carried out at intervals not exceeding 3 years. However, annual testing is recommended if:

(a) assessed representative patient doses exceed the DRL

(b) image quality analysis indicates that greater than 10 per cent of images are unacceptable for a diagnosis, or

(c) the QA programme identifies some other significant performance weakness.

In any of these events, it is recommended that the equipment be subsequently tested at annual intervals until there is full confidence that acceptable performance is being maintained.

5.24   Until national DRLs are available for dental work, values published by the NRPB as reference doses (Napier, *Reference Doses for Dental Radiography* [56]) should be used as a starting point on which to base local DRLs. It will be adequate for representative patient doses to be assessed as a part of each routine test, provided that the QA programme is able to confirm an acceptable ongoing quality of radiographs.

5.25   Electrical and mechanical faults could give rise to inadvertent radiation exposure, e.g. a faulty cable to a hand switch or failure/malfunction of the rotational movement mechanisms on panoramic equipment. It is expected that these kinds of faults will be identified and rectified by the employer's overall programme of managing work equipment safely. For further advice, see Safe Use of Work Equipment, ACoP and Guidance on the Provision and Use of Work Equipment Regulations (PUWER) [57].

5.26   A record of maintenance, including any defects found and their repair, should be kept for each item of X-ray equipment and relevant auxiliary equipment. Following maintenance, the service engineer should provide a written report prior to handing the equipment back for clinical use. This should detail any changes that may affect radiation dose (to patient or staff) or image quality. The RPA and/or MPE should be consulted as necessary. When a maintenance log is provided, there is a legal duty to keep it up to date.

5.27   All departments carrying out dental radiography should institute a routine QA programme. An appropriate QA programme for departments (e.g. oral surgery and orthodontics) that do not have access to sophisticated testing equipment would be that outlined in chapter 5 of the *Guidance Notes for Dental Practitioners* [8]. Dental equipment under the control of a radiology department should be included in their QA programme (see paragraph 3.30) and should include those equipment tests as recommended in national guidance [20 and 55].

General procedures

5.28 The tube housing should never be held by hand during an exposure. The operator should stand well outside the controlled area and, preferably, at least 2 m away from the X-ray tube and patient, making use of the full length of cable to the exposure switch. Where a protective panel is provided the operator should stand behind it.

5.29 If it is necessary to provide assistance by supporting a handicapped patient or a child during radiography, this should only be done in accordance with the advice of an RPA (see paragraph 3.42).

5.30 Where equipment provides a choice of beam or field sizes, the smallest reasonably practicable size should be used consistent with the radiographic procedure.

5.31 The operator should check that the exposure warning light and, where provided, any audible warning signal, operates at each exposure and ceases at the end of the intended exposure. If the exposure does not appear to have terminated as intended, the unit must immediately be disconnected from the mains electricity supply. The RPA should be consulted and a preliminary investigation should be undertaken to ascertain whether the incident warrants further investigation and possible reporting (see paragraphs 1.100 to 1.106).

5.32 If there is reason to think that the exposure control is defective, the exposure warning does not operate or that there may be some other fault (e.g. signs of damage, excessive X-ray tube temperature), the equipment should be disconnected from the supply and not used again until it has been checked and repaired by a service engineer.

5.33 The exposure settings should be chosen and checked by the operator on each occasion before an examination is made. This is especially important where available options necessitate the use of different exposure settings (e.g. to make allowance for the use of a long or short cone, variable kV and mA settings, different film speeds or exposure programmes).

Classification of staff and personal dosimetry

5.34 Sensible application of radiation protection measures should ensure that all staff involved in dental radiography receive an annual effective dose of considerably less than 6 mSv. Consequently, it will seldom, if ever, be necessary for staff to be designated as classified persons solely because of work involving dental radiography. However, any staff who enter a controlled area must be subject to suitable written arrangements, or they will have to be designated as classified persons.

5.35 Personal monitoring is recommended if the risk assessment indicates that individual doses could exceed 1 mSv year^{-1}. In practice, this should be considered for those staff whose weekly workload exceeds 100 intra-oral or 50 panoramic films, or a pro-rata combination of each type of examination. The dosemeter wear period may be up to 3 months; results should be recorded and periodically discussed with an RPA to ensure that doses are being kept ALARP.

Detectors, processing and viewing, and digital detectors

Intra-oral film

5.36 The fastest available films consistent with satisfactory diagnostic results should be used. Intra-oral films of ISO speed group E, or faster, are preferred. The use of 'instant process films' should be limited to specific essential situations (e.g. during surgery or endodontics). It should be noted that, in situations where 'rapid images' are routinely required, conventional film with rapid processing chemistry will generally give better results than instant process films.

Extra-oral, panoramic and cephalometric film

5.37   The fastest available film and intensifying screen combination consistent with satisfactory diagnostic results should be used. The speed of the system should be at least 400. The light sensitivity of the film should be correctly matched with the intensifying screens. The condition and effectiveness of the screens should be confirmed at regular intervals as part of the QA procedures. Provided that screens are handled carefully during routine use, cleaning should only be required infrequently. When cleaning is necessary it should be in accordance with the manufacturer's instructions.

Film processing

5.38   Strict attention should be paid to correct and consistent film processing so as to produce good quality radiographs and avoid the necessity for examinations to be repeated. Where automatic processing is used, the processor should be properly cleaned and maintained. In the case of manual processing, the temperature of the developer should be checked prior to film processing and the development time adjusted in accordance with the film manufacturer's instructions. The developer should be changed at regular intervals in accordance with the manufacturer's instructions.

Film viewing

5.39   In order to extract full diagnostic information from the films it is essential to have dedicated viewing facilities. A specially designed light-box should be installed in an area where the ambient lighting can be adjusted to appropriate levels. Suitable film masking should be used to optimise the viewing conditions by cutting out stray light. For viewing dense areas of a radiograph the incorporation of a high intensity light source in the light-box is recommended. The provision of magnification by a factor of two would be beneficial.

Digital imaging systems

5.40   In selecting digital equipment, it is necessary to ensure that the chosen system offers the field sizes that are clinically required. Field sizes should be available in a range that is comparable with dental film.

5.41   The sensitivity of the detector system must be compatible with the X-ray unit(s) for which it is to be used. Ideally the X-ray unit used should have an effectively constant operating potential with the ability to set sufficiently low exposure settings to realise the full extent of the possible dose savings.

5.42   Exposure settings should be reduced to the minimum compatible with the diagnostic quality of the image.

5.43   Because of the ease with which radiographs can be retaken, it is essential to ensure that all retakes are properly justified, recorded and included in QA statistics.

Intra-oral film radiography

5.44   This section applies to the use of intra-oral films or digital detectors wholly (periapical or bitewing) or partly (occlusal) in the mouth, and also to the use of extra-oral films with similar X-ray equipment.

5.45   Whenever practicable, techniques using film holders incorporating beam-aiming devices should be adopted for bitewing and periapical radiography. If rectangular collimation is being used, a beam-aiming device is essential for accurate alignment with the intra-oral film. Attention is drawn to the probable need for additional operator training in the use of film holders when moving from circular to rectangular collimation.

5.46   The equipment should have open ended beam collimators/directors conforming to the recommendations of paragraph 6.14. When a choice of beam collimators/directors is provided, the one most suited to the technique to be employed should be fitted ideally just covering the film or image receptor. The open end of the collimator/director should be placed as close as possible to the patient's head to minimise the size of the incident X-ray beam. If it is desired to use a longer focus to skin distance (FSD), a longer collimator/director should be employed.

5.47   The dental film or digital detector should only be held by the patient when it cannot otherwise be kept in position. It should not normally be hand-held by anyone else. Exceptionally it may be held by someone other than the patient using a pair of forceps, or other appropriate holder, to avoid direct irradiation of their fingers, e.g. when a child or a handicapped person cannot hold the film themselves. In such cases advice should be sought from an RPA and will be based on similar principles to that contained in paragraphs 3.42 to 3.44, and 5.29.

5.48   Extra-oral and vertex occlusal views should always be taken with cassettes incorporating appropriately matched film and intensifying screen combinations. It is recommended that a left and/or right marker be used on the cassette to confirm which side of the patient has been imaged.

Panoramic radiography

5.49   Where panoramic equipment features a cephalometry mode of operation, a check should be made before every exposure to ensure that the correct collimator is in place for panoramic operation (see *Reduction of the Dose to Patients During Lateral Cephalometric Radiography* [58]). Some designs provide an interlock to ensure that this is the case. Additionally, where the equipment features a number of different rotational modes (e.g. TMJ mode), a check should be made before every exposure to ensure that the correct mode has been selected.

5.50   If the rotational movement fails to start, or stops before the full arc is covered, the exposure switch should be released immediately to avoid any high localised exposure of the patient. The reason for any such failure should be investigated, and any faults rectified by an engineer before the equipment is used again for clinical purposes.

5.51   It is not acceptable to undertake panoramic radiography using an X-ray tube placed inside the patient's mouth.

Cephalometry

5.52   To minimise magnification effects, the FFD should be greater than 1 m and ideally within the range 1.5 m to 1.8 m.

5.53   The patient should be positioned in relation to the X-ray field by means of a cephalostat. To ensure correct orientation of the cassette, positioning markers for the film/cassette should be incorporated for all available apertures.

5.54   An intra-oral dental X-ray unit should not be used for cephalometry, other than with specially designed ancillary equipment. Even then, the ongoing suitability of the equipment for cephalometry should be confirmed with an RPA and/or MPE.

Protective clothing

5.55   There is no justification for the routine use of lead aprons for patients in dental radiography. Lead aprons do not protect against radiation scattered internally within the body, and only provide a practicable degree of protection in the case of the infrequently used vertex occlusal projection. Even in this case, the use of the lead apron could only be regarded as prudent for a female patient who is, or may be, pregnant. Thyroid collars should be used in those few cases where the thyroid may be in the primary beam, based on advice from an MPE.

5.56   Protective aprons (lead equivalence not less than 0.25 mm) should be available for any person who provides assistance by supporting a patient (see paragraphs 5.29 and 5.47).

5.57   Protective aprons and thyroid collars should be stored and inspected as indicated in paragraphs 3.117 to 3.122.

6 Equipment for dental radiography

General recommendations

6.1 This chapter applies to equipment specifically designed for radiography of the teeth or jaws. This includes equipment for intra- and extra-oral radiography, panoramic tomography and cephalometric radiography.

6.2 Dental X-ray equipment should be designed, constructed and installed to comply with recognised British, European or international standards of construction that will enable the recommendations in this chapter to be met. Medical devices placed on the market in the European Community should meet the relevant essential requirements for safety and performance of the Medical Devices Directive [44], transposed into United Kingdom law by the Medical Devices Regulations [45], and be CE-marked as appropriate (also see paragraphs 4.2 to 4.5).

6.3 All newly installed or reinstalled fixed X-ray installations must comply with the current edition of the IEE Wiring Regulations [48] (or subsequent revisions) and the requirements of TRS89 [49] (or subsequent revisions), if the latter is specified in the equipment purchase specification or tender documentation. Prior to installation, the supplier should supply a pre-installation specification to the purchaser (to include mechanical and electrical safety and installation requirements) to facilitate the safe installation, use and maintenance of the equipment. The purchaser should identify who does the necessary pre-installation work, and confirm that it is done to specification as part of the acceptance process.

X-ray source assembly

6.4 Every X-ray source assembly (comprising an X-ray tube, an X-ray tube housing and a beam-limiting device) should be constructed so that, at every rating specified by the manufacturer for that X-ray source assembly, the air kerma from the leakage radiation at a distance from the focal spot of 1 m averaged over an area not exceeding 100 cm^2 does not exceed 0.25 mGy in 1 h for intra-oral radiography equipment, or 1 mGy in 1 h for all other equipment [50].

6.5 The X-ray source assembly should be marked to identify the nominal focal spot position [50].

Beam filtration

6.6 The total filtration of the beam (made up of the inherent filtration and any added filtration) should be equivalent to not less than the following [50]:

(a) 1.5 mm aluminium for X-ray tube voltages up to and including 70 kV, or

(b) 2.5 mm aluminium, of which 1.5 mm should be permanent, for X-ray tube voltages above 70 kV.

6.7 The advice of an MPE should be sought if considering the use of a dose reduction or optimisation strategy incorporating filtration levels significantly greater than those in paragraph 6.6, and when considering the use of rare-earth filters such as erbium. The use of filtration significantly greater than these values will be undesirable if it creates the need for exposure times greater than 1 s for an intra-oral examination.

6.8 The value of the permanent filtration should be marked clearly on the tube housing, preferably in millimetre aluminium (mm Al) equivalent [50]. Every added filter should also be clearly marked with its filtration in aluminium equivalent. Where materials other than aluminium have been used as filters, the X-ray tube should be clearly marked with the chemical symbol and thickness in mm of the filter or marked with the equivalent filtration in mm Al.

X-ray tube operating potential

6.9   Equipment for dental radiography should incorporate adequate provision for adjustment of exposure factors (a suitable range of kV, mA) and exposure time, to allow for the required range of views, patient size and modern film/screen combinations. Medium frequency dental X-ray generators with an effectively constant potential (DC) output are preferred to one and two pulse (AC) generators.

6.10   For intra-oral radiography the nominal tube potential should not be lower than 50 kV. New equipment should operate within the range 60–70 kV.

6.11   For panoramic and cephalometric radiography with manual control, a range of tube potential settings should be available, preferably from 60 kV to 90 kV. There should be provision for the selection of a range of tube currents so that full advantage can be taken of the sensitivity of modern film/screen combinations (see paragraph 5.37).

6.12   All equipment should operate within ± 10 per cent of the stated or selected tube potential (allowing for measurement uncertainties). It is recommended that intra-oral units operating at less than 50 kV be withdrawn from use as soon as is reasonably practicable. Any units still in use that operate at less than 45 kV should be withdrawn immediately from use.

6.13   It is further recommended that, whatever their operational tube potential, units that cannot attain representative patient doses at or below the national DRL (see paragraph 5.24) be withdrawn from use as soon as is reasonably practicable. Any units still in use that deliver representative patient doses in excess of double the DRL should be withdrawn immediately from use.

Beam size and distance control

Intra-oral radiography

6.14   Rectangular collimation should be provided on new equipment and should be retro-fitted to existing equipment at the earliest opportunity. Rectangular collimation should be combined with beam-aiming devices and film holders, since this not only reduces patient dose but will also improve the diagnostic quality of radiographs and reduce the proportion of rejected films. Rectangular collimators should be designed so that the beam size at the tip of the collimator does not exceed 40 mm by 50 mm (i.e. does not overlap the dimensions of the standard ISO film size 2 by more than 5 mm at any edge) and preferably does not exceed 35 mm by 45 mm (i.e. no more than a 2.5 mm overlap at any edge).

6.15   Where circular X-ray beams continue to be used, the beam diameter should not exceed 60 mm at the end of the beam collimator/director, with a maximum tolerable error of +3 mm. It is stressed that beam diameters less than this, and rectangular collimation, will reduce patient dose.

6.16   Beam collimators/directors should be open ended and should provide a minimum FSD of 200 mm for equipment operating at 60 kV or greater and an FSD of at least 100 mm for equipment operating at below 60 kV (*Guidelines on Radiology Standards for Primary Dental Care* [59]). Where X-ray output permits, FSDs larger than this can produce radiographs with improved geometrical unsharpness and lower patient dose.

Panoramic radiography

6.17   Equipment must be provided with patient positioning aids, which need to incorporate the use of light beams if they are to be effective.

6.18   Field limitation can significantly reduce patient exposure when specific diagnostic information is required. New equipment should be provided with automatic selection of beam limitation, although manual selection is acceptable.

6.19   The beam height at the received slit or secondary collimator should be restricted (automatically or manually) to no greater than that required to expose the area of diagnostic interest and certainly no greater than the film or detector in use (normally 125 mm or 150 mm). The beam width should be no greater than 5 mm. All primary slits (more than one may be selectable) should be accurately aligned with the receiving slit.

Cephalometry

6.20   Equipment must be capable of ensuring the precise alignment of X-ray beam, film cassette and patient. An LBD, or other suitable means, should be provided so that the beam can be accurately collimated (BS EN 60601-1-3:1995 *Medical Electrical Equipment* [43]) to include only the diagnostically relevant area.

6.21   To facilitate the imaging of soft tissues, a wedge filter should be provided at the X-ray tube-head, in preference to one at the film cassette.

6.22   Use of intra-oral equipment adapted for cephalometry should be positively discouraged. However, where such equipment is in use, it should be so only with the specific approval of an appropriately qualified RPA or MPE.

Warning signals

6.23   There should be a light on the control panel to show that the mains is switched on. This indicates a state of readiness to emit radiation.

6.24   All dental equipment should be fitted with a light that gives a clear and visible indication to the operator that an exposure is taking place. The light should be triggered by conditions associated uniquely with the commencement and termination of the emission of radiation, but arranged to be seen irrespective of the exposure duration. Audible warnings, provided in addition to the visual warning, should be triggered by the same conditions.

Exposure control

6.25   The exposure should be terminated automatically when a predetermined condition, such as a pre-set time, has been attained. Systems allowing AEC, e.g. on some modern cephalometric radiography systems and digital detectors, should incorporate a suitable guard timer circuit to prevent excessive exposure in the event of failure of the automatic means. Such AEC systems should give a post-exposure indication of the mAs or time given.

6.26   Exposure switches on all dental X-ray equipment should be arranged so that an exposure continues only while continuous pressure is maintained on the switch and terminates if pressure is released. To guard against timer failure, an additional means of termination should be provided which is independent of the normal means. The release of the exposure switch may be regarded as the additional means when this action overrides the timer. Exposure switches relying on a remote control to initiate the exposure must contain all the safety features of conventional exposure switches, with regard to exposure control and release.

6.27   Exposure switches should be designed to prevent inadvertent production of X-rays. If resetting is automatic it should be ensured that pressure on the switch has to be released completely before the next exposure can be made.

6.28   The exposure switch should be arranged so that the operator can remain outside the controlled area and, preferably, at least 2 m away from the tube and the patient during exposure. It should be located or arranged so that inadvertent or unauthorised use should not be possible.

6.29   The X-ray output from intra-oral X-ray equipment should be able to be adjusted such that the range of dental films to be used can be exposed correctly and consistently. This requires the provision of a suitable film speed control and suitably fine adjustment of appropriate exposure time settings.

6.30   When purchasing new panoramic equipment it is recommended that equipment be chosen which is designed to abort the exposure automatically, on sensing a failure or interruption of rotational movement, thereby avoiding an unnecessary and high localised skin dose to the patient. Additionally, the immediate release of the exposure switch should also abort the exposure. When an exposure is interrupted, the unit should be unable to restart the exposure from the interrupted position.

7　Radiotherapy

Introduction

7.1　This chapter describes the duties and responsibilities of staff in the radiotherapy department, the written procedures required for clinical radiotherapy, and the design of radiotherapy treatment rooms in relation to the following techniques:

(a) external beam radiotherapy using a collimated beam of ionising radiation (X-rays, gamma rays, beta rays or electrons), and

(b) brachytherapy using remotely controlled after-loading equipment which transfers sealed sources from a storage container into applicators pre-positioned at a treatment site and withdraws the sources after treatment.

7.2　For the purposes of these guidance notes, remotely controlled after-loading equipment is divided into two classes, high (HDR) and low dose rate (LDR), giving an instantaneous absorbed dose rate, with the source in the patient, greater or less than 10 mGy h^{-1} at 1 m respectively. Pulsed dose rate (PDR) after-loading equipment is classed as HDR in terms of the potential hazard involved; however, risk assessments should take account of the special control systems involved.

7.3　The installation, management and safe operation of radiotherapy equipment for these techniques is described in Chapter 8. Particular arrangements for equipment on loan are detailed in paragraph 1.113. A list of British Standards relating to radiotherapy equipment is given in Appendix 13.

Roles and responsibilities of duty holders in radiotherapy

7.4　The referrer in the radiotherapy process will usually be a medical practitioner. The referrer for concomitant exposures (see paragraph 2.22) will depend on local procedures. The referrer should provide sufficient information about the patient for the radiation oncologist acting as IR(ME)R practitioner to decide if radiotherapy is an appropriate treatment for the patient. The referrer should be identified in the patient's notes. A list of referrers should be available, but note that this can include reference to generic groups of referrers where the individual identity of referrers is unlikely to be known.

7.5　The IR(ME)R practitioner in the radiotherapy process will normally be a radiation oncologist. A list of practitioners should be recorded in the local protocols for radiotherapy treatment. The IR(ME)R practitioner should:

(a) assess the information provided by the referrer and, if necessary, ask for more information from the referrer

(b) decide if radiotherapy is an appropriate treatment for the patient, and

(c) justify in writing the medical exposures necessary to deliver the course of radiotherapy treatment, if indeed radiotherapy is the appropriate treatment.

7.6　The IR(ME)R practitioner will also prescribe the course of radiotherapy treatment (in most cases according to an agreed local protocol). The justification and prescription should be recorded in the patient's notes. Justification of a course of radiotherapy treatment will generally imply justification of all the medical exposures involved, including CT localisation, simulator localisation or verification and portal imaging. In situations where CT localisation scans are carried out in another department (e.g. a radiology department), local agreements should be made either for the oncology practitioner to also be the IR(ME)R practitioner for the CT scans or for a member of the radiology department to be the IR(ME)R practitioner with the oncologist as referrer. These responsibilities must be made clear in the appropriate local protocols.

7.7 Operators in the radiotherapy process will be those appropriately trained members of staff who initiate the exposure in either treatment or simulation, carry out or check treatment planning, calibrate, service or repair radiotherapy equipment, or carry out any other task which could affect the safety of the radiotherapy treatment. An operator should be responsible for each step within the radiotherapy process. Staff in training should be under the direct supervision of an operator. Any treatment aids (such as beam direction shells, compensators or shielding blocks) manufactured within the radiotherapy department should be checked by an operator before being used in the treatment of a patient. Operators in a radiotherapy department may be medical staff, radiographers, nurses, physicists or technical officers. A list of operators should be recorded in the local protocols for radiotherapy treatment.

7.8 MPEs in radiotherapy should be closely involved in all procedures related to the radiotherapy techniques described in this chapter. This will involve providing advice on all aspects of patient dosimetry, on the optimisation and safety of treatment and treatment planning, on the QA programme (including QC procedures) and on any other matters relating to the safety of the radiotherapy equipment or treatment. An MPE should also be consulted before complex radiotherapy equipment or new treatment techniques are introduced. A list of MPEs should be recorded in the local protocols for radiotherapy treatment. MPEs will also be responsible for the acceptance testing of new or modified radiotherapy equipment, its commissioning and definitive calibration (see Appendix 15), and for countersigning ARSAC certificate applications for brachytherapy procedures. The MPE will be involved with the RPA when the installer undertakes the critical examination of new equipment, or major upgrades of existing equipment.

7.9 An RPA for the radiotherapy department should have appropriate experience in the application of radiation protection principles in radiotherapy. The RPA should be consulted on all matters specified in Schedule 5 of IRR99 [1] relevant to the radiotherapy department, including the local rules for the use of ionising radiation required for all designated areas within the radiotherapy department. The local rules must be appropriate for the radiotherapy equipment and practices used in the areas and should contain contingency plans relating to the equipment or operations, as appropriate, in the event of a radiation incident or emergency (see also paragraph 7.61). One or more RPSs should be appointed by the employer to ensure that everyone is aware of the local rules and that these are observed. The RPSs should be involved in preparing the local rules for designated areas and should establish and maintain a communication channel with the RPA. A list of RPSs and their areas of responsibility should be recorded in the local rules.

Procedural requirements for radiotherapy

7.10 Written procedures are required for the radiotherapy techniques specified in paragraph 7.1. For clinical radiotherapy techniques there may be several written procedures, to allow for differences in procedure between different treatment sites, different complexities of treatment technique, etc. Clinical procedures should include:

(a) details of procedures to identify patients correctly
(b) lists of individuals entitled to act as referrers, IR(ME)R practitioners and operators
(c) details of how treatment and simulation exposures are to be recorded
(d) details of how clinical QA procedures are to be implemented, and
(e) procedures for providing appropriate information and written instructions to patients.

7.11 Written procedures are also required for some of the equipment-related procedures described in Chapter 8, such as equipment acceptance, calibration and equipment QC.

7.12 Where IR(ME)R practitioners justify a course of radiotherapy according to a generic local clinical protocol for a particular tumour type or treatment site, that protocol shall provide general details of the dose, fractionation scheme, specific treatment techniques to be implemented and treatment aids which might be used. The IR(ME)R practitioner will also provide and sign a radiotherapy prescription for each patient. The clinical protocol should specify any circumstances which might arise where an operator must refer to the IR(ME)R practitioner, or consult an MPE, before proceeding with the treatment.

7.13   Where a local clinical protocol does not exist, or is not appropriate for a specific patient, the IR(ME)R practitioner must ensure that written instructions are available for all operators in the radiotherapy process. These written instructions should also specify any circumstances which might arise where an operator must refer to the IR(ME)R practitioner, or consult an MPE, before proceeding with the treatment.

7.14   Particular care should be taken to ensure that all IR(ME)R practitioners, operators and MPEs are fully informed and trained when new techniques or protocols are introduced, or when there are any changes in these protocols.

Radiotherapy treatment rooms

7.15   This section applies to equipment for external beam radiotherapy and HDR remotely controlled after-loading. This section does not apply to LDR remotely controlled after-loading equipment which is designed for use in a ward or adjoining room. Guidance on treatment rooms for this latter type of equipment is given in paragraphs 7.46 to 7.58.

7.16   Radiotherapy equipment should be installed in a treatment room designed for the purpose within a radiotherapy department. Information on the design of treatment rooms is available in IPEM75 *The Design of Radiotherapy Treatment Room Facilities* [60].

7.17   Normally two or more items of therapy equipment should not be installed in the same treatment room. If, however, a second item of therapy equipment is installed in a treatment room (e.g. an HDR remotely controlled after-loader installed in a megavoltage accelerator treatment room), then there must be suitable engineering controls to ensure that only one item of equipment can operate at a time. If appropriate design precautions are implemented, and a suitable risk assessment is undertaken, it may be reasonable to operate two LDR systems or an LDR and a PDR system in the same room when the room has been designed to the higher specification.

7.18   The treatment room should be designed with adequate shielding as described in paragraphs 1.55 and 1.56. The IDR for collimated beam equipment should be measured outside each primary barrier, with the radiation beam pointing directly at that barrier. The thickness of shielding should allow for the fact that the area of wall, floor or ceiling which produces scattered radiation is much greater when the useful beam is uncollimated (as is the case for after-loading equipment). In estimating adequate protection at the design stage, the following possible future developments should be considered:

   (a) increases in dose rates

   (b) increases in number of beams per hour and in dose per beam

   (c) increase in use of higher energy photon beams

   (d) increases in the number of total body and hemi-body treatment techniques involving beam projection against a specific wall, and

   (e) changes in use and occupancy of adjacent areas.

   Further advice on the design of radiotherapy treatment rooms is available [60].

7.19   Adjacent areas where there may be a radiation risk while equipment is in use, such as roofs, basements and upper parts of external walls, may not need to be considered as controlled or supervised areas if they are declared as prohibited areas and if effective arrangements have been made that physically prevent access whenever the equipment is, or may be, in operation (L121 paragraph 259 [2]). Adjacent plant or equipment rooms which are designated as controlled or supervised areas may also be declared prohibited areas, with access for servicing following a system of work detailed in the local rules. All systems of work for access, and arrangements for prohibiting access, should be regularly reviewed in consultation with the RPA in conjunction with the appropriate RPS.

7.20   All treatment rooms should be controlled areas. The control panel should be located outside the treatment room. Ideally the control panel should be positioned so that the treatment operator can view the entrance to the treatment room. Where this is not possible, a closed circuit television system should be used to view the entrance to the treatment room. For the special case where the control panel for kilovoltage equipment used for superficial therapy, operating at no more than 50 kV, is inside the treatment room, there should be a protective panel installed to provide adequate protection (see paragraphs 1.55, 1.56 and 7.18) for the treatment operator. The local rules should detail procedures to ensure that all staff not excluded from the treatment room are behind this protective panel before radiation is initiated.

7.21   In the special case of a PDR machine it may be appropriate to have the programming console within the treatment room, with the start and stop controls outside the room.

7.22   If a maze entrance is designed, the protection provided by the door to the treatment room may be reduced or the door may be replaced by another type of barrier. Shielded doors in treatment rooms should be clearly marked with the equivalent thickness of lead. It may also be appropriate to fix a notice advising caution in any maintenance procedure, because of the weight of the door.

7.23   Electrically operated doors in treatment rooms should have an emergency mechanical mechanism for opening them in the case of electrical power failure. This mechanism should be tested regularly and appropriate staff training provided.

7.24   Normally, observation windows should not be installed in external beam radiotherapy treatment rooms. Observation windows in kilovoltage treatment rooms, or HDR after-loading equipment treatment rooms, should provide the same degree of protection as that required of the walls or doors in which they are located.

7.25   Effective interlocks should be provided to restore equipment to a safe state when doors are opened, or other access barriers interrupted or passed. These interlocks should not be reset simply by closure of the door or restoration of the barrier.

7.26   A door interlock reset switch should be provided near the exit from the treatment room, at a position from which a person leaving the treatment room has a clear view of the room. This switch should have a delayed action, sufficient to permit the person to exit from the room. During this time delay a second action has to be completed, either by closing the room door or operating a switch outside the room. The local rules should make it clear that the last person to leave the treatment room should check visually that no one but the patient is in the room, only then should that person operate both these switches in series as described.

7.27   The access interlock, when reset, should return the equipment from the safe state to a preparatory state and not to a radiation state. These states are defined in the appropriate part of BS EN 60601 (see Appendix 13). Advice on the design of interlocks for equipment safety is given in BS 5304 (now replaced by PD5304: 2000) [61].

7.28   Means should be provided, normally by a closed circuit television system, for the treatment operator to observe the patient from the control panel during treatment. Where parts of the radiotherapy equipment move during treatment, it may be necessary to have more than one television camera to ensure that the patient is visible at all times during treatment. It should also be possible for the treatment operator to hear and speak to the patient during treatment. This may be by means of a switched intercom system.

7.29   Warning notices, indicating that the room is a controlled area and the nature of the radiation source (Appendix 12), should be fixed to treatment room doors or clearly displayed at maze entrances.

7.30   Illuminated warning signs should be installed at the entrance to the treatment room. These signs should be controlled by the radiation equipment (or, in the case of some after-loading equipment, by an independent radiation detector as discussed in paragraph 7.42) and should normally indicate two states of the radiation equipment: (i) when the equipment is in a preparatory or ready state, and (ii) when radiation is being emitted (the beam-on state). The preparatory or ready state should be indicated by the radiation trefoil and, where appropriate, a 'Controlled Area' or 'Radiation Hazard' legend. This circuit can use fluorescent or tungsten bulbs. The radiation beam-on state should be indicated as 'Radiation On' or 'X-rays On', in red lettering on a black background, using tungsten bulbs rather than fluorescent bulbs to ensure immediate indication. One possible arrangement for these signs is shown in Appendix 12. The legend on an illuminated sign should not be visible when the lamp is off.

7.31   Similar warning signs should be installed within the treatment room (and any adjacent designated area), operating in conjunction with those at the entrance to the treatment room. These should be augmented with a continuous audible indication of the radiation state. The audible signal may be a sound that is produced by the equipment when in the radiation beam-on state, or may be an independent audible signal modulated at a frequency of 500–800 Hz. The operation of these illuminated signs and audible signals should be checked before clinical treatments commence every day. If these signs or audible signals fail to operate, the treatment operator should stop and report the situation to the operator responsible for the technical maintenance of the equipment. The equipment should not be used until the signs and audible signals are operational again.

7.32   Emergency stop switches should be provided at the control panel, at the entrance to the treatment room, within the treatment room and in any adjacent controlled area. Operation of these switches should cause the equipment to stop emitting radiation and also stop any dynamic motions of the equipment that might put the patient at risk. The switches within the treatment room should be located so that any person accidentally in the room when radiation commences can reach an emergency stop switch without passing through the radiation beam. Emergency stop switches should be of the lock-on type, so that the equipment remains in a safe state until the switch is released by an appropriate operator who will ensure that it is safe to return the equipment to the preparatory state. The procedure to be followed after an emergency stop switch has been used should be clearly identified in the local rules. Emergency stop switches should be regularly tested as part of the equipment QC procedures.

Additional requirements for treatment rooms containing electron beam equipment

7.33   Normally, a treatment room designed to provide adequate protection for X-ray generating equipment and satisfying the recommendations in the preceding paragraphs will provide adequate protection for electron beam generating equipment. The shielding of the treatment room barriers in the directions in which the useful electron beam can be directed should, however, take into account the production of bremsstrahlung in the shielding barrier. Consideration should also be given to the need for a solid barrier, such as a wooden door, at the external maze entrance because of bremsstrahlung radiation scattered into the maze.

7.34   Treatment rooms designed for electron beam therapy should be well ventilated, with adequate air flow to remove ozone formed by irradiation of oxygen in the air. This is particularly important for whole body electron treatments using long treatment distances and high electron dose rates. In general, ventilation systems providing 14–16 air changes per hour will be appropriate for radiotherapy treatment rooms. The exposure limits for ozone are given in the HSE publication EH40/2000 *Occupational Exposure Limits* [62]. Advice on the health hazards of ozone is given in HSE publication EH38/96 *Ozone: Health Hazards and Precautionary Measures* [63].

Additional requirements for treatment rooms operating with X-ray energies over 10 MeV

7.35   Neutrons may be produced adventitiously by X-rays of energy exceeding about 10 MeV and by bremsstrahlung from electron beams of similar energy. They may, consequently, form a significant fraction of the stray radiation from megavoltage equipment. This should be taken into account in the design of the treatment room, to ensure that adequate protection as defined in paragraphs 1.55 and 7.18 is achieved. Neutron-absorbing materials can produce gamma rays and this may require additional shielding.

7.36   Induced radioactivity may occur in accelerators. Materials used for collimation and shielding should be chosen to avoid long-lived activity. Following appropriate measurements and a risk assessment it may be necessary to delay entry into the room or parts of the room, or to restrict service access to the equipment, to avoid a hazard from short-lived activity. These restrictions should be included in the local rules.

Additional requirements for treatment rooms containing gamma-beam teletherapy equipment

7.37   Treatment rooms containing teletherapy sources should have a radiation monitor permanently installed in the room. The radiation monitor should have a 'supply on' indicator and should be independently connected to the electricity supply, rather then directly to the radiotherapy equipment. Ideally, it should also have a battery supply that automatically provides electrical power in the event of a supply failure. An audible indication of HDRs is advisable. Installed radiation monitors should be tested at least weekly, as part of the equipment QC procedures.

7.38   Details of the immediate action to be taken if a radiation emergency occurs, such as the source transfer mechanism sticking or the shutter failing to operate, should be described in the local rules as a local equipment contingency plan. The local rules should also provide a list of people who must be informed and their contact details. The RPA, RPS and an MPE with knowledge of gamma beam teletherapy equipment must always be consulted. A summary of the procedure and contact information should be clearly displayed at the control panel and at the entrance to the treatment room. All treatment operators should be conversant with this procedure, which should be rehearsed at least monthly and whenever the operating team changes.

7.39   Any equipment or tool required for use in a radiation emergency must be kept outside the treatment room, close to the control panel and in a clearly marked location. The equipment or tool should only be used by the RPS, MPE or those staff trained in its use and identified in the contingency plan. Every day, before clinical use of the machine commences, a check must be made that this equipment or tool is in the correct location and that the operator has been trained in its use.

7.40   A portable radiation monitor should be available, outside the treatment room, for use in locating the source in the event of a failure of the source return mechanisms. The monitor should only be used by the RPS, MPE or those staff trained in its use and identified in the contingency plan. The portable monitor should be battery operated and the battery should be tested on a regular basis. Every day, before clinical use of the machine commences, a check should be made that this monitor is in the correct location and is working.

Additional requirements for treatment rooms containing high dose rate after-loading equipment

7.41   HDR after-loading equipment, even that designed as mobile equipment, should always be used in a properly shielded and designated treatment area.

7.42   Treatment rooms containing after-loading sources should have an installed radiation monitor. The radiation monitor should have a 'supply on' indicator and should be independently connected to the electricity supply rather than directly to the radiotherapy equipment. Ideally it should also have a battery supply which automatically provides electrical power in the event of a supply failure. An audible indication of HDRs is advisable. Installed radiation monitors should be tested at least weekly, as part of the equipment QC procedures.

7.43   The action to be taken if a radiation emergency occurs, such as the source transfer mechanism sticking or failing to operate, should be specified in the local rules as a local equipment contingency plan. The local rules should also provide a list of people who must be informed and their contact details. A summary of the procedure and contact information should be clearly displayed at the control panel and at the entrance to the treatment room. All treatment operators should be conversant with this procedure. The RPA, RPS and an MPE with knowledge of after-loading equipment must always be consulted about the plan. The emergency plans should be rehearsed as part of staff training, whenever the operating team changes and at least once a year for all staff.

7.44   Any equipment or tool required for use in a radiation emergency must be kept outside the treatment room, close to the control panel and in a clearly marked location. The equipment or tool should only be used by the RPS, MPE or those staff trained in its use and identified in the contingency plan. Every day, before clinical use of the machine commences, a check must be made that this equipment or tool is in the correct location and that the operator has been trained in its use.

7.45   A portable radiation monitor should be available and should be used to locate the source in the event of a failure of the source return mechanisms. The portable monitor should be battery operated and should be tested on a regular basis. The monitor should only be used by the RPS, MPE or those staff trained in its use and identified in the contingency plan. Every day, before clinical use of the machine commences, a check must be made that this monitor is in the correct location.

Treatment rooms containing low dose rate after-loading equipment

7.46   LDR after-loading equipment should be installed in a room or ward designed for the purpose, normally within a radiotherapy department. Normally no more than two items of after-loading equipment should be installed in the same treatment room, particularly if the absorbed dose rate from either of the items is greater than 2 mGy h^{-1} from a source within a patient.

7.47   The treatment room should be adequately protected as defined in paragraphs 1.55 and 1.56. If a second item of after-loading equipment is installed in the room then there must be appropriate shielding between the beds. Care should also be taken to ensure that adjoining rooms are adequately protected. The thickness of shielding should allow for the fact that the area of wall, floor or ceiling which produces scattered radiation is much greater when the useful beam is uncollimated (as is the case for after-loading equipment).

7.48   Where mobile shielding is used, either within or at the door of the treatment room, its correct location should be clearly marked on the floor and described (perhaps with the aid of diagrams) in the local rules. The radiation integrity of mobile shielding should be regularly checked as part of the QC programme.

7.49   Effective interlocks should be provided to restore equipment to a safe state when doors are opened or other access barriers interrupted or passed. Simply closing the door or restoring the barrier should not reset the interlocks. The access interlock, when reset, should return the equipment from the safe state to a preparatory state and not to a radiation state. These states are defined in the appropriate part of BS EN 60601 (see Appendix 13). Advice on the design of interlocks for equipment safety is given in BS 5304 (now replaced by PD5304: 2000) [61].

7.50   Means should be provided, either via a window or by a closed circuit television system, for the treatment operator to observe the patient from a safe location outside the room. It should also be possible for the treatment operator to hear and speak to the patient during treatment. This may be by means of a switched intercom system.

7.51   Warning notices indicating a controlled area and the nature of the radiation source (Appendix 12) should be fixed to treatment room doors.

7.52   Illuminated warning signs should be installed at the entrance to the treatment room. These signs should be controlled by the radiation equipment and normally indicate two states of the radiation equipment: (i) when the equipment is in a preparatory or ready state, and (ii) when radiation is being emitted. The preparatory or ready state should be indicated by the radiation trefoil and, where appropriate, a 'Controlled Area' legend. This circuit can use either fluorescent or tungsten bulbs. The radiation state should be indicated as 'Radiation On' or 'X-rays On', in red lettering on a black background, using tungsten bulbs rather than fluorescent bulbs to ensure immediate indication. The legend on an illuminated sign should not be visible when the lamp is off. One possible arrangement for these signs is shown in Appendix 12.

7.53   The operation of these illuminated signs should be checked before clinical treatments commence. If these signs fail to operate, the treatment operator should stop and report the situation to the operator responsible for the technical maintenance of the equipment. The equipment should not be used until the signs are operational.

7.54   Emergency stop switches should be provided at the control panels, at the entrance to the treatment room (if this is not the location of a control panel) and in any adjacent controlled area. Operation of these switches should cause the equipment to stop emitting radiation. Emergency stop switches should be of the lock-on type, so that the equipment remains in a safe state until the switch is released by an appropriate operator who will ensure that it is safe to return the equipment to the preparatory state. The procedure to be followed after an emergency stop switch has been used should be clearly identified in the local rules. Emergency stop switches should be regularly tested as part of the equipment QC procedures.

7.55   Treatment rooms containing after-loading sources should have an installed radiation monitor. The radiation monitor should have a 'supply on' indicator and should be independently connected to the electricity supply rather than directly to the radiotherapy equipment. Ideally, it should also have a battery supply which automatically provides electrical power in the event of a supply failure. An audible indication of HDRs may be advisable.

7.56   Details of the action to be taken if a radiation emergency occurs, such as the source transfer mechanism sticking or failing to operate, should be specified in the local rules and the contingency plan. The local rules should also provide a list of people who must be informed and their contact details. A summary of the procedure and contact information should be clearly displayed at the control panel and at the entrance to the treatment room. All treatment operators should be conversant with this procedure. Contingency plans should be rehearsed as part of staff training, whenever the operating team changes and at least once a year for all staff. The RPA, RPS and an MPE with knowledge of after-loading equipment must always be consulted about the plan.

7.57   Any equipment or tool required for use in a radiation emergency must be kept outside the treatment room, close to the control panel and in a clearly marked location. The equipment or tool should only be used by the RPS, MPE or those staff trained in its use and identified in the contingency plan. Every day, before clinical use of the machine commences, a check must be made that this equipment or tool is in the correct location and that the operator has been trained in its use.

7.58   A portable radiation monitor should be available and should be used to locate the source in the event of a failure of the source return mechanisms. The portable monitor should be battery operated and should be tested on a regular basis. Every day, before clinical use of the machine commences, a check must be made that this monitor is in the correct location.

Radiotherapy simulator rooms

7.59   The radiotherapy simulator room should be designed with adequate protection as defined in paragraph 1.54, following the relevant guidance given in Chapters 3 and 4. Particular attention should be given to the differences in equipment parameters and operational procedures between a radiotherapy simulator and a diagnostic fluoroscopic unit.

Treatment rooms for other types of radiotherapy equipment

7.60   Guidance on treatment rooms for radiotherapy equipment involving neutron or proton beams and neutron activation analysis has not been included in this chapter. For any project involving these techniques appropriate advice should be sought from the RPA, RPS and MPE. Advice may also be available from the relevant Health Department and the appropriate professional bodies.

Risk assessments and contingency planning for radiotherapy accidents

7.61   A risk assessment to identify all hazards with the potential to cause a radiation accident within the radiotherapy department must be undertaken before any new activity involving radiation equipment or sources. This should be undertaken by the employer and the management of the radiotherapy department in co-operation with the RPA and the appropriate MPEs. The risk assessment should be reviewed in co-operation with the RPA at regular intervals. Detailed guidance on risk assessment is available in Chapters 1 and 19 and in the HSE publication *5 Steps to Risk Assessment* [15].

7.62   Where the prior risk assessment shows that a particular type of radiation accident is reasonably foreseeable, such as a source sticking, a shutter failure or a fire outbreak, the employer and the management of the radiotherapy department in co-operation with the RPA, RPS and the appropriate MPEs should prepare a contingency plan for the radiotherapy department. The contingency plan should be designed to limit the consequences of any accident that does occur. The contingency plan may comprise different sections relating to different types of equipment or operations, as mentioned in paragraphs 7.38, 7.43 and 7.56, and should detail the immediate action to be taken to limit the consequences of the accident. Appropriate details of the contingency plan should be incorporated into the local rules. Rehearsals of the arrangements in the plan should be undertaken at suitable intervals, depending on the probability and severity of the accident. The contingency plan should be reviewed in co-operation with the RPA at regular intervals, at least annually.

Radiotherapy accidents and incidents

7.63   Accidents or incidents where the radiotherapy or brachytherapy patient receives an exposure significantly greater than intended may have to be reported to HSE and the appropriate Health Department. The guideline multiplying factor for radiotherapy and brachytherapy to be used in deciding when an incident has to be reported is given in table 1 of HSG226 [10], along with the guidance on the appropriate investigation and reporting procedure. However, HSG226 is being revised for issue in 2002 and the multiplier indicated for radiotherapy fractions may be changed to take into account the overall effects of the treatment rather than each single-fraction event. Incidents where the radiotherapy or brachytherapy patient is underexposed can also have serious consequences. While these are not notifiable under IRR99 [1] or IR(ME)R [3], a full investigation involving the IR(ME)R practitioner, RPA, RPS, MPE responsible for the QC of the equipment and any other operators or external service staff involved in the incident should be undertaken. Further guidance is given in Chapter 19 and in HSG226 [10].

7.64   Accidents, incidents or potential incidents involving either an exposure significantly greater than intended or an underexposure of a radiotherapy or brachytherapy patient which can be attributed to failure of the radiotherapy equipment should be reported to the appropriate authority, the Incident Reporting and Investigation Centre (IRIC) of the MDA, the Scottish Healthcare Supplies or the Department of Health, Social Services and Public Safety for Northern Ireland. Details of the reporting procedure are given in the Safety Action Notices MDA SN2000(01), SAN(SC)00/01 (see http://www.medical-devices.gov.uk/) and the equivalent for other parts of the United Kingdom.

8   Radiotherapy and brachytherapy equipment

Introduction

8.1   This chapter is concerned with the following radiotherapy equipment:

     (a) accelerators for megavoltage X-ray and electron radiotherapy
     (b) kilovoltage X-ray equipment for superficial and orthovoltage radiotherapy
     (c) gamma-beam teletherapy equipment
     (d) HDR remotely controlled after-loading equipment
     (e) LDR remotely controlled after-loading equipment, and
     (f) radiotherapy simulators.

8.2   For the purposes of these guidance notes, remotely controlled after-loading equipment is divided into two classes, HDR and LDR, giving an instantaneous absorbed dose rate greater or less than 10 mGy h^{-1} at 1 m respectively. PDR after-loading equipment is classed as HDR (see paragraph 7.2).

8.3   The guidance in this chapter also applies when equipment intended primarily for therapy is being tested or calibrated at its place of use or used for *in vitro* irradiation.

8.4   Guidance on other types of radiotherapy equipment (such as those involving neutron or proton beams) and on some specialised radiotherapy techniques (such as intraoperative and intracavity radiotherapy) has not been included in this chapter. For advice on these types of equipment or techniques, appropriate advice should be sought from the RPA, RPS and MPE. Advice may also be available from the HSE, the relevant Health Department and the appropriate professional bodies.

Equipment inventory

8.5   An inventory of all radiotherapy equipment must be maintained by the radiotherapy department. For each piece of radiotherapy equipment the following information should be recorded:

     (a) type of equipment (following the classification of paragraph 8.1)
     (b) name of manufacturer
     (c) model number
     (d) serial numbers or other unique identifiers
     (e) year of manufacture, and
     (f) date of acceptance.

8.6   For equipment containing a radioactive source, details of the source, source strength and date of installation should be recorded, along with a copy of the RSA93 registration [7]. A copy of this information should be displayed at the treatment room. This information will usually be available on the supplier's calibration certificate. For equipment controlled by computer software or firmware, details of the software modules, versions and dates of installation should be recorded.

8.7   The inventory information should be updated whenever a major upgrade or source change is undertaken. When equipment is decommissioned or removed from the department, this should also be recorded in the inventory. The inventory for the radiotherapy department must be available for inspection by the appropriate authority (see addresses in Appendix 16).

General radiation equipment safety recommendations

8.8   Radiotherapy equipment should comply with all sections of BS EN 60601 that are relevant to the safe operation of the equipment. Appendix 13 lists the relevant sections of BS EN 60601 (note that BS 5724 has been retitled BS EN 60601).

8.9   For all types of radiotherapy equipment it should only be possible to commence an exposure from the control panel. The control panel should give a clear and unambiguous indication of the treatment mode selected. The treatment operator should be required to confirm that the correct mode has been selected. The operational state of the equipment should also be clearly and unambiguously indicated on the control panel. Operational states are defined in the appropriate section of BS EN 60601 (Appendix 13). The control panel should also indicate the choice and correct location of optional treatment accessories such as wedge filters, electron applicators, etc. Where there is a choice of available accessory, a select and confirm system should be provided. The control panel should provide means of initiating the radiation exposure, interrupting the radiation exposure and terminating the radiation exposure.

8.10   It should be possible to inhibit or disable the facility to initiate a radiation exposure from the control panel by means of either a key switch with a removable key or a password entered via a keyboard at the control panel. A clear indication should be available at the control panel if the treatment has been terminated by any event other than the operation of the primary dosimetry or timer system.

8.11   The control panel should indicate the dose delivered during the emission of radiation. In order that the magnitude of any exposure should be obvious to the treatment operator, all dose indicators should count up from zero. All equipment should be provided with two or more detectors, for monitoring and displaying dose and dose rate, and a back-up timer. This requirement is not appropriate for after-loading equipment. Details of the requirements for these systems for different types of radiotherapy equipment are given in the relevant sections of BS EN 60601 (see Appendix 13).

8.12   Wherever practicable, interlocks and safety tripping mechanisms should be designed so that their operation or non-operation is evident. Facilities should be provided by the manufacturer so that the operation of interlocks and safety tripping mechanisms can be tested.

8.13   Suppliers and manufacturers of equipment should provide appropriate operating manuals for the equipment. They should also provide technical manuals and, where appropriate, circuit diagrams, giving details of calibration and QC procedures. These manuals, or other documents provided, must contain adequate information about safe use, testing and maintenance of the equipment. Manuals and circuit diagrams should be updated when appropriate as part of the QA programme.

Prior risk assessment

8.14   A new activity involving the therapeutic use of radiation may not begin until a risk assessment has been made and recorded in writing. This assessment must be kept up to date where there is any significant change in the equipment or its operational use. Further guidance on risk assessments is available in *Work with Ionising Radiation* L121 [2] and in *Management of Health and Safety at Work* [64] (see paragraph 1.16).

Prior authorisation

8.15   Prior authorisation from HSE is required before equipment intended to produce X-rays for medical treatment (i.e. kilovoltage therapy equipment and linear accelerators) is used. However, HSE have published a list of conditions which, if satisfied, will be taken as fulfilling the requirements for prior authorisation and specific authorisation from HSE will not be required. Details of the conditions for this generic authorisation are given in Appendix 18. Equipment containing radioactive sources may require registration under RSA 93 [7]. Before new equipment is used for the first time the employer has the responsibility for checking that the conditions of generic authorisation are met; this is usually delegated to the RPA, RPS or MPE. It may be appropriate to file a copy of these conditions with the local rules. Note that prior authorisation, which by definition relates to practices and not to the equipment as such, is not required for the use of gamma beam teletherapy equipment, after-loading equipment or radiotherapy simulators (see paragraph 1.22).

Notification

8.16   When a radiotherapy department on a new site is to be opened, HSE must be notified of this intention in writing at least 28 days before work starts with ionising radiation. The details required by HSE are listed in Schedules 2 and 3 of IRR99 [1]. A new development on the same site will not require notification unless there is a material change in the nature of the radiation work. HSE must be notified if radiation work ceases at a site (see paragraph 1.29).

Installation and commissioning of radiotherapy equipment

8.17   An MPE should be responsible for the acceptance testing of new or modified radiotherapy equipment (see paragraph 1.42). Radiotherapy equipment should comply with these guidance notes, publication HSG226 [10] and the appropriate sections of BS EN 60601 (see Appendix 13) relevant to the safety of equipment. If the manufacturer or supplier has an acceptance testing protocol this should also be followed. Further guidance on the acceptance testing and commissioning of radiotherapy equipment is given in IPEM54 *Commissioning and Quality Assurance of Linear Accelerators* [65] and IPEM81 *Physics Aspects of Quality Control in Radiotherapy* [66].

8.18   All available combinations of treatment mode and treatment accessory should be tested as part of the acceptance procedure. If any combination is not tested or accepted then the MPE should ensure that all operators are informed that these combinations cannot be used clinically until they have been accepted. Equipment such as treatment planning systems and dosimetry equipment, which can affect the safety of radiotherapy treatment, should also undergo acceptance testing.

8.19   Data from acceptance testing should be used as a reference baseline from which to monitor the performance of equipment during subsequent QC testing.

8.20   An MPE should be responsible for the commissioning of the necessary data for planning radiotherapy treatments. Appropriate testing should be undertaken to ensure the integrity of equipment data transferred to subsidiary equipment such as treatment planning systems.

8.21   Where equipment can be customised by modifying accessories or the control system software, an MPE should be responsible for ensuring that details of all customisation is recorded. All the appropriate operators should be informed by the MPE of the implications of any customisation both for treatment techniques and for patient safety.

Critical examination and quality control baselines

8.22   Before new equipment is used clinically, a representative of the manufacturer or supplier should carry out a critical examination in the presence of an MPE or RPA. Specific attention should be addressed to leakage from the radiation head, operator-controlled beam and motion termination, machine-controlled beam and motion termination, visible and audible indications of the operational state of the radiation equipment, and the operation of safety-critical interlocks. A report of the examination should be made to the employer and should be kept for reference during the working life of the equipment. The critical examination should be repeated after any major upgrade to the equipment.

8.23   Before the equipment is brought into clinical use, adequate testing of the equipment must be carried out to establish a QC baseline for the QA programme; all appropriate data should be recorded. All safety-related features of the equipment should be examined and where appropriate demonstrated or tested, including those associated with the treatment room.

Calibration

8.24 Two independent MPEs should undertake a definitive calibration before the equipment is first used clinically. One of the MPEs should be responsible for procedure and its recording. The second independent MPE may come from a different radiotherapy department. This may be particularly appropriate when additional expertise in new techniques or equipment is required. Details of the procedure for carrying out a definitive calibration are given in Appendix 15. When source changes are undertaken in after-loading equipment appropriate measurements should be undertaken to confirm source strength and properties. These measurements should be checked by an MPE who will then be responsible for issuing appropriate source data for clinical use.

8.25 The appropriate Code of Practice for radiotherapy dosimetry should be used for all measurements. These Codes of Practice are produced by the IPEM (see Appendix 16) which will update and reissue them as necessary. In general a department should adopt new Codes of Practice within 3 years of their date of publication. Details of the present Codes of Practice for the dosimetry of megavoltage X-rays, kilovoltage X-rays and electrons are listed in Appendix 14. The responsibility for definitive calibrations within a department should be vested in an MPE with a minimum of 6 years relevant experience in radiotherapy. The measurements for each definitive calibration should be undertaken by two physicists with at least 4 years relevant experience in radiotherapy. Details of the procedure for carrying out a definitive calibration are given in Appendix 15.

8.26 An MPE should be made responsible for ensuring that the calibration of all radiotherapy equipment is checked at regular intervals. Advice on minimum frequencies of dosimetry calibration is given in Appendix 15. Date and results of calibration measurements and recalibrations should be entered in a calibration record as part of the QA system. These records should be signed or countersigned by an appropriate physics operator and should be available for inspection by the appropriate authority as given in Appendix 16.

8.27 As part of the QC system, an inventory of radiotherapy dosimetry equipment should be maintained. This should include all dosemeters, chambers and check sources. For each piece of equipment the following information should be recorded:

(a) type of equipment
(b) name of manufacturer
(c) model number
(d) serial number or other unique identifier, and
(e) year of manufacture.

The MPE responsible for radiotherapy dosimetry should ensure that a record of calibration data (including calibrated energies) is maintained for all dosimetry equipment.

8.28 The causes of any significant changes in output absorbed dose rate should be reported to and investigated by an MPE, who should ensure that any necessary action is taken before the equipment is used clinically again [67]. This is particularly important for any equipment that does not have an integrating dosemeter, such as some equipment for superficial therapy.

8.29 An MPE should ensure that all gamma-ray equipment is checked for correct operation and the applicability of the output data in use, at least once every month or before use if use is infrequent or intermittent.

8.30 Whenever service or maintenance procedures or repairs have been undertaken which might have involved adjustments or changes to the equipment which could alter the output calibration for any reason, the equipment should be recalibrated before it is again used clinically.

8.31 Dosemeters and dosimetry equipment used for calibrations and output checks must be maintained in good condition and appropriate tests made to ensure that their sensitivity remains constant. The operation and sensitivity (traced to a national primary standard) should be checked at least annually over the range of radiation qualities normally used within the department. Further guidance on the QC of dosimetry equipment is given in IPEM81 [66].

Quality assurance

8.32   QC testing of all radiotherapy equipment should be included in the radiotherapy department QA programme. An MPE should be responsible for ensuring that appropriate QC tests are undertaken at suitable frequencies. Guidance on QC programmes and the frequency of testing is given in IPEM54 [65] and IPEM81 [66] and the World Health Organization (WHO) document on *Quality Assurance in Radiotherapy* [68] http://www.who.int/home-page/.

8.33   The MPE should ensure that appropriate corrective action is taken if the results of any test indicate that the safety of the patient or the accuracy of the treatment may be compromised. Records of QC testing should be signed or countersigned by an appropriate physics operator and be available for inspection by the appropriate authority as given in Appendix 16.

8.34   The QC testing programme should include programmable electronic control systems that control the operation of radiotherapy equipment. Guidance on programmable electronic systems in safety-related applications is available in BS IEC 61508 [69]. Particular attention should also be given to the QC of systems such as treatment record and verify systems, computer media and networks which manipulate, store or transfer radiotherapy data used for specifying patient treatments [67].

8.35   The QC testing programme should also include any non-radiation equipment, such as treatment planning systems, which can affect the safety of radiotherapy treatment. Guidance on the QC of treatment planning equipment is given in IPEM68 *A Guide to the Commissioning and Quality Control of Treatment Planning Systems* [70] and IPEM81 [66].

8.36   Sealed radioactive sources for gamma-beam therapy or remotely controlled after-loading equipment should have been tested by the manufacturer before delivery and should be accompanied by a leakage test certificate. If this is not so, the source should be tested for leakage before it is loaded into the equipment or the equipment is brought into clinical use. Sources should be retested at least once every 2 years, but for those that are in frequent use for remotely controlled after-loading, leakage tests should be made at least once a year. These sources may be subject to mechanical wear and there would be a particular hazard to a patient or staff if leakage occurred. A test should be made immediately if any damage to a source is suspected. It is usually unnecessary, and likely to be more hazardous, to make direct leakage tests on installed gamma sources. Instead the equipment should be tested for leakage at the sites indicated in Table 8.1. Where equipment contains components made from uranium (see paragraph 8.57), there is a need to carry out leakage tests for these components, using an instrument able to detect alpha-emitting material.

Table 8.1 Leakage testing

Equipment	Place to be wipe-tested
Gamma-beam therapy equipment	The surface of the radiation head including the beam aperture
Remotely controlled after-loading equipment	The internal surfaces of the transit tubes after ensuring that all the sources have recently passed through the transit tubes

8.37   If, in a leakage test, the activity measured on the swab is less than 200 Bq the source(s) may be considered to be leak free. Immediate steps should be taken to prevent the spread of contamination if the measured activity is greater than 200 Bq, followed later by the removal of the leaking source and decontamination of the equipment. All leakage tests should be recorded as part of the QC testing programme.

8.38   Radiotherapy simulators should be included in the QC testing programme. Special attention should be paid to the accuracy of the mechanical parameters as well as fluoroscopic and radiographic parameters.

Maintenance and servicing of radiotherapy equipment

8.39   Treatment operators should report all faults that could compromise the safety or accuracy of patient treatments to the appropriate staff. These should be investigated and, if necessary, corrected before the equipment is used clinically again. The local rules should identify the action to be taken and the conditions under which clinical use of the equipment should stop.

8.40   A record of defects and maintenance should be kept for each item of equipment. This record should be examined regularly to identify degradation in equipment performance or systematic faults. Further information on maintenance logs is available in the guidance for PUWER [57].

8.41   Clear indication should be available at the control panel when equipment is being serviced or repaired. This may be by means of a notice clearly indicating that the equipment is being serviced. The local rules should specify clear handover arrangements between treatment and service staff. Safety precautions for maintenance and repair procedures should also be described in the local rules.

8.42   When gamma-beam teletherapy equipment is being maintained or repaired, the source or shutter should be locked in the 'off' position. As the source is still emitting in this position the room should be entered only by staff, for the minimum time associated with the maintenance or repair of the equipment.

8.43   When maintenance or repair work has been done in the vicinity of the electron path, the X-ray target, the flattening filter or scattering foils, or the magnet system of any accelerator operating above 10 MeV, monitoring for possible induced radioactivity should be carried out. Such monitoring should take account of any components present in the equipment that are made from uranium (see paragraph 8.57). If significant activity is detected, protective measures should be taken such as remote handling and the use of PPE or clothing, or further work should be postponed until short-lived activity has decayed. Equipment and components for which these precautions are required should be identified in the local rules, which should also detail the appropriate safety procedures.

8.44   Any maintenance or service operation that might alter the radiation output, or quality of the radiation or the shielding of the radiation source, should be notified to the staff responsible for the technical operation of the equipment. The procedure for this notification should be described in the local rules. The equipment should not be used clinically until the appropriate parameters have been checked. A local QC procedure should be available for ensuring that these checks are undertaken and that the machine is not used clinically until the appropriate calibration testing has been undertaken and recorded in the calibration record.

8.45   When maintenance or repair work is carried out by external service engineers, great care should be taken to ensure that the equipment is safe for use when this work is completed. A local QA procedure for the handover of equipment should be available. It is of particular importance that the appropriate procedures discussed in paragraph 8.43 are undertaken. It may be appropriate for a form to be completed and signed by the external service engineer and by an appropriate representative of the department. This form should clearly indicate the work undertaken (perhaps by reference to the service engineer's report), and should indicate if the equipment may require recalibration. If handover forms are used, they should be kept for future reference.

8.46   Before treatments are commenced following any maintenance or experimental work, a test exposure should be made to ensure that the equipment is functioning correctly and that all safety interlocks are operational.

Loading or exchanging sources in therapy equipment within a hospital

8.47   Great care is essential when loading or exchanging sources in beam therapy equipment, in view of the high activity of these sources and because it is usually necessary to override safety interlocks. A system of work for this procedure should be set out in writing, taking into account the following paragraphs. A radiotherapy MPE should be appointed as the RPS to supervise radiation safety during such a procedure.

8.48   The procedure to be adopted should be drawn up by the employer responsible in consultation with the RPA. The operation should be supervised by the RPS to ensure compliance with the written procedure. Any technical instructions provided by the equipment manufacturer should be strictly followed.

8.49   Before the work is commenced a risk assessment should be carried out. Based on this a written contingency plan should be drawn up in consultation with the RPA and, if appropriate, the RPS supervising the procedure.

8.50   Loading and unloading should be carried out by at least two persons (who should be designated as classified radiation workers) who are properly trained and experienced. They should be the only people authorised to enter or remain in the room during the procedure, apart from the RPS as discussed in paragraph 8.54.

8.51   If the work is carried out by an external contractor, either with his or her own engineers or in collaboration with hospital staff, responsibility should be clearly defined in writing. These operations are not frequently carried out in some departments and they require good co-ordination between individuals who do not usually work together (i.e. contractors and hospital staff).

8.52   The transfer container should be positioned close to the radiation head, in such a position that the source remains shielded throughout the transfer operation.

8.53   Each person involved in source changing should wear a direct-reading personal dosemeter covering the anticipated dose range and a range one order of magnitude higher, in addition to the normal personal dosemeter and any audible alarm.

8.54   The RPS supervising the operation should be additional to those concerned in the actual loading or unloading. The operation should be monitored and timed and, in case of difficulty, instructions should be given for a pre-arranged contingency plan to be followed.

8.55   As part of the critical examination required when the operation has been completed, a check should be made to ensure that all interlocks function and that all other safety features are fully operational.

Decommissioning of radiotherapy equipment

8.56   The target and collimators in accelerators operated above 10 MeV may become activated during use. However, the amount of induced activity is such that they fall within the provisions of the Radioactive Substances (Testing Instruments) Exemption Order 1985 [71].

8.57   Steps should be taken to ascertain whether accelerators or gamma-beam teletherapy equipment contain depleted uranium shielding or collimators. If depleted uranium is present, the items concerned should be registered under the Radioactive Substances Act 1993 [7] and disposed of according to the guidance in Chapter 18.

The safe operation of radiotherapy equipment

8.58   The treatment operators and all other persons except the patient should normally be outside the treatment room when the equipment is about to be used. If, for compelling clinical reasons, it is necessary for a person other than the patient to be in the treatment room, during kilovoltage treatment, the RPA should be consulted before the treatment course commences. A written system of work identifying the person, other than the patient, who is to be in the treatment room, and any associated restrictions or precautions which must be observed (based on appropriate dose constraints), should be available at the treatment room for this specific case. A person other than the patient should never be in the treatment room during megavoltage treatments.

8.59   The treatment operator should make sure that only the patient is in the treatment room and that the maze entrance is unoccupied before setting the door or entrance interlock. Particular care is needed if there are areas within the treatment room or maze in which a person could be hidden from view.

8.60   To avoid errors in patient treatment, a strict procedure for the operation of the equipment is essential. This may be by means of a work instruction in the QA programme. The work instruction should clearly define the extent of the responsibility of the different operators. The work instruction should include the checking of the identity of the patient and the operating conditions and set-up parameters by the treatment operator before each treatment. Before treatments are commenced following any maintenance or experimental work, a test exposure should be made to ensure that the equipment is functioning correctly and that all safety interlocks are operational.

8.61   If there is a potential hazard to the treatment operator from activated treatment accessories, e.g. removable wedges in accelerators operated at high photon energies, then the hazard and any necessary precautions should be identified in the local rules.

8.62   The treatment operator(s) should report immediately to the person specified in the local rules any of the following circumstances:

   (a) if the treatment is terminated or interrupted by any event other than the primary dose-integrating system (or primary timer in the case of gamma-beam teletherapy equipment), unless the reason is obvious

   (b) if any interlock or trip switch is observed not to function correctly

   (c) if any emergency stop switch is activated, and

   (d) if any other parameter falls outside locally defined limits.

8.63   The equipment should not be used again until the circumstances have been investigated and a safe mode of operation confirmed or re-established.

8.64   Where a back-up timer is provided it should be pre-set, to a time 10 per cent greater than the estimated duration of treatment, or on the advice of the MPE, to an appropriate value which takes into account variations in source transit times.

8.65   Whenever radiotherapy equipment is left unattended it should be left in a safe state. The local rules should describe arrangements for access to treatment rooms by cleaners and hospital building maintenance staff.

8.66   All radiotherapy doses and treatment parameters should be recorded. Details of the length of time for which treatment records must be kept are given in Appendix 9.

Additional considerations for whole body electron treatments

8.67   Where an accelerator is used for whole body HDR electron therapy, it should incorporate appropriate design features and interlocks to ensure safe operation. The control panel should give a clear and unambiguous indication when an HDR electron mode is selected. The treatment operator should be required to confirm that this mode has been selected.

8.68   Before whole body electron treatments involving extended treatment distances and high electron dose rates, a dummy run should be performed to check that the dose rate is within acceptable limits.

The safe operation of kilovoltage equipment

8.69   Where a dose rate monitor is not fitted, the output under standard conditions should be checked at least once each working day. This is particularly important for sets operating below 50 kV as small spectral changes can lead to significant output changes. Any variations from the standards specified in Appendix 14 should be reported to the operator identified in the local rules.

8.70   The treatment operator, and any other person who needs to be in the treatment room during kilovoltage therapy up to 50 kV, should wear a protective apron and, if the hands are likely at any time to be close to the radiation beam, protective gloves. They should also make use of protective panels.

8.71   The X-ray tube or associated support or stand should never be held by any operator while high voltage is applied.

8.72   For kilovoltage equipment, an interlocked system should be employed to control the maximum and minimum kilovoltage that may be used with a particular filter thickness.

8.73   Great care should be taken in the identification and positioning of all filters, especially wedge filters, and any other beam modifying devices if the equipment has no electrical facility to check and indicate the selection of these devices.

The safe operation of gamma-beam teletherapy equipment

8.74   There must be a clear indication to any person about to enter the treatment room if the source is not in a safe position. In addition to normal personal dosemeters, treatment operators should wear audible, personal alarms unless a radiation monitor operating an audible signal has been installed in the treatment room. Such alarms give further indications of the source positions as well as the room and equipment warning signals. The personal monitors should be switched on throughout the working period and should be capable of giving a recognisable signal up to the maximum possible dose rate for the source being monitored. The audible indication should preferably be dose rate dependent.

8.75   All operators should know how to use the emergency manual means to return the source to the 'off' position with the least practicable exposure of themselves and the patient. A daily check should be made that any tool required for this operation is in the proper accessible position near the entrance to the room.

8.76   If it is not possible, even by the emergency manual means, to return the source to the 'off' position, it will be necessary to enter the treatment room in order to remove the patient. The patient should be removed as quickly as possible, the greatest care being taken to avoid any exposure to the radiation beam. If it is possible to close the collimators from the control panel this should be done before entering the room; otherwise, it may be advisable to rotate the head away from the route of entry and then close the collimators immediately after entering the room. This action should be practised from time to time.

8.77   All operators should be conversant with the emergency procedure displayed at the entrance to the treatment room (see Chapter 7). Further information on emergency procedures is given in Chapter 19.

8.78   As a teletherapy source is still emitting radiation when in the 'off' position, the room should be entered only by staff, for the minimum time associated with the maintenance or repair of the equipment and other essential activities.

8.79   The shutter or source should be locked in the 'off' position when the equipment is not in use, to protect persons who may enter the treatment room while the equipment is unattended.

The safe operation of remotely controlled after-loading equipment

8.80   To minimise the possibility of sources sticking in transfer tubes and applicators, excessive bends should be avoided and the manufacturer's recommendation on the minimum radius of curvature should be followed. Transfer tubes and applicators should be examined for kinks before each treatment.

8.81   Operators should know how to use the emergency manual means provided on HDR equipment to return sources to the storage container with the least practicable exposure of themselves and the patient. A daily check should be made that any tool required for this operation is in the proper, accessible position near the entrance to the treatment room.

8.82   In the event of failure of all the systems provided on the equipment for the return of sources, it may be necessary to enter the treatment room and to withdraw the loaded applicators from a patient manually, using long-handled forceps or other instruments if necessary. Details of the action to be taken if such a radiation emergency occurs should be specified in the local rules. The local rules should also provide a list of people who must be informed and their contact details. A summary of the procedure and contact information should be clearly displayed at the entrance to the treatment room. All treatment operators should be conversant with this procedure. The RPA, RPS and an MPE with knowledge of the after-loading equipment must always be consulted after a failure or near miss to identify and report the equipment fault, to estimate any additional exposure to patients or staff and to re-evaluate the emergency procedure.

8.83   Any tool and protected receptacle required for use in a radiation emergency must be kept at the entrance to or just outside the treatment room, close to the entrance and in a clearly marked location. A check must be made that this tool is in the correct location every day before clinical use of the machine commences.

8.84   A portable monitor should be available and should be used to locate the source in the event of a failure of the source return mechanisms. The portable monitor should be battery operated. In the case of LDR equipment, the portable monitor should be used after each treatment if it is not otherwise possible to check that all sources have been returned to the source container.

8.85   Medical, nursing and auxiliary ward staff should not remain unnecessarily in the vicinity of patients during treatment. Where it is clinically acceptable, after-loading treatment should be interrupted and the sources withdrawn during nursing procedures. Patients should only have visitors when the sources are withdrawn.

8.86   As the sources are still emitting radiation even when in the storage container, the room should be occupied only for necessary purposes associated with the operation of the apparatus and other essential activities.

The safe operation of radiotherapy simulators

8.87   DRL and dose constraints to the patient will not apply to radiotherapy simulators or CT scanners when used for radiotherapy simulation. The principle of ALARP must still be applied. The guidance given in paragraph 2.22 relating to concomitant exposures should be noted and the general guidance given in Chapter 4 will apply (see also paragraph 3.116).

8.88   Operators should ensure that the beam is collimated to protect the patient so far as is compatible with the simulation process. Care should be taken that the image intensifier intercepts the primary beam at all times.

8.89   Operators should minimise fluoroscopic exposure times to protect the patient so far as is compatible with the simulation process. It is not appropriate for radiotherapy simulators to be fitted with DAP meters as the imaging field is necessarily larger than the treatment field with organs adjacent to the treatment field being identified and exposed during simulation to avoid subsequent exposure during treatment. An estimate of time and exposure rate is sufficiently accurate when concomitant exposures are compared with subsequent therapy exposures (see paragraph 2.25).

9 Brachytherapy sources

Scope

9.1 This chapter presents the necessary precautions to be taken in the use of small sealed sources, or other solid sources, for intracavitary or interstitial radiotherapy, other than by remotely controlled after-loading. This chapter includes the preparation, sterilisation, testing and use of these sources. Chapter 17 should be consulted for guidance on storage arrangements for, and Chapter 18 on disposal of, these sources. The sources considered include ^{137}Cs and ^{60}Co needles and tubes, ^{198}Au grains, ^{192}Ir wire, ^{125}I and ^{103}Pd seeds, ^{90}Sr and other beta ray plaques and neutron sources such as ^{252}Cf. The clinical use of ^{226}Ra and ^{182}Ta has been discontinued in the United Kingdom.

9.2 A sealed source is a radioactive substance whose structure is such as to prevent, under normal conditions of use, any dispersion of radioactive substances into the environment. 'Solid source' in these guidance notes means any non-dispersible solid source (e.g. ^{192}Ir wires) other than a sealed source. Note that non-dispersible sources (such as iridium wire and sealed sources whose radioactive cores are non-dispersible under emergency conditions) are exempt from the requirements of REPPIR [28].

Sources for brachytherapy

9.3 All sealed sources used for brachytherapy should conform to BS 5288 *Sealed Radioactive Sources* [72]. If any source that does not conform to the standard is to be used, the RPA should be consulted before it is used and the clinical justification for its use recorded in writing.

9.4 Procedures for the use of all sources should take into account the supplier's recommendations on working life and environment of use. Copies of these recommendations should be referenced in the local rules and available to all staff involved in their use.

Preparation and cleaning room

9.5 A dedicated room should be provided for the preparation and cleaning of sources and applicators. This room should only be used for this work and should only be occupied during such work. Arrangements for restricted access should be specified in the local rules. The room should be designated as a controlled area because of the radiation hazard. Dose rates can often be reduced significantly by the use of appropriate local shielding and this should be considered in the design of the room. The design should also take account of the possibility of contamination from the handling of sealed sources and be designed for easy cleaning and decontamination. Work benches, floors and walls should have smooth impervious surfaces and flooring material should be coved at all walls to avoid the possibility of contamination leaking under coverings. Sinks should have suitable traps so sources cannot be lost. It is advisable, when designing new rooms, to identify the location of drainage pipework in case lost sources need to be traced. The condition and integrity of these safety features should be checked preferably monthly, e.g. by the RPS, and confirmed annually by the employer who could delegate this to the RPA.

9.6 The entrance of the room should be marked with an appropriate warning sign to indicate both the presence of radioactive sources and the existence of a controlled area (see Appendix 12).

9.7 Sources should be stored in a shielded safe, preferably in the preparation room to minimise radiation doses arising from the movement of sources. Information on the storage of sources is given in Chapter 17.

Roles and responsibilities of duty holders in brachytherapy

9.8   The referrer for a brachytherapy procedure will always be a medical practitioner. The referrer should provide sufficient information about the patient for the radiation oncologist acting as the IR(ME)R practitioner to decide if radiotherapy is an appropriate treatment for the patient. The referrer should be identified in the patient's notes. A list of referrers should be recorded in the local protocols for radiotherapy treatment.

9.9   The IR(ME)R practitioner in the brachytherapy process must be a person authorised under MARS78 [5] and MARS95 [6] (i.e. the holder of an ARSAC certificate) and will normally be a radiation oncologist. A list of practitioners should be recorded in the local protocols for brachytherapy treatment. The practitioner should:

     (a)   assess the information provided by the referrer and if necessary ask for more information from the referrer

     (b)   decide if brachytherapy is an appropriate treatment for the patient, and

     (c)   justify in writing the medical exposures necessary to deliver the course of brachytherapy treatment, if indeed radiotherapy is the appropriate treatment.

9.10   The IR(ME)R practitioner will also prescribe the brachytherapy treatment (in most cases according to an agreed local protocol). The justification and prescription should be recorded in the patient's notes. Justification of a course of brachytherapy treatment will generally imply justification of all the medical exposures involved, including any localisation and verification films.

9.11   Sources may only be administered to patients by a person authorised under MARS78 [5] and MARS95 [6], or by an appropriately trained operator under the direction of that person. The IR(ME)R practitioner (or in some circumstances the operator) should explain to the patient, and if appropriate their relatives, prior to treatment the possible need to remove permanent implants surgically in the unlikely event of their death, or to accept burial rather than cremation, and should obtain their written consent. In some circumstances the IR(ME)R practitioner may decide it is more appropriate for a relative to give written consent. The precautions necessary in the event of death should be recorded in the patient's notes and communicated to the patient's GP (see paragraph 16.30).

9.12   Operators in the brachytherapy process will be those members of staff who initiate the treatment exposure or take localisation or verification films, carry out or check treatment planning, calibrate, service or repair brachytherapy equipment, or carry out any other task which could affect the safety of the brachytherapy treatment. An operator should be responsible for each step within the brachytherapy process. Staff who are not operators should be under the direct supervision of an operator. Any treatment aids manufactured within the radiotherapy department should be checked by an operator before being used in the treatment of a patient. Operators in a brachytherapy department may be medical staff, radiographers, nurses, physicists or technical officers. A list of operators should be recorded in the local protocols for radiotherapy treatment.

9.13   MPEs in radiotherapy should be closely involved in all procedures related to the brachytherapy techniques described in this chapter. This will involve providing advice on all aspects of source and patient dosimetry, on the optimisation and safety of treatment and treatment planning, on the QA programme (including QC procedures) and on any other matters relating to the safety of the radiotherapy equipment or treatment. An MPE should also be consulted before new treatment techniques are introduced. A list of MPEs should be recorded in the local protocols for radiotherapy treatment. MPEs will also be responsible for the acceptance testing of new or modified brachytherapy equipment, its commissioning and definitive calibration. The MPE will be involved with the RPA in the critical examination of new or modified equipment.

9.14   The RPA for the radiotherapy department should have appropriate experience in the application of radiation protection principles in brachytherapy. The RPA should be consulted on all matters specified in Schedule 5 of IRR99 [1] relevant to brachytherapy within the radiotherapy department. One or more RPSs should be appointed by the employer to ensure that all staff are aware of the local rules and that the local rules are observed. The roles of the RPA and RPS are discussed in paragraph 7.9.

Source calibration and testing

9.15   Sealed radioactive sources will usually have been tested by the manufacturer or supplier and be accompanied by a leakage test certificate. Test certificates must be filed for future reference. If there is no certificate, the source should be tested for both leakage and surface contamination before it is used clinically for the first time. Sources should be retested at least once per year and whenever damage or leakage is suspected. This is necessary because brachytherapy sources are subject to wear through frequent use, cleaning and sterilisation procedures, and because of the particular hazard to a patient if leakage should occur, pathways for intake being comparatively short. Advice on wipe testing can be found in BS 5288 [72] and ISO 9978 *Sealed Radioactive Sources. Leakage* [73].

9.16   The activity of all sources should be measured, and compared with the calibration certificate supplied by the supplier, before being administered to a patient. Sources should be measured individually, but those that have been produced collectively in a common irradiation container, with each source having all dimensions less than 5 mm, may be measured collectively. The activity of sources containing long-lived radionuclides need not be checked on each occasion of use. All sources and calibration certificates should be kept and controlled as described in Chapter 17.

9.17   A record should be kept of the issue, distribution and return of all sources and also of the administration of permanent implants. Further advice on record keeping is given in Chapter 17 and Appendix 9.

9.18   If, in a leakage test, the activity measured on the swab (or in the liquid used for an immersion test) is less than 200 Bq the source may be considered leak free. Activity greater than 200 Bq can also be due to surface contamination arising from a different source, therefore the source should be decontaminated and retested before a leak is confirmed. In carrying out leakage tests of beta sources care is essential to avoid damaging the window, if there is one, through which beta radiation is emitted.

9.19   Whenever it is believed that a source is, or might be, leaking, it should be sealed in an airtight container and kept separate from other sources. The RPS and RPA should be informed and an inspection by a competent authority should be arranged as soon as possible. Arrangements should then be made for repair or disposal. The RPA and RPS should investigate the possibility of staff and other persons having been contaminated as a result of the leak, including the possibility that some contamination may have occurred prior to detection.

General operating procedures and local rules

9.20   Special tools or surgical instruments should always be used when sources are being prepared for, or administered to, patients. These should be constructed so as to provide the maximum handling distance or shielding compatible with effective manipulation. All operators should be trained not to pick up sources or loaded source applicators by hand under any circumstances and this should be emphasised in the local rules and any work instructions. Methods of work and work instructions should be reviewed regularly by the RPS and operators, and at least annually by the RPA.

9.21   The local rules should emphasise that work on equipment and applicators should be carried out, as far as possible, before the insertion of the source. If work has to be carried out on equipment or appliances with a source inserted then precautions to minimise the exposure of any staff must be taken. The local rules should also provide detailed guidance on arrangements for monitoring during source preparation, with particular reference to hand monitoring.

9.22   The local rules should explicitly prohibit the placing of objects in the mouth, eating, drinking or the application of cosmetics within the preparation and cleaning room. The local rules should also only permit the use of disposable handkerchiefs. These precautions are necessary because the tools for handling sources may become contaminated, creating a risk of contamination entering the body.

9.23   All appliances should be capable of being handled easily and speedily. For example, needle eyes should be easily threaded (frayed thread ends should be waxed) and screw threads should be of the optimum size and pitch to allow fast 'jam proof' operation. The operator should regularly examine screw thread and other mechanical fixings.

9.24   When needles, capsules or other applicators of the same appearance but of different activity are used, they should be made easily distinguishable, e.g. by different coloured threads, beads or markings. Details of any colour code used should be clearly displayed wherever the sources are handled. Copies of any colour code should also be in the local rules. These should be checked regularly by the RPS.

9.25   In intracavitary radiotherapy a thread should be passed through the source eyelet or attached to the applicator to provide an emergency method of removal from the patient. An operator should be responsible for ensuring that this is done.

9.26   Flexible tubes into which sources are to be loaded should be inspected by an operator, before use, to ensure that they are in good condition.

9.27   The number and position of removable sources in or on the patient should be regularly checked by an operator, using a procedure that minimises doses to staff. A radiation monitor should be used to confirm that no sources remain in the patient, or in the treatment area or ward, at the conclusion of treatment. The operation of the monitor should be tested by placing it close to the patient before the sources are removed. Dressings, wipes and excreta from patients receiving treatment should not be disposed of until monitoring has shown that they are not contaminated by radioactive material and that all sources have been accounted for. To reduce the possibility of sources being mislaid, they should be inspected, cleaned and returned to storage (or identified as sent for disposal) without delay. Advice on inspection is given in this chapter and Chapter 17 and on source disposal in Chapter 18. These procedures should be the responsibility of a specific operator or the RPS.

9.28   A shielded container should be placed near the bed of a patient being treated with removable sources. If a source becomes accidentally displaced it should immediately be transferred to the container using forceps. The incident should be reported immediately to the IR(ME)R practitioner (ARSAC certificate holder), clinician in charge of the patient and to the RPS. This incident procedure should be described in detail in the local rules. Details of the incident should be recorded.

9.29   Steps should be taken to ensure that sources which might be mislaid or lost from a patient do not leave the ward or treatment area, e.g. for the hospital laundry or refuse incinerator. All containers such as rubbish bins, soiled dressings bins and laundry baskets, coming from a ward or other area where such sources are employed, should be tested for radioactivity with a monitoring instrument. An additional check can be provided using a permanent alarm installed in a doorway or corridor through which outgoing bins, baskets and trolleys have to pass. Where permanent alarms are installed, the person responsible for ensuring they are regularly checked and recording that they are functioning correctly should be the RPS.

9.30   Sources used for brachytherapy should be cleaned before being returned to the store so as to minimise subsequent sterilisation and disinfection difficulties.

Sterilisation, disinfection and cleaning of small sources

9.31   When sterilising or disinfecting small sources, the manufacturer's or supplier's instructions should be consulted. Appropriate precautions should be taken to avoid:

      (a) unnecessary radiation exposure of nursing and other staff

(b) damage to sources, and

(c) loss of sources.

9.32   If autoclaves, hot air ovens and other equipment are used for sterilising or disinfecting sources they should be adequately shielded and designed to prevent damage to or the loss of a source from the equipment during use.

9.33   The following special precautions need to be taken when sterilising or disinfecting sources:

(a) sterilisers should be fitted with a cutout that will prevent the temperature of the source rising above 180°C

(b) applicators containing sources should not be sterilised or disinfected if found to be damaged, and

(c) disinfecting solutions that do not attack identification marks should be used.

9.34   When sources need to be cleaned before being returned to the storage, particular care should be taken with thin-walled sources.

9.35   Before sources are cleaned the manufacturer's or supplier's instructions should be consulted. Abrasive substances (such as metal cleaners and polishes) should never be used and sources should never be allowed to come into contact with mercury or mercury salts, iodine, solutions of hypochlorites or corrosive substances. Immersion in a solution such as normal saline will aid the removal of blood and tissues from appliances. The following cleaning methods are particularly suitable for sealed sources:

(a) soaking for at least an hour in a suitable disinfectant, or in a solution of hydrogen peroxide, to remove dried blood, or in an organic solvent (such as xylene) to remove moulding material

(b) thorough rinsing in warm or boiling water, and

(c) ultrasonic cleaning using a low power generator.

9.36   Following sterilisation, disinfection or cleaning, an operator should check that identification marks or colour coding have not been damaged.

Loss or breakage of a source

9.37   Procedures for action to be taken in the case of the suspected loss or breakage of a radioactive source should be detailed in the local rules and contingency plan. Notices outlining the procedure should be displayed in each room, theatre or ward where such sources are handled or used (see the guidance in Chapter 19). Contingency plans should be rehearsed at appropriate intervals, normally annually.

9.38   Special care should be taken with sources of long half-life radionuclides with high or medium toxicity. The RPA should be consulted about the appropriate action to take in the event of any suspected leak or contamination.

Beta sources

9.39   Suitable shields or baffles should be provided to ensure adequate protection when manipulating beta radiation sources. A transparent plastic plate, e.g. polymethylmethacrylate (PMMA), of adequate thickness should be mounted, or worn, between the source and the face of the operator, in order to prevent the head of the operator from being placed too near the source, and to protect the eyes and face from beta radiation. Particular care should be taken when using high-activity beta sources (3 GBq or greater), such as for the treatment of pterygia. A plastic shield should be in position on the handling rod to protect the operator's hands, as the beta surface dose rates from such sources can be very high.

9.40   In the case of large activity beta sources, bremsstrahlung, characteristic X- and annihilation radiation may present a hazard that should be evaluated and the necessary precautions taken; e.g. sources should be kept well away from material of high atomic number. Some beta sources also emit gamma radiation (see paragraphs 9.42 and 9.43). The RPA should be consulted about suitable precautions.

9.41   Most sources intended for the utilisation of beta radiation outside the container have a thin window. When the sources are not in use, this window should be covered using a low atomic number or plastic shield of sufficient thickness to stop all beta radiation, minimise bremsstrahlung radiation and protect the window. When cleaning the sources, the precautions referred to in paragraphs 9.31 to 9.36 should be observed and care should be taken to avoid damage to the window.

Gamma sources

9.42   Benches used for the preparation, assembly and cleaning of gamma radiation source capsules and appliances should be provided with adequate protection for the operator and for other persons either associated with the work or in adjacent areas. The RPA should be consulted on the protective measures required.

9.43   Mobile protective barriers, mounted on wheels and provided, where necessary, with sterile drapes, should be used in operating theatres and other treatment rooms. These barriers should be so designed as to give protection in all directions where persons are usually stationed during brachytherapy procedures. Where possible, the optimum positions for the shields should be clearly marked on the floor of the room. In some situations, however, the precise position of shields will depend on the specific source or procedure employed. Gamma sources should remain behind protective shielding as long as possible and be removed only when required for application to the patient. In all cases, expeditious handling and the use of suitable instruments (see paragraph 9.20) will reduce the hazard. Mobile barriers should be clearly identified for use with specific sources and marked with their shielding properties in millimetres of lead equivalent. Mobile protective barriers should be regularly examined to ensure the integrity of the protection and the mechanical stability of the barrier's transport mechanism. The RPS will usually be the appropriate person to do this, as the way in which barriers are to be used must be specified in the local rules.

Neutron sources

9.44   Where neutron sources, such as ^{252}Cf, are used for brachytherapy, shielding against both neutron and gamma radiation should be provided.

9.45   Personal dosemeters and area monitoring instruments should be suitable for fast and thermal neutrons.

Protection of persons in proximity to patients undergoing brachytherapy

9.46   Most areas in which patients are treated will need to be designated as controlled areas, except where only low activity beta sources are used.

9.47   Wherever possible, treatment should be carried out in rooms having only one bed, or at most two beds. People in adjoining rooms (whether on the same level or on floors above and below) should be protected using adequate shielding (see paragraphs 1.55 and 1.56).

9.48   Where treatment with low activity sources is carried out in a general ward, the beds of patients under treatment should be positioned according to advice given by the RPA to minimise radiation doses to other patients, particularly those not undergoing radiotherapy treatment. In general this would require that any patient not being treated is at least 2.5 m from the centre of any bed occupied by a patient under treatment. Written arrangements should be available in the local rules for nursing access and for restricting access to these patients by other patients or visitors. For beta plaques, the nursing staff should confirm the presence of the source at shift handovers using an appropriate detector.

9.49   Mobile protective shielding should be used around the beds of patients being treated with gamma or neutron sources, except possibly for ^{192}Ir wires and ^{125}I grains. It is advisable that their optimum shielding position around a treatment bed be clearly marked on the floor. Circumstances where protective shielding cannot be used should be included in a written system of work, detailed in the local rules, together with the alternative precautions to be undertaken. Guidance on the use of mobile shielding is given in paragraph 9.43.

9.50   Beds in which there are patients undergoing treatment with radioactive sources should carry a notice that includes a radiation warning sign (see Appendix 12). The nursing staff should be given written details of the number and nature of sources, their total activity, the time and date of application and intended removal, and relevant nursing instructions. The RPS should ensure that these details are kept up to date.

9.51   The maximum dose rate at a distance of 1 m from each patient undergoing treatment should be determined and recorded as part of the risk assessment conducted in consultation with the RPA.

9.52   The local rules should include:

(a) safe working procedures for all staff involved in the treatment of the patient

(b) written arrangements providing entry to the controlled area for staff (with particular attention to domestic and housekeeping staff), and

(c) written arrangements for visitors.

9.53   Patients with sources in or upon their bodies should not normally leave the ward or treatment room without the approval of the medical staff responsible for their treatment and the RPS. The nursing staff should keep records in the patient's notes of when patients leave the ward, and if or when they return. Guidance on when patients may leave hospital after administration of radioactive substances is given in Chapter 15. Guidance on the actions necessary in the event of the death of a patient is given in Chapter 16.

9.54   Nursing staff and any other persons, including visitors, should not remain unnecessarily in the vicinity of patients undergoing treatment with gamma or neutron sources. Where possible, nursing procedures should be postponed until after the sources have been removed. Guidance on the role of the patient's comforters and carers is given in Chapter 1.

9.55   It may be considered desirable to reallocate duties of staff who are known to be pregnant. The RPA should be consulted for advice.

10 Diagnostic uses of unsealed radioactive substances

Scope

10.1 This chapter applies to:

(a) the use of unsealed (dispersible) radioactive substances that are administered to human subjects for diagnosis, health screening or research into diagnostic techniques

(b) the use of unsealed radioactive substances for *in vitro* studies made for the purpose of clinical diagnosis or research, and

(c) the use of radioactive substances for testing and calibrating equipment used under (a) and (b), whether sealed (e.g. commercially available ^{57}Co flood phantoms) or unsealed (e.g. refillable ^{99}Tc^m flood phantoms).

For information on leak testing of sealed sources, see paragraph 14.8. The use of transmission sources and anatomical marker sources is covered in Chapter 14.

10.2 Much of the guidance in this chapter may not be relevant to work involving quantities of radionuclides less than or similar to those listed in column 3 of Schedule 8 of IRR99 [1]. A table of these quantities for some commonly used radionuclides is given in Table 10.1. In medical practice, it is the total quantity that is most likely to be the limiting factor. The table gives limits for this exemption from notification under IRR99. Exemption is also given in the case of sources of low radioactive concentration, see column 2 of the same Schedule 8. Often, hospital laboratories such as haematology or pathology only perform tests involving these exempt levels of activity. Chapter 13 has been written for these users. Specific advice on work with tritium is also given there.

Table 10.1 Quantity for notification of some commonly used radionuclides under regulation 6 of IRR99

Radionuclide	MBq	Radionuclide	MBq	Radionuclide	MBq	Radionuclide	MBq
^{3}H	1000	^{51}Cr	10	^{81}Kr^m	10000	^{99}Tc^m	10
^{14}C*	10	^{57}Co	1	^{81}Rb	1	^{111}In	1
^{18}F	1	^{58}Co	1	^{89}Sr	1	^{125}I	1
^{32}P	0.1	^{59}Fe	1	^{90}Y	0.1	^{131}I	1
^{35}S**	100	^{67}Ga	1	^{99}Mo	1	^{201}Tl	1

*not monoxide or dioxide
** organic

10.3 This chapter does not apply to the rare use of unsealed alpha-emitting radionuclides for medical purposes. The advice of the RPA should be sought on the additional precautions and special procedures needed when handling such materials before any decision concerning their use is taken.

Hazards from unsealed radioactive substances and principles for their control

10.4 A radiation hazard may arise from unsealed radioactive substances, either through external irradiation of the body or through the entry of radioactive substances into the body. The main precautions required in dealing with external irradiation are similar for both sealed sources and unsealed substances and depend on the physical characteristics of the radiation emitted, the total activity and the physical half-life of the radionuclide. Unsealed radioactive substances may produce a further external radiation hazard as a result of contamination.

10.5   When unsealed radioactive substances enter the body, the internal radiation dose will depend on factors such as the physical and chemical form of the material, the activity, the mode of entry and the biokinetics.

10.6   The design of all rooms in which unsealed radioactive substances are used, the design of all equipment required in their use, and the procedure involved in work with such substances should be aimed at:

   (a) minimising the irradiation of persons in the course of their work or training

   (b) limiting the irradiation of patients to that consistent with medical requirements

   (c) minimising the irradiation of members of the public (such as visitors and patients who are not being examined), and

   (d) avoiding radioactive contamination and controlling the spread should it occur.

10.7   The risk to any person from any work with unsealed radioactive substances should be assessed prior to the start of the work and kept under review. General information on risk assessments and setting dose constraints is given in Chapter 1 and Appendix 6. More specific guidance relating to the use of unsealed sources is given in this and the following chapters.

10.8   Work with unsealed radioactive substances should be governed by clearly understood and documented rules of procedure, so that efficient practices can be organised and the control of hazards becomes an established routine. These rules of procedure will include local rules, protocols and other types of instructions. A clear indication of the roles and responsibilities of staff must also be set out in procedures wherever unsealed radioactive substances are administered to patients.

10.9   Staff involved in the use of unsealed radioactive substances must receive training to ensure they can undertake their duties safely. Requirements for information, instruction and training under regulation 14 of IRR99 [1] are discussed in L121 paragraphs 234 to 240 [2]. Staff undertaking procedures involving the administration of radioactive substances to patients should have received appropriate practical training (see paragraphs 2.73 to 2.76).

Pregnant or breastfeeding staff

10.10   Employers should assess the likely dose to the fetus of a pregnant employee from each work activity [11]. The risk assessment should examine previous staff dose measurements and the likelihood of incidents leading to external or internal irradiation of the fetus. Doses should always be ALARP but, if the fetus might receive more than 1 mSv (from internal and external sources combined) over the declared term of pregnancy (see paragraph 1.91), a change of work activity should be discussed and agreed with the pregnant employee. For external irradiation from $^{99}Tc^m$ or ^{131}I, a dose of 1 mSv to the fetus can be assumed if the dose measured at the surface of the maternal abdomen is 1.3 mSv [74]. For external irradiation from positron emitters, the dose to the fetus may be similar to the dose at the surface of the maternal abdomen. Pregnant staff should not take part in any work activity involving significant risk of body contamination, including internal uptake [75].

10.11   If a member of staff is breastfeeding she should not take part in procedures or work in areas where there is a significant risk of bodily contamination, e.g. cleaning up a large spill of radioactivity, particularly of a longer-lived radionuclide. An assessment should be undertaken of the potential radiation dose to the infant resulting from a chance inhalation by the mother (as a member of staff) of radioactive gases or aerosols arising from her work. Appropriate action should then be taken to restrict this dose as necessary. Until told otherwise, it should be assumed that a woman is breastfeeding for 6 months after delivery.

Roles and responsibilities of duty holders in nuclear medicine

10.12   Paragraphs 10.13 to 10.22 should be read in conjunction with Chapter 2, which gives a general overview of IR(ME)R [3]. Duty holders under IRR99 [1] are described in Chapter 1.

10.13   Employers must develop recommendations for referral criteria for all their standard nuclear medicine investigations by consultation with and taking advice from the professionals involved. The British Nuclear Medicine Society (BNMS) procedure guidelines available on the web at http://www.bnms.org.uk/ and the booklet *Making Best Use of a Department of Clinical Radiology* [29] may help departments define their criteria. Two other useful web sites are the European Association of Nuclear Medicine (EANM) at http://www.eanm.org/ under EANM Service/Guidelines and the Society of Nuclear Medicine (SNM) guidelines at http://www.snm.org/ under Policy and Practice/ 1999. The latter set is comprehensive but it should be borne in mind that some of the activity levels used in the USA are much higher than the ARSAC recommended levels.

10.14   Referrers should be informed of the criteria that apply to the investigations they may request, including information on radiation doses and associated risks, particularly for use in the case of child patients or female patients who might be pregnant. The information should be given to referrers in writing but should also be disseminated through appropriate training and update sessions.

10.15   The referrer to a nuclear medicine facility will usually be a medical practitioner. The referrer should provide sufficient information about the patient for the IR(ME)R practitioner to decide if nuclear medicine is the appropriate diagnostic procedure for the patient. Referrers should be identified in the employer's procedures.

10.16   IR(ME)R practitioners should take account of data provided by the referrer when justifying examinations. Referrals should be clear and unambiguous and the IR(ME)R practitioner should consult the referrer if insufficient clinical information has been provided to enable him or her to justify the medical exposure involved in the examination. Relevant clinical information may include previous diagnostic information, medical records, images from other investigations, or that a female patient is known to be pregnant. Employers should have adequate systems to provide IR(ME)R practitioners with previous images. Referrers should discuss requests not covered by the normal referral criteria directly with the IR(ME)R practitioner.

10.17   The IR(ME)R practitioner in nuclear medicine must have an appropriate certificate from ARSAC for each procedure undertaken. The IR(ME)R practitioner should:

(a) assess the information provided by the referrer and, if necessary, ask for more information from the referrer

(b) decide if nuclear medicine is an appropriate modality for the patient, and

(c) justify in writing (see paragraph 10.19) the medical exposures necessary to fulfil the clinical request.

10.18   All examinations must be justified by an IR(ME)R practitioner and authorised by either the IR(ME)R practitioner or an operator who has the responsibility for authorisation under pre-arranged procedures and following prescribed referral and other criteria (see paragraphs 2.19 and 2.29). Employer's procedures should be designed to assist IR(ME)R practitioners with justification, particularly in:

(a) the case of medicolegal exposures
(b) where the exposure is part of medical research
(c) where a female patient may be pregnant, and
(d) where the patient is a child.

10.19   Before an examination can proceed, it is necessary to identify that it has been justified (see paragraph 2.33). The IR(ME)R practitioner may, for example, record the authorisation by signing the request form or the prescription for the radioactive medicinal product to be used. Alternatively, in circumstances in which justification is made through a pre-arranged procedure, the operator can authorise it by recording that the request complies with that procedure. Employer's procedures may also require operators to record on the request form that other checks have been performed for individual patients, e.g. patient identification and whether female patients may be pregnant.

10.20   All staff involved in the practical aspects of nuclear medicine procedures (operators) must be adequately trained (see paragraphs 2.73 to 2.76) and undertake continuing education in accordance with the employer's procedure for the task(s) they undertake. Tasks to be performed by operators must be specified in an employer's procedure and will include:

(a) authorisation of an exposure

(b) QC and calibration of any instrumentation (e.g. radionuclide calibrator, gamma camera)

(c) QC and preparation of the radioactive medicinal product including labelled autologous cells

(d) the unique identification of the patient prior to administration

(e) questioning of female patients as to the possibility of pregnancy or whether they are breastfeeding

(f) administration of any radioactive material to the patient, and

(g) the clinical procedure, including imaging, analysis and display of results.

If the ARSAC certificate holder performs any of the tasks above, they take on the role of an operator. Persons who may generate the report of an investigation must be specified in an employer's procedure although, under IR(ME)R, the task itself is not reserved to the IR(ME)R practitioner or an operator.

10.21   Operators are directly responsible for the practical aspects of any part of a nuclear medicine procedure that they perform. In addition to following the employer's procedures and protocols, they should ensure that the radioactive medicinal product administered to the patient is the one that is intended and that the activity administered is within the range required by the IR(ME)R practitioner. Allowance may have to be made for dead space or adherence of the material to the delivery system. If the IR(ME)R practitioner wishes to exceed the DRL (see paragraph 10.27) in an individual case, the reasons for this should be fully documented. Operators should select the practical methods and, where possible, the equipment to ensure that as much diagnostic information as may be necessary is obtained once the radioactive medicinal product has been administered to the patient. Operators should clearly understand the extent of their own responsibilities. A trainee operator must be supervised by an operator who is adequately trained.

10.22   An MPE should either be present, available on site or, at least, contactable to advise on the scientific aspects of all the diagnostic procedures being undertaken (Williams *et al.* [76]). The MPE helps to ensure the overall scientific and technical quality of the investigations by providing advice on a range of issues, such as the form and frequency of QA checks, patient dosimetry (including dosimetry assessments in research protocols), analysis, display and presentation of results, including images. MPEs would normally also be responsible for, or at least heavily involved in, the specification of new equipment, the acceptance testing or commissioning of new or modified equipment (including equipment on loan, see paragraph 1.113) and optimisation of parameters and techniques for all studies undertaken. The role of the MPE is separate from that of the RPA, although each informs the other. The qualifications of MPEs are given in Appendix 5 together with the roles they may undertake on behalf of an employer.

10.23   The RPA for the nuclear medicine facility should have appropriate experience in the application of radiation protection principles to unsealed sources. The RPA should be consulted on all matters specified in Schedule 5 of IRR99 [1] relevant to the facility (see Appendix 4). These matters will include the correct designation of areas as controlled or supervised, the content of local rules and other matters as detailed in the appendix. Note that the RPA may be the same person as the MPE.

10.24   The employer must ensure that all staff are aware of the local rules. The task may often be delegated to the RPS although the responsibility cannot. At least one RPS should be appointed to supervise the arrangements set out in the local rules. The RPSs can also provide a communication channel with the RPA (see Appendix 3).

Protection of the patient

10.25   There must be an employer's procedure concerning the provision of any required written or verbal advice on radiation protection to patients (see paragraphs 2.71 and 2.72 and also 10.76), relatives, nursing staff or anyone likely to be exposed as a result of the clinical procedure undertaken.

10.26   The advice given in the ARSAC *Notes For Guidance* [35] concerning the performance of clinical procedures on pregnant or breastfeeding patients should be followed. There must be an employer's procedure for making enquiries of females of childbearing age to establish whether the individual is or may be pregnant or breastfeeding. Only those investigations that are imperative should be conducted during pregnancy. Specific written instructions must be given to breastfeeding mothers to minimise the radiation dose to the infant through the ingestion of milk. These should be discussed with the mother as soon as practicable and certainly prior to the test. A risk assessment should be made for procedures where a specific recommendation is not available [35], employing a dose constraint of 1.0 mSv to the breastfeeding baby.

10.27   The national DRL for each procedure is tabulated in the ARSAC *Notes For Guidance* [35]. Departments should set their own DRLs taking local circumstances into account. These DRL may be lower than those quoted in [35] but higher levels may only be used with specific ARSAC approval. All the dispensed activities should be checked prior to administration to the patient to ensure that the locally set DRL is not being exceeded. (It may be helpful to define a range of acceptable activities within the DRL since attempting to dispense to better than 10 per cent is likely to increase finger doses for questionable benefit.) Higher values can be administered locally in individual cases, with the permission of the ARSAC certificate holder, however the need for the increase should be defendable and fully documented. The activities administered should be reviewed periodically as part of the QA programme, to ensure that the optimum balance between maximising information (benefit to the patient) and minimising dose (risk to the patient) is being maintained.

Design of nuclear medicine departments

10.28   The requirements for medical establishments using unsealed radioactive substances vary with the type of medical procedures being undertaken. The RPA should be consulted about the design of laboratories and other work areas and detailed plans should be drawn up in collaboration with the clinician responsible for the service and the MPE. Changes that may become necessary from time to time should also be discussed with the RPA. Advice on the design of equipment and facilities is given in ICRP52 *Protection of the Patient in Nuclear Medicine* [77] and ICRP57 *Radiological Protection of the Worker in Medicine and Dentistry* [78]. HBN6 *Facilities for Diagnostic Imaging and Interventional Radiology* [79] also gives guidance.

10.29   Where unsealed radioactive substances are administered to patients, a risk assessment specifying the nature and extent of the clinical procedures to be undertaken should be made. It should include an assessment of the need for the following areas:

(a)   radiopharmacy
(b)   blood cell labelling facility
(c)   radioactive waste storage and disposal
(d)   radionuclide administration to patients
(e)   separate patient waiting and changing areas and toilets
(f)   clinical measurements or imaging
(g)   sample measurements, and
(h)   area for decontamination of articles or people

as well as office and reporting areas and staff facilities such as cloakroom, shower and toilets.

10.30 Where radioactive substances are used solely for *in vitro* diagnostic tests, Chapter 13 may be more helpful. The design of radiopharmacies is discussed in Chapter 11.

10.31 Special consideration should be paid to ensuring that activities in one area do not interfere with work in adjoining areas. For example, radioactive samples or waste should not be handled or stored where they might interfere with imaging or counting procedures, or cause fogging of film stored nearby.

10.32 The appropriate designation of areas where unsealed radioactive substances are stored or handled should be determined by risk assessment (see also paragraphs 1.16 to 1.20). The risk assessment must be reviewed if there is a reason to suspect that it is no longer valid or there has been a significant change in the matters to which it relates (L121 paragraph 52 [2]), and should be reviewed periodically, normally by the radiation protection committee. The specific circumstances of the area that need to be taken into account are:

(a) whether special procedures must be followed to restrict significant exposure

(b) the external radiation hazard, both in terms of dose rate averaged over 1 min (IDR) and the working day (TADR) (see paragraph 1.56)

(c) the risk and level of contamination hazard (see paragraph 1.57)

(d) the control of access

(e) whether staff untrained in radiation protection need to enter

(f) the length of time over which persons need to remain in the area, and

(g) whether the only radioactive substances present are within the body of a person, in which case restrictions based on IDR may be relaxed.

Measurements of actual doses received by individuals waiting in a typical diagnostic nuclear medicine waiting room have shown that designation of the area as controlled is not merited. Supervision of such areas by staff is normally sufficient to ensure that patients and accompanying persons are not exposed to unnecessary dose or contamination. Written instructions for patients, accompanying persons and other visitors to waiting areas could simply be a notice saying 'Supervised Area: please let the receptionist know you have arrived'. Written arrangements in local rules will only be needed for staff working regularly in such areas. Periodic review of use and environmental monitoring will be necessary to confirm the appropriate designation.

10.33 All surfaces of the room where radionuclides are used or stored, benches, tables and seats, should be smooth and non-absorbent, so that they can be cleaned and decontaminated easily. (This is often difficult to implement fully, particularly in clinical areas. In such cases, articles that become contaminated must be removed from use. Further guidance is given in paragraphs 10.93 to 10.104.) Materials not affected by damp, chemicals or heat should be chosen. Bench surfaces should be coved against walls and lipped at the edges. Floor coverings should be 'non-slip' even though this will limit the degree of decontamination that can be achieved. They should (after welding if necessary) be in one continuous sheet, coved against walls. The choice of surface materials should take account of the effects of solvents and cleaning materials likely to be used.

10.34 The floor and benches, including worktops inside enclosures, should be strong enough to support the weight of any necessary shielding materials or of radionuclide generators. A square metre of lead brick wall 50 mm thick weighs 570 kg. The Manual Handling Operations Regulations [80] require lifting tasks to be assessed and lifting equipment to be supplied for heavy loads, e.g. radionuclide generators. Remote handling equipment may be required under the Lifting Operations and Lifting Equipment Regulations [81].

10.35 Work, other than clinical ventilation studies (see paragraph 10.75), that may cause airborne contamination should be carried out under conditions such as to prevent inhalation of radioactive substances. A risk assessment will determine whether or not local exhaust ventilation should be provided. The work should be done in a contained workstation if significant contamination may occur (see paragraphs 11.13 to 11.17).

10.36   One or more wash-hand basins fitted with foot, knee or elbow operated taps and with hot and cold water supply should be provided close to and preferably at the exit from each area where radioactive substances are handled. Disposable towels (and a nearby waste bin) should be provided. In radiopharmacies, these hand-washing and drying facilities will have to be provided in a way that does not contravene aseptic regulations, see paragraph 11.9. There should also be a means of monitoring persons and items upon leaving the area.

10.37   In designing an area where radioactive substances are to be handled, the need for the following special features should be considered initially and independently of the likely and final designation of the area:

(a)   the need to prevent entry by unauthorised persons

(b)   adequate storage space so that essential equipment used in the laboratory is kept there, thus minimising the risk of spreading contamination to other areas

(c)   one or more contained workstations designed for ease of decontamination

(d)   an entry lobby, or an area near the entrance, where protective clothing (see paragraphs 10.61 and 10.62) can be put on, taken off and kept when not in use

(e)   a secure and shielded store for radioactive substances (see paragraph 17.7)

(f)   a shielded temporary store for solid radioactive waste; it is convenient to use disposable plastic liners of distinctive colours and suitably marked to aid disposal; sharp waste should be kept separately

(g)   a limited number of places, designated and clearly marked, for the disposal of radioactive liquid waste; where direct disposal of low activity waste to drains is authorised, the drain should be connected as directly as possible to the main sewer; drainage system materials should take account of the possible build-up of contamination on surfaces; U-bends flush more completely than traps but, if traps are used, they should be small and accessible for monitoring

(h)   depending on the type and activity of radionuclide to be handled, shielding in order to protect the worker from unnecessary exposure to external radiation; persons in adjacent rooms or corridors need to be adequately protected from external radiation that penetrates the floor, walls or ceiling (see paragraphs 1.54 to 1.57)

(i)   a wash-up area for contaminated articles such as glassware; the drainage should comply with (g) above; subject to the approval of the RPA, the wash-up area may be combined with (g) above, but not used for hand-washing, and

(j)   pipework through which radioactive materials flow should be clearly marked to ensure that monitoring precedes any maintenance.

10.38   In hospitals, excreta are not normally collected for specific disposal as radioactive waste; however, collection of samples is sometimes needed for diagnostic tests. The store used to contain them should be locked and conform to the guidance in Chapter 17.

10.39   Occasionally, some specimens of blood, urine or tissue that are sent for analysis (e.g. to a pathology laboratory) cannot be disregarded for the purposes of radiation protection. A risk assessment should be undertaken for each type of situation and take into account:

(a)   the external dose rate and ease of shielding
(b)   the risk of contamination from the procedures to be performed
(c)   the time for which the sample must be worked, and
(d)   the storage and disposal conditions.

Even when hazards to staff are minimal, the radioactivity in samples may still interfere with the analysis. Appropriate labelling of the sample will be required and should be used to warn other staff of this possibility. Even fairly small activities will be above the level at which work with unsealed substances must be notified to the HSE (see paragraph 10.2 for a list of values for commonly used radionuclides). If the laboratory is on a site not covered by an existing notification, then the employer at that site should be advised that such notification is required. The initial risk assessment should include a recommendation as to whether or not the receiving hospital needs to consult an RPA and any legislative requirements under RSA93 [7] (see paragraph 13.24). The proper disposal of any radioactive waste generated should also be addressed (see Chapter 18). Radioactive samples may occur as a result of surgery (see paragraph 10.83) and radiation safety after sentinel node localisation has been investigated extensively (Waddington *et al.* [82]).

10.40   In addition to those of the general requirements listed in paragraph 10.37 that are considered necessary, the area for administration of radioactive substances to patients should be large enough to provide ample space, not only for the patient, any escort and staff, but also for any trolleys of equipment required. This also applies where radioactive substances are administered to patients in areas used for clinical measurements or imaging (e.g. in renography). Shielded storage may be needed for radioactive substances prior to administration, and for surplus substances, waste and contaminated equipment afterwards.

10.41   Where an area for decontamination of persons is provided, a large wash-hand basin with detachable spray head may be useful for carrying out procedures discussed in paragraphs 10.87 to 10.92. The design of decontamination areas in casualty departments for use in major incidents is discussed in paragraphs 19.24 to 19.27.

10.42   In addition to the warning signs required for controlled areas, all work areas where unsealed radioactive substances are present should be marked with a sign indicating ionising radiation (see Appendix 12).

Enclosures and extract systems

10.43   For details on the requirements for enclosures and extract systems, including those used for aseptic work and iodination procedures, see Chapter 11.

Equipment: installation, maintenance and quality assurance

10.44   All medical devices must carry the CE mark to indicate that they conform to the Medical Devices Directive [44]. The enforcement authority for this directive in the United Kingdom is the MDA. The most common items of equipment in nuclear medicine facilities are the gamma camera and the radionuclide calibrator. The MDA supports the independent Gamma Camera Assessment Team (GCAT); more information can be found on the MDA web site (see Appendix 16). The National Physical Laboratory (NPL) provides services to ensure that the performance of radionuclide calibrators is traceable to national and international standards.

10.45   All equipment that emits radiation will require a critical examination in accordance with the IRR99 [1]. This includes such items as the radioactive line sources or CT equipment attached to gamma cameras in order to generate attenuation maps. This examination ensures that safety features and warning devices function correctly and that the radiation protection arrangements for the installation are satisfactory (see paragraphs 1.30 to 1.48 and 13.4). The installation of radionuclide calibrators and gamma cameras implies that radioactive sources and radioactive patients will be brought to such equipment and the radiation protection arrangements of the designated areas where such equipment has been installed should be checked.

10.46   Before any piece of nuclear medicine equipment enters clinical use, it should undergo acceptance testing to ensure that it operates safely and performs to specification. Manufacturers of gamma cameras specify performance in relation to standards laid down by the National Electrical Manufacturers' Association (NEMA). The International Electrotechnical Commission (IEC) and the British Standards Institution (BSI) have harmonised their standards and include more clinically relevant performance parameters than NEMA (BS EN 60789 *Methods of Test for Anger Type Gamma Cameras* [83]). Detailed information on QC of gamma cameras and associated computer systems is given in IPSM66 *Quality Control of Gamma Cameras and Associated Computer Systems* [84] (under revision).

10.47   Further commissioning tests should aim to provide baseline results for subsequent QA tests and will provide information that can be used to define optimum acquisition parameters for all clinical procedures.

10.48   All departments should undertake QA to ensure the continual production of optimum quality images and diagnostic information using the minimum administered activity to the patient. QA programmes should include checks and test measurements on all parts of the imaging and computing system, at appropriate time intervals. There must be a QA programme in place to check the performance of the radionuclide calibrator. A QA programme must also be in place to review administered activities to patients, see paragraph 10.27. An RPA and MPE should be consulted when planning these programmes and they should be involved in regular reviews of their effectiveness. QA of radiopharmaceuticals is discussed in Chapter 11. Guidance on all aspects of quality in nuclear medicine is provided in IPSM65 *Quality Standards in Nuclear Medicine* [85] (under revision).

10.49   All equipment should be maintained to the specification and at the frequency recommended by the manufacturer.

10.50   A record of maintenance including QA should be kept for each item of equipment: this should include information on any defects found by users (fault log), interim remedial action taken, subsequent repairs made and results of testing before equipment is reintroduced to clinical use.

10.51   A person who carries out modifications or maintenance which could affect image quality or the assay of radioactivity, should immediately inform the person responsible for the use of the equipment before it is returned to clinical use. Where this is not possible, e.g. when the work is performed out-of-hours, a notice drawing attention to the modification or maintenance should be attached to the equipment. In all cases, a clear written report of the changes and current operational status should be given, including the name of the person concerned and the date, either in the maintenance log or in the form of a hand-over questionnaire. This should include details of any changes affecting image quality or assay of radioactivity that may require further measurements.

10.52   After work affecting equipment performance (see paragraph 10.51), staff must perform any in-house testing required by their QA programme before the equipment is returned to clinical use. In some cases, the programme may indicate that advice must be obtained from the RPA or MPE before proceeding. If alterations in procedures, clinical protocols or local rules are required, the responsible person must communicate the changes to all users.

Provision of protective equipment and clothing

10.53   Laboratories and other work areas used for manipulation of unsealed radioactive substances should be provided with equipment kept specifically for this purpose. This equipment may need to include:

  (a) apparatus for maximising the distance of the worker from the source, e.g. tongs, forceps

  (b) containers for radioactive substances that incorporate the necessary shielding as close to the source as possible

  (c) double-walled containers (the outer wall being unbreakable) for liquid samples

  (d) a drip tray (see paragraph 10.57)

  (e) disposable tip automatic pipettes; alternatively, hypodermic syringes to replace pipettes (see paragraph 10.63)

  (f) syringe shields

  (g) lead walls or 'castles' for secondary shielding

  (h) lead barriers with lead glass windows

  (i) barriers incorporating Perspex™ for work with beta emitters

(j) radiation and contamination monitoring equipment

(k) equipment for the assay of stock solutions and radioactive substances prepared for administration to patients (radionuclide calibrators – see paragraph 10.72)

(l) carrying containers, wheeled if necessary, for moving radioactive substances from place to place, and

(m) equipment and materials to deal with spills.

10.54   Protective clothing should be used in work areas where there is a likelihood of contamination, both to protect the body or clothing of the wearer and to help to prevent the transfer of contamination to other areas. The clothing should be monitored and removed before leaving designated areas. When moving between supervised areas such as the camera room and the injection area, it may not be necessary to change the protective clothing unless a spill is suspected. In any case, protective clothing should be removed prior to leaving the designated areas, e.g. when visiting the staff room. The clothing may include:

(a) laboratory coats or protective gowns

(b) gloves which are waterproof and, where low-energy beta emitters are handled, thick enough to protect against external beta radiation

(c) overshoes, and

(d) caps and masks for aseptic work.

10.55   Respirators are not normally needed for medical work, though they may be required for some emergencies. The respirators must be adequately maintained and records of maintenance must be kept. Persons who may need to wear them should be suitably trained in their use.

General procedures in nuclear medicine departments

10.56   The advice of the RPA and MPE should be sought before new procedures are introduced or major changes are made to existing procedures. The procedures should be reviewed from time to time in consultation with the RPA. Extremity monitoring may be of particular use in planning and reviewing operational procedures. New or changed procedures should be rehearsed, where possible, without using radioactive substances.

10.57   Working procedures should be designed to prevent spillage occurring and, in the event of spillage, to minimise the spread of contamination from the work area. This is necessary not only in the interests of the safety of persons but also to prevent interference with assay of samples containing radioactivity. Dispensing of radioactive substances should be done in a contained workstation, especially if particulates, aerosols, vapours or gases are involved. For the specific case of ventilation imaging, refer to paragraph 10.75. All manipulations should be carried out over a drip tray, in order to minimise the spread of contamination due to breakages or spills. No object should be introduced into a contained workstation if it interferes unacceptably with the pattern of airflow. Contingency plans for reasonably foreseeable incidents (IRR99 regulation 12 [1]) should be drawn up and referred to or included in the local rules (see also paragraphs 11.39 and 12.21).

10.58   No food or drink (except that used for medical purposes), cosmetics or smoking materials should be brought into an area where unsealed radionuclides are used, neither should they be stored in a refrigerator used for unsealed radioactive substances. In addition, crockery and cutlery (except that used for medical purposes) should not be brought into the laboratory either for washing or storage.

10.59   Handkerchiefs should never be used in these areas; an adequate supply of paper tissues should be provided (unless in an aseptic area, see paragraph 11.19).

10.60   Any cut or break in the skin should be covered before a person enters an area where unsealed radioactive substances are handled. Dressings should incorporate a waterproof, adhesive strapping. If a cut or break in the skin is sustained while in the area, refer to paragraph 10.91.

10.61   When an area is designated as controlled on account of the potential for contamination, anyone working in or visiting the area should wear any protective clothing identified as necessary in the prior risk assessment. (Protective clothing is unlikely to be necessary for persons accompanying patients into gamma camera rooms.) On leaving a controlled area, all protective clothing should be monitored and placed in an appropriate container if contaminated (but see paragraphs 10.37 and 10.54). The method of removing gloves should be based on the surgical technique, in order to avoid transferring activity to the hands. If a risk assessment has shown that reusable gloves are acceptable, the same technique of removal will avoid contaminating the inner surfaces of the gloves. There are different considerations where the reusable gloves are attached to an isolator, see paragraph 11.19.

10.62   Staff leaving a controlled area, designated on account of the potential for contamination, should, after removing protective clothing, wash their hands and then monitor their hands, clothing and body, as appropriate. Mild liquid soap should be provided unless aseptic considerations require an alternative cleaner. Non-abrasive single-use nailbrushes should only be used if contamination persists after simple washing. Further advice is given in paragraphs 10.87 to 10.92.

10.63   Equipment provided specifically for the safe handling of unsealed radioactive substances should always be used. Such equipment should not be moved from the work area. Pipettes should never be operated by mouth. The hazards of recapping needles (needle-stick injury leading to contamination or infection of staff) will usually outweigh the hazards of not recapping them (contamination incidents from dripping needles). Special procedures will be necessary if assessment of residual activity in the syringe is required. Remote-handling equipment should be provided and used where it can be effective in reducing radiation dose.

10.64   The work area should be kept tidy and free of articles not required for the work. It should be cleaned often enough to ensure minimal contamination. Cleaning methods should be chosen in order to avoid raising dust or spreading contamination. Articles used for cleaning controlled or supervised areas should be restricted to these areas. They should be monitored periodically, and, if found to be contaminated, reference should be made to paragraphs 10.93 to 10.104. Cleaning and contamination control may be simplified by using disposable items and (except where this conflicts with aseptic requirements, see Chapter 11) by covering benches and the interior of drip trays with disposable material such as plastic-backed absorbent paper.

10.65   Shielding should always be considered for any radioactive source. The prior risk assessment should identify what shielding is required and what type and form it should take. Figure 10.1 may be helpful in this process. Appropriate shielding may be obtained using a variety of materials such as lead, lead glass, lead composite, tungsten or aluminium. Shields incorporating acrylic materials such as Perspex™ may be more suitable for beta emitters. Lead should be painted with a suitable gloss finish or encased to provide a safe, cleanable surface.

10.66   Syringes used for handling radioactive liquids should be shielded wherever practicable. Suitable shielding materials are discussed in paragraph 10.65. The distance between the fingers and the radioactive substance should be as large as can be achieved safely. The radioactive liquid should not normally exceed 50 per cent of the syringe capacity. Consideration should be given to the need for extremity monitoring, particularly in the case of new techniques, inexperienced staff and increased workloads. Further information is given in paragraph 1.94.

10.67   The activities of each radionuclide handled or stored in a particular work area should not exceed the values for which the area has been designed. These activity limits should be specified in the local rules. The RPA should be consulted in particular cases where it is desired to use larger activities than those specified. In all cases the activities used must be within the Certificate of Registration issued under RSA93 [7] (see Chapter 17).

Figure 10.1 Shielding decision chart

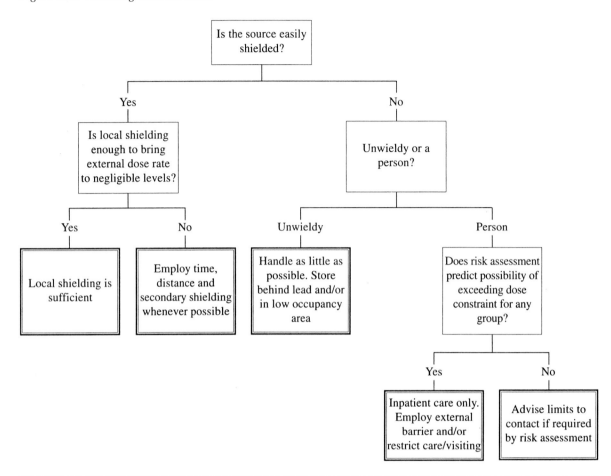

- Vials of most radiopharmaceuticals are easily shielded by being placed in lead pots, but the pots themselves may still need to be kept behind lead walls when the vials are not being used.
- It is generally impossible to avoid some direct handling of large flood phantoms (sealed or unsealed) used for testing gamma cameras or to avoid using them while unshielded. Protection of staff is optimised by handling as little as possible and not lingering near the source when it is unshielded.
- Recommended values for dose constraints are given in paragraphs 1.56, 1.62, 1.73 and 15.12.
- Additional shielding may be required for sources kept near low level counting areas or film stores

10.68   Radioactive substances should be clearly labelled, indicating the radionuclide, chemical form, and activity at a given date and time. Batch number and expiry date and time should be added if appropriate. Records of stocks, administrations and disposals should be kept (see paragraphs 10.71 and 10.79, Chapter 17 and Appendix 9).

10.69   Systems must be in place to detect when maintenance work is to be performed on equipment that might be contaminated, particularly enclosures for controlling airborne activity, ventilation trunking, sinks and waste pipes. In hospitals, this might take the form of information on potential areas being provided to the estates department and an instruction to inform the RPS whenever such work is planned. The radiation employer should carry out a risk assessment that takes account of the dose rate or activity likely to be encountered in the work and the nature of the necessary precautions to keep exposures ALARP. This will enable a decision to be made on a suitable system of work and the level of supervision needed. Direct supervision of the work may be required if, for example, the dose rate or activity is likely to be high, or complicated instructions are needed to keep exposures ALARP. Otherwise, it will be sufficient to issue a permit to work detailing the precautions to be taken by the maintenance staff. The maintenance staff must sign that they have read and understood the precautions before work can start.

Administration of radiopharmaceuticals

10.70   The activity administered to a patient, whether for diagnosis or research, must be determined by a person holding an appropriate ARSAC certificate or under a protocol authorised by such a person. Any advice necessary to restrict the exposure of other persons (see paragraphs 2.71, 2.72 and 10.76) should be discussed with the patient in advance (see paragraph 12.17 for fuller details). Operators who administer the activity must be suitably trained.

10.71   Records should be kept of all administrations of radioactive substances as indicated in paragraph 10.68. These records must be kept in such a way as to:

(a)   facilitate accounting of stock under RSA93 [7] and IRR99 [1] (see Chapter 17)

(b)   allow all components of any individual administration to be traced retrospectively (as required by the Medicines Act [18])

(c)   allow review of DRLs, clinical audit and estimation of the effective dose to an individual patient as required under IR(ME)R [3], and

(d)   ensure that information on the administration is made available to persons who need to be advised, as part of the procedure adopted to restrict their exposure (see paragraph 10.76).

10.72   The activity should be checked before administration. Equipment used for this purpose should be checked daily using a test sealed source and should be calibrated at regular intervals with sources traceable to national standards (see paragraph 10.44). In situations where calibration of activity is difficult (e.g. in the case of ^{51}Cr, ^{125}I and some beta emitting radionuclides) users should make every effort to ensure that the system they adopt is as robust as possible. Users may have to rely on calculation by volume, making the necessary decay corrections to the radioactive concentration printed on the vial by the manufacturer.

10.73   If it is suspected that a patient has received a radiation dose significantly greater than intended, an investigation of the circumstances must be undertaken immediately (see 1.100 to 1.109). The RPA may need to be involved. If the investigation confirms the suspicion, a detailed report must be made and action should be taken to prevent a recurrence. If the incident is notifiable, the appropriate bodies should be contacted. If the patient procedure was compromised or the exposure was significantly greater than intended (see HSG226 [10] and Table 10.2), the patient should be informed if appropriate. The ARSAC certificate holder will normally perform this task but it can be delegated if specified in the employer's procedure. If the exposure was significantly greater than intended and was due to equipment malfunction, the incident must be reported to the HSE and to the appropriate Health Department: Adverse Incident Centre at MDA, Incident Reporting and Investigation Centre at Scottish Healthcare Supplies or the Department of Health, Social Services and Public Safety for Northern Ireland (see Appendix 16). If the exposure was significantly greater than intended (as defined above) and was due to reasons other than equipment malfunction, the incident must be reported under IR(ME)R [3] to the relevant enforcing authority.

Table 10.2   The maximum ratio of actual dose to expected dose before mandatory notification to the relevant authority.

Expected effective dose	Guideline factor
Greater than 5 mSv	3
Between 0.5 mSv and 5 mSv	10
Less than 0.5 mSv	20

10.74   To reduce the radiation dose to the patient's thyroid, the use of a thyroid blocking agent should be considered if radioiodine in certain forms is to be administered, provided this will not interfere with the procedure, as advised in the ARSAC *Notes for Guidance* [35].

10.75   When radioactive gases such as ^{133}Xe or aerosols are administered, a build-up of airborne activity within the room should be avoided by conducting exhaled breath directly out of the building if this is permitted by the waste disposal authorisation under RSA93 [7], or by trapping it in a shielded leak-free container or filter. With very short half-life gases (e.g. ^{81}Kr^m), these precautions may not be necessary. Adequate ventilation should be provided for all rooms where radioactive gases and aerosols are stored, released or used. The need for, or frequency of, air monitoring should be decided with advice from the RPA and described in the local rules.

10.76   Persons to whom unsealed radioactive substances are administered (and/or their carers, as appropriate) should receive instructions and information, as appropriate, on precautions to be taken and, if necessary, on any hazards involved (see also Chapter 15). This is always necessary for administrations of ^{131}I greater than 30 MBq [35]. The instructions and information may be given verbally and/or in written form (see paragraphs 2.71 and 2.72). The persons responsible for taking the necessary actions must be identified in the employer's procedures.

10.77   In most cases, the radiation dose sustained by family and friends due to diagnostic procedures is small, particularly if the patient is still in hospital and they are only visiting. Chapter 15 gives more information on prior assessment of risk to these groups and any precautions that need to be taken when the patient goes home.

10.78   Protection against external contamination should be provided for patients who receive oral administrations of radioactive materials or inhale radioactive aerosols. A plastic apron is normally sufficient to protect clothes.

Procedures in wards and clinics

10.79   If radionuclides are administered to inpatients, the need for advice to staff on wards and in other departments should be considered as part of the risk assessment. Information, advice and training must be provided as necessary for ward staff. It may also be necessary to record the administration and any advice regarding radiation protection in the patient's notes so that ward staff are fully informed.

10.80   Ward staff will usually be sufficiently protected from contamination from body fluids if standard hygiene precautions are followed, e.g. use of gloves and plastic aprons. The staff on the ward should be issued with storage and handling instructions to be followed if bedding or clothing becomes contaminated. In most situations involving diagnostic levels of activity, a risk assessment will show that contaminated items can be sent directly to the hospital laundry. Where higher activities or longer-lived radionuclides have recently been administered to a patient, the items may need secure storage in a plastic bag for an appropriate period to reduce the contamination to a level at which the items can be sent to the laundry (see paragraphs 10.96 to 10.99).

10.81   The external radiation dose received from the nursing of these patients will not normally be such that any special precautions will be required unless the patient needs intensive nursing. A prior risk assessment should be made to identify the situations in which sharing of nursing duties may be required in order to address this problem. Advice should be sought from the RPA if pregnant nurses are to be involved.[1] Ideally, pregnant nursing staff should not be involved in escorting patients who require intensive nursing to the nuclear medicine department. Ward staff should be alerted to the inadvisability of this and asked to contact the nuclear medicine department for advice in such situations.

---

1   The need for such advice is suggested particularly for nurses on general wards where staff are unlikely to have much experience of work with radiation and where an RPS is unlikely to have been appointed. The situation is therefore different from that of nurses who are employed in nuclear medicine departments. However, both situations should have been covered in a prior risk assessment.

10.82   If radionuclides are to be administered outside the nuclear medicine department, such as on wards or in clinics, the local rules for the department must be extended to cover these areas. The ward or clinic area should where possible, meet the requirements of paragraphs 10.33, 10.35 and 10.36. If this is not the case, special precautions should be taken. Consideration should be given to covering surfaces that may become contaminated as detailed in paragraph 10.99(a). Following the administration, the area should be monitored for contamination if there has been a suspected spill of radioactive material, and decontaminated if necessary. A decontamination kit should be available. Procedures to deal with any contamination of the ward or clinic area should be contained in the local rules.

Procedures in operating theatres

10.83   When an operation takes place on a patient who is undergoing an investigation (e.g. sentinel node localisation) or has recently undergone a diagnostic nuclear medicine test (e.g. bone scan), the external radiation risk will not normally be such that any special precautions are required. The risk of contamination will depend upon the distribution of the radiopharmaceutical within the body. Standard procedures in operating theatres should protect the staff from any contamination. If a significant risk is identified from the prior assessment, staff should be monitored. If, exceptionally, no prior risk assessment exists, the RPA should be consulted for advice. Paragraph 10.39 gives information on procedures to be adopted if contaminated samples or tissues are to be transferred to a laboratory for examination. Normal cleaning and sterilisation procedures should be adequate to remove any contamination from equipment. If any potentially contaminated waste is generated, it should be collected in a clearly labelled plastic bag and removed by trained staff for disposal by an authorised route (see Chapter 18).

Monitoring of work areas

10.84   Laboratories and other areas in which work with unsealed radioactive substances is undertaken should be monitored, both for external radiation and for surface contamination, on a systematic basis. For each controlled or supervised area there should be a suitable monitoring schedule; for other areas occasional monitoring is acceptable. Monitors used must be suitable for the task and regularly tested. Action levels must be determined. The person who undertakes the monitoring must be adequately trained. Records of the monitoring must be kept for at least 2 years and should include the date, type of monitor, person undertaking the task, areas, results and what action was taken if action levels were exceeded.

10.85   Contamination should be kept ALARP. Normal monitoring and decontamination procedures should aim to keep the level of contamination below levels that are detectable with the most sensitive method available. Procedures must be developed to deal with the situation if contamination is detected (see paragraphs 10.93 to 10.104).

10.86   Contamination monitoring will be required for:

(a)   all working surfaces (including the interior of enclosures), tools, equipment, the floor and any items removed from the area; also during maintenance of contained workstations, ventilation systems and drains; direct monitoring should be used in preference to wipe testing unless HDRs in the area would limit unacceptably the level of contamination that would be detected by direct monitoring; unless other information is available, it should be assumed that wipe testing will only remove 10 per cent of the total contamination present on the swabbed area

(b)   protective and personal clothing, including shoes, particularly when persons leave an area that is controlled due to the risk of contamination; a monitoring instrument should be placed near the exit

(c)   clothing and bedding of patients where contamination is suspected, and

(d) the hands of staff before leaving an area where they have been handling unsealed radioactive substances;[2] an instrument for monitoring the hands should be available where the hands are washed; this monitoring should extend to other skin areas, e.g. the face, if there is any reason to suspect that these areas may have become contaminated; low levels of skin contamination can be difficult to detect against even fairly modest background levels, depending on the design of the monitor; care should be taken to monitor in an area where the background is suitably low.

Decontamination of persons

10.87   Hands should be washed if contamination is suspected, on completing work with unsealed radioactive substances and on leaving an area that is controlled due to the risk of contamination. Swabbing may be more effective if the contamination is confined to a relatively small area. If detectable contamination remains on the hands after simple washing, using a surfactant[3] or chelating agent specific to the chemical form of the contaminant may be more successful. The hands should not be rubbed or brushed vigorously, nor should harsh chemical treatments be attempted, as this might injure the skin and allow the radioactivity to enter the body.

10.88   When contamination of parts of the body, other than the hands, is suspected, or when the procedures described above for decontamination of the hands are ineffective, the line manager and the RPS must be notified and consideration given to any further action. Some pointers are given below. The RPA may need to be contacted for advice

10.89   Special care needs to be taken in the decontamination of the face to restrict entry of radioactive material into the eyes, nose, ears or mouth. Decontamination of skin is best achieved as detailed for the hands in paragraph 10.87. Hair should be decontaminated similarly before being washed in shampoo. In all cases, care should be taken not to spread the contamination further.

10.90   Contaminated clothing should be removed as soon as practicable, taking care not to spread the contamination. If it cannot be left securely for the radioactivity to decay, the clothing should be dealt with as detailed in paragraphs 10.96 to 10.98. If the contamination is long-lived, the clothing may have to be treated as radioactive waste (see Chapter 18).

10.91   If the skin is broken or a wound is sustained in conditions where there is a risk of radioactive contamination, the injury should be irrigated with water as soon as appropriate, taking care not to wash contamination into the wound, or spread contamination to other areas of the body. As soon as the first aid measures have been taken, the person should seek further treatment, including decontamination if necessary. In such cases it is essential that details of the incident are recorded and the head of department informed. The RPA should be contacted for advice. It is usual to keep the RPS informed. Further guidance on the procedures to be adopted in the case of serious incidents (including those involving members of the public and under the NAIR scheme) is given in Chapter 19.

10.92   All staff working with unsealed sources should be trained in the locally agreed procedures for dealing with accidents, spills or contaminated persons, with refresher training provided at appropriate intervals. A copy of the procedures should be readily available in the work area for reference. The procedures, a summary of them or an indication of where they are kept, must be included in the local rules.

Decontamination of areas, surfaces and equipment

10.93   If buildings, fittings or articles become contaminated prompt action should be taken to prevent dispersal of the activity, particularly its transfer to the clothing or body of any person. Contaminated equipment

---

2   This may be difficult to achieve in clinical areas. However, monitoring devices should be available in the vicinity and used if contamination is suspected and before leaving the wider area or eating or drinking.

3   Undiluted Fairy Liquid™ has been shown to be particularly effective (C. Griffiths, personal communication).

and areas of walls and floors should be isolated and small objects transferred to containers using tongs and gloves. An assessment of the amount of activity involved and the associated radiation hazard must be made.

10.94 Once as much contamination as practicable has been removed, the remaining radioactivity and the hazards of it remaining there should be assessed. Acceptable levels of contamination are not specified. The existing derived limits for surface contamination can be used as a starting point[4] to assess whether further action needs to be considered. For publicly accessible areas, these limits are 300 Bq cm^{-2} for ^{3}H and ^{51}Cr; 30 Bq cm^{-2} for ^{14}C, ^{35}S, ^{57}Co, ^{67}Ga, ^{99}Tc^m, ^{123}I, ^{125}I and ^{201}Tl; and 3 Bq cm^{-2} for most other radionuclides in common medical use, including ^{131}I. Measurements should be averaged over the most appropriate area, not exceeding 1000 cm^2 for floors, walls and ceilings and 300 cm^2 for all other surfaces (except body surfaces, where 1 cm^2 is more likely to be appropriate, but see previous section). Further guidance is given in the following paragraphs. The advice of the RPA may have to be sought.

10.95 Care should be taken to ensure that the proposed action is in full compliance with the requirements of RSA93 [7] for the accumulation or disposal of radioactive waste (see Chapter 18). If the possibility of contravention of RSA93 does arise, the RPA should be contacted immediately for advice.

10.96 When contamination is due to short-lived radionuclides and the risk of biological contamination is insignificant,[5] it may be feasible to close off the area or store the article in an impermeable bag for a sufficient time to allow the radioactivity to decay away naturally. In any other circumstance, positive action to decontaminate will be necessary.

10.97 When storage is not practicable but suitable laundering facilities are available (see footnote referred to in paragraph 10.96), any washable articles contaminated with short- or long-lived radionuclides may be given a series of washes in a proprietary cleansing agent, alternating with rinses (as provided by an automatic washing machine). Hot water may bind the contamination into the material. Machines may need to be checked for and rinsed clear of residual contamination afterwards and outflow pipes should be marked as in paragraph 10.37(j).

10.98 Contaminated clothing or bedding should not be sent to public laundries unless the activities are below the limits given in paragraph 10.94.

10.99 Proprietary cleaning agents are normally adequate for removal of contamination. Agents that will not damage the material or interfere with its essential properties (e.g. non-slip or anti-static) should be chosen. Water and any other agent used for decontamination should be treated as radioactive waste (see Chapter 18). If cleaning fails to decontaminate adequately, the following actions should be taken:

(a) for short-lived radionuclides, the surface should be covered with impermeable coated paper: tar paper is not robust in wet conditions; strong polythene sheet may substantially increase the risk of slipping when used as a floor covering; the temporary covering should be clearly marked as radioactive and a date given for removal; this date should be after the radioactivity will have decayed below the limits given in paragraph 10.94, and

(b) for longer-lived radionuclides, surfaces may have to be removed and replaced.

10.100 Glassware and porcelain can usually be cleaned with a suitable proprietary agent (e.g. Decon™, Milton™) or bleach. They are best cleaned immediately after use. The solutions used for cleaning should never be returned to the stock bottle.

10.101 Dilute nitric acid can be used to clean some plastics, since it will usually be effective without damaging the material. Care should be taken to avoid the use of ketonic solvents and certain chlorinated hydrocarbons, which will dissolve some plastics. No organic solvent has any effect on polythene.

---

4 The derived limits [86] have not been reduced because there has been no evidence that any worker or member of the public exceeded the IRR99 dose limits [1] when working to the previous derived limits. There are indeed reasonable arguments for increasing surface contamination action levels.

5 The RPA and/or Infection Control officer may be approached for advice.

10.102   Washing with a heavy-duty detergent, followed if necessary by specific chelating agents, may clean contaminated metal tools, trays, sinks and equipment.

10.103   If articles cannot be decontaminated satisfactorily, or stored, they must be treated as radioactive waste.

10.104   Articles should be monitored before reuse to ensure that decontamination has been successful.

11 Preparation of radiopharmaceuticals

Scope

11.1 This chapter applies to the production and preparation of radiopharmaceuticals for subsequent administration to human subjects for the purpose of diagnosis, treatment or research. This includes the labelling of commercially available kits or other pharmaceuticals and labelling of autologous blood components. Also included are those radiopharmaceuticals that may be purchased as ready-to-use products or products requiring dilution or sub-division. The particular precautions necessary for iodination are also covered.

Hazards from unsealed radioactive substances and principles for their control

11.2 The hazards from unsealed sources and the principles for their control are the same as for diagnostic (see paragraphs 10.4 to 10.9) and therapeutic uses (see paragraphs 12.4 and 12.5). However, the activities handled by radiopharmacy staff are often much greater than those encountered by staff in individual nuclear medicine departments. Additional radiation protection measures are almost always required.

Staff dose issues

11.3 Constant vigilance is required to ensure that doses are kept ALARP. Optimisation of procedures, rigorous attention to technique and the use of remote handling equipment should enable the radiation doses sustained by radiopharmacy staff to be kept below the levels at which classification is required (IRR99 regulation 20 [1] and L121 paragraphs 367 to 370 [2]). In particular, if finger doses in excess of 25 mSv year^{-1} are anticipated (1/20 of annual limit by analogy with L121 paragraph 386 [2]), monitoring is recommended. This should demonstrate that the procedures designed to keep doses ALARP are preventing the dose averaged over any 1 cm^2 of the fingers from approaching 150 mSv year^{-1} (see paragraph 1.94). The frequency of dosemeter change should be determined by risk assessment, taking into account the activities handled, facilities available and previous dose measurements. The wearing of EPDs is particularly useful in the training of new staff and assessment of the impact of new procedures and equipment. Using an external fixed or hand-held monitor to assess internal contamination of the thyroid may be indicated for staff performing radioiodinations. If any of the relevant 3/10 dose levels are likely to be exceeded, in spite of full radiation protection measures, the staff must be classified (although see also paragraph 1.76).

11.4 The risks to the fetus or breastfeeding infant must be assessed where radiopharmaceuticals are prepared by pregnant or breastfeeding staff [11]. Paragraphs 10.10 and 10.11 apply. It may be necessary to adjust systems of work or reallocate duties for such staff, particularly if radioiodine is dispensed in liquid form.

Protection of the patient

11.5 The use of radioactive substances for medical exposures is covered by MARS78 [5] and MARS95 [6] and IR(ME)R [3]. Further details are given in paragraphs 10.12 to 10.27. Staff who prepare radiopharmaceuticals for clinical use are defined as operators under IR(ME)R (see Chapter 2 for their general duties).

Design of radiopharmacies

11.6   The two over-riding, and sometimes conflicting, principles applied to the design of a radiopharmacy are protection of the operator from ionising radiation and protection of the radiopharmaceutical, and hence the patient, from microbial contamination and pyrogens.

11.7   The design process should be primarily concerned with the safe production of radiopharmaceuticals in terms of good manufacturing, aseptic dispensing and radiation protection practices. The pharmacist providing specialist advice, the regional QC pharmacist and the RPA should be involved from an early stage.

11.8   The accommodation required by a radiopharmacy will depend on local arrangements, the range and type of procedures undertaken and the likely designation of the area. The need for the following areas should be considered:

(a) cleanroom suite or facility, including a changing area
(b) blood labelling facility, including a changing area
(c) laboratory
(d) radionuclide store
(e) reception area for radioactive materials, and
(f) storage and disposal facilities for radioactive waste

as well as office space and staff facilities such as a cloakroom, shower and toilet.

11.9   The general provisions of paragraphs 10.28 to 10.42 apply to all areas where radionuclides are handled although, as indicated, where aseptic procedures take place, there are some further considerations:

(a) sinks or drains should not be sited in the aseptic area or in the changing area, however, there must be adequate cleaning and decontamination facilities for persons and equipment, taking into account contingency arrangements; in particular, hand-washing and drying facilities should be available as close as aseptic requirements will allow

(b) classification of areas will be required in terms of grade of air as well as the associated radiation hazard, and

(c) since the area will require a positive pressure differential with respect to adjacent areas, radiation protection is best provided by a workstation that operates at a negative pressure to its surroundings to prevent release of radioactive materials.

11.10   Radiopharmacies must be designed to conform to the requirements of the Medicines Act [18]. Units must either be licensed under the Act or claim a section 10 exemption from the Act, as non-licensed units. In the latter case, they should comply with equivalent standards. Licensed units are inspected to the Orange Guide *Rules and Guidance for Pharmaceutical Manufacturers and Distributors* [87] by Medicine Control Agency (UK) (MCA) inspectors and non-licensed units are inspected by NHS Pharmaceutical Quality Controllers as required by HBN29 *Accommodation for Pharmaceutical Services* [88], for aseptic preparation as described in *The Quality Assurance of Aseptic Preparation Services* [89], and for radiopharmaceuticals as described in *Quality Assurance of Radiopharmaceuticals* [90]. Design features required for a radiopharmacy are covered in these documents and in several others [91–94].

11.11   Blood component labelling is classed as a clinical procedure. It is not subject to the requirements of the Medicines Act [18] although many of the design features are similar. Further information is given in paragraphs 11.27 to 11.32. The Medicines Inspectorate will only scrutinise the procedure if the labelling might interfere with the work of the radiopharmacy.

11.12   Work involving volatile radioactive materials such as iodination may be undertaken without the product being administered to patients. In this case, the requirements of the following section should be met. Iodinated products for administration to patients should be prepared in a facility conforming to the standards referenced in paragraph 11.10.

Enclosures and extract systems

11.13   All aseptic manipulations, including generator elution, must be performed in a workstation or isolator sited in a room conforming to the specifications referenced in paragraph 11.10 (although also see paragraph 17.16).

11.14   A workstation for non-aseptic work involving volatile radioactive materials should conform to the requirements of BS 5726 *Microbiological Safety Cabinets* [95] for general protection of the operator. The workstation may be a microbiological safety cabinet, or an isolator [91], or a fume cupboard.

11.15   Where the exhaust from contained workstations cannot be discharged safely within the laboratory, because of a risk of radioactive or other contamination, it should be separated from the normal ventilation system and should be discharged through ducting which is at an adequate height and not in close proximity to windows or air intakes. A discharge point 2 m or 3 m above the roof and well away from any point of re-entry to the building is usually sufficient. Provided that each outlet point is well selected, a risk assessment should show that filters to trap radioactive contamination will not be necessary for the amounts normally handled in hospitals and other medical establishments (although iodination may be an exception; and note that filters may be expected on aseptic facilities). The extractor fan should be positioned close to the outlet, in order to maintain a negative pressure throughout the duct, and the motor should be outside the duct.

11.16   The local exhaust ventilation system should be inspected and tested at least annually (every 14 months) by a competent person under PUWER [57] and for compliance with BS 5726 [95], to ensure that it is adequate in adverse circumstances, e.g. when windows and doors are open and the wind conditions are unfavourable. It should prevent radioactive dust and vapours escaping from the enclosure into the work area, or into the air of neighbouring rooms through the external vent. Smoke tests are one useful method for checking airflows.

11.17   It may become necessary to decontaminate the exhaust ducting, e.g. if maintenance work is required or the unit is being decommissioned. Ducting should be labelled if any hazard is likely. The need for decontamination or labelling is most likely if long-lived radioactive substances are used in the enclosure. Ducting should be made of non-absorbent and fire resistant material and be removable in sections.

Equipment and clothing

11.18   Reference should be made to paragraphs 10.44 to 10.55 and 11.10. There are usually more stringent clothing requirements (e.g. for non-shedding material) to comply with the Medicines Act [18].

General procedures in radiopharmacies

11.19   The advice in paragraphs 10.56 to 10.69 is also applicable to the handling of unsealed radioactive substances in radiopharmacies and in blood labelling and radioiodination facilities except that:

(a) paper tissues must not be brought into an aseptic area because of the probability of particulate contamination from them, and

(b) care must be taken that the reusable gloves found in isolators do not become contaminated since this will increase the finger dose to staff.

11.20   The person(s) responsible for procuring radionuclides need(s) to be aware of the limitations imposed by the certificates of registration and authorisation granted under RSA93 [7], or the conditions of a certificate of exemption, so as not to exceed the limits on holdings or radioactive waste (see Chapter 18). If radionuclides are to be transferred off-site, this should also be verified for the receiving establishment.

11.21   Only the minimum number of personnel required should be present in areas set aside for aseptic work. Wristwatches and jewellery should not be worn. Entry to the room must be restricted to essential materials and trained personnel (or those undergoing training). Entry of materials or people, staff changing and washing must follow written procedures designed to minimise the entry of particulate contamination and the spread of radioactive contamination in or out of the area.

11.22   If radiopharmaceuticals are dispatched to other sites, the employer becomes a consignor and, if in-house vehicles and/or drivers are used, the employer also acts as a carrier. In either case, the employer, in consultation with the RPA, should ensure compliance with the requirements of road transport regulations [96]. A safety adviser may be required to advise under the regulations on the transport of dangerous goods [97]. Transport of radioactive substances is covered in more detail in paragraphs 17.42 to 17.51.

Quality assurance of radiopharmaceuticals

11.23   Radiopharmaceuticals are considered to be medicinal products under section 130 of the Medicines Act [18] (see paragraph 11.10). A key requirement of the manufacture of medicinal products is a system of QA covering all matters concerned with the quality of the product. Guidance on the level of QA deemed to be acceptable is given in two publications [89 and 90]. The *Textbook of Radiopharmacy Theory and Practice* [98] describes in some detail the parameters by which the quality of radiopharmaceuticals may be checked. A quality management system such as BS EN ISO 9001 *Quality Management Systems* [99] may be used to demonstrate compliance with the various statutory requirements.

11.24   Acceptable radionuclide and radiochemical purity of the radiopharmaceutical is essential in the minimisation of the radiation dose to the patient and the optimisation of the quality of the diagnostic test or efficacy of therapeutic treatment. Purity tests should be conducted in a form, and at a frequency, agreed between the regional QC pharmacist and the MPE. They will include:

(a)   assessment of ^{99}Mo breakthrough into the initial elution from each ^{99}Tc^{m} generator

(b)   radiochemical purity determination on sample vial(s) of radiopharmaceutical reconstituted from each batch of a commercial kit with a United Kingdom product licence, and

(c)   radiochemical purity determination on every vial of an unlicensed product.[1]

11.25   As many of the tests are not completed before the product is released for use, a greater emphasis is placed on process controls to ensure the continued quality of the radiopharmaceuticals produced. This is achieved by:

(a)   all operating procedures being documented and strictly observed

(b)   the keeping of accurate and up-to-date records

(c)   routine monitoring of the production environment with respect to microbiological, particulate and radioactive contamination, and

(d)   planned preventative maintenance on equipment and instruments routinely used, including a full QA programme on e.g. radionuclide calibrators (see paragraphs 10.44 to 10.55).

11.26   If QC samples have to be sterility-tested outside the radiopharmacy, they must be stored to allow the radioactivity to decay before release. In order not to underestimate non-sterility due to the failure of any contaminants to survive, the samples must be incubated while being stored. The procedure adopted should be agreed between the radiopharmacist, microbiologist and MPE.

---

1   Unlicensed products should only be used if there is no alternative licensed product.

Blood cell labelling

11.27   Generally in radiopharmacy practice the problems of ensuring the sterility of the product as well as protecting the environment are resolved as described above. When handling blood components, however, there is an additional risk of viral contamination (hepatitis B and HIV) of other products as well as the potential for the accidental infection of the operator. The radiation hazard, however, is generally relatively small because of the limited amount of radioactivity involved.

11.28   Although closed[2] procedures should be used wherever practicable, open procedures are often preferred for blood labelling, particularly for white cells and platelets. Open procedures can save time, thereby reducing radiation dose, and can also eliminate the risk of needle-stick injury. However, note that stringent monitoring for contamination is required.

11.29   It is preferable, especially when cell labelling is carried out frequently, to have a dedicated facility. For infrequent use it is considered permissible (Monger [100]) to carry out labelling procedures in the same cleanroom as other aseptic operations, if separate workstations are used at different times, and only closed procedures [89] are used (although see paragraph 11.11). The advice of the regional QC pharmacist should be sought.

11.30   A dedicated workstation of the type referenced in paragraph 11.10 must be reserved for all stages of blood labelling using open procedures, and should be considered for those using closed procedures. Simultaneous labelling of blood from more than one person should not be carried out in the same workstation.

11.31   All work should be carried out in a drip tray large enough to contain any spillage. Centrifuges with sealable buckets are required, to contain blood if the primary container leaks or breaks.

11.32   The surfaces of the workstation, benches and all equipment used in the process must be disinfected after use to prevent cross-contamination. It is essential to use a disinfectant that is active against hepatitis B and HIV taking due notice of the COSHH Regulations 1999 [101], as such agents can be both toxic and corrosive.

Monitoring of persons

11.33   Routine measurement of radiation doses to the body, hands and eyes of radiopharmacy staff will be necessary (see paragraph 11.3). Frequent monitoring for personal contamination is also required, especially on leaving the radiopharmacy. External monitoring of the thyroid may be indicated for staff performing radioiodinations (see paragraph 11.3). Monitoring schedules should be established as part of the risk assessment, taking activity levels, working conditions and procedures into account.

Monitoring of work areas

11.34   The advice in paragraphs 10.84 to 10.86 applies to all rooms in the radiopharmacy in which work with unsealed radioactive substances is undertaken.

11.35   The frequency of monitoring should be decided on the basis of the risk assessment, taking account of the advice of the RPA, The monitoring programme should be able to detect changes in radiation and contamination levels and to ensure that these levels are ALARP. Monitoring will also be required for particulate contamination of the air in the aseptic suite. Radiation dose levels in adjacent rooms should be monitored at appropriate intervals.

---

2   A closed procedure includes opening a vial of saline for immediate use. An open procedure is one during which an ingredient or semi-finished product is at some stage after sterilisation, open to the atmosphere.

11.36   Transport containers should be checked for damage and/or radioactive contamination prior to each use. If radiation dose rates are not negligible, the presence of contamination will have to be assessed by wipe testing rather than using a contamination monitor directly.

11.37   Before returning radionuclide generators to the manufacturer for recycling, external surfaces should be swabbed to check for contamination (see Chapter 18 if to be disposed). No authorisation is needed to accumulate spent $^{99}Tc^m$ generators if they are simply awaiting collection (the open source registration should have sufficient capacity to cover them).[3] However, an authorisation is needed for accumulation and disposal if the generators are being held for decay to recover the lead before subsequent disposal as waste.

11.38   It may be necessary to monitor filters removed from the ventilation system and the ventilation ducting before disposal (see paragraph 11.17). Personal protective equipment, such as gloves, overalls and disposable masks, should be used as necessary.

Decontamination

11.39   Decontamination procedures detailed in paragraphs 10.87 to 10.104 are applicable although it can be difficult to cope with radioactive spills in aseptic areas because of the general prohibition on materials that might shed particles. However, it is possible to find absorbent materials that are non-shedding. Contingency plans for potentially serious incidents such as cracked generator columns, broken eluate vials, etc., may have to include instructions to bring large quantities of absorbent material into the area. In this case, aseptic work cannot restart until the resulting particulate count is below the appropriate level.

---

3   Note that registration as a closed source is required for the depleted uranium used to shield high activity $^{99}Tc^m$ generators.

12 Therapeutic uses of unsealed radioactive substances

Scope

12.1 This chapter applies to the use of unsealed (dispersible) radioactive substances that are administered to people as patients for treatment or for research into treatment.

12.2 Most of the information on the diagnostic uses of unsealed radioactive substances given in Chapter 10 is also applicable to therapeutic uses, including that in relation to the designation of areas (paragraphs 1.52 to 1.57 and 10.32). Additional information specific to therapy administrations will be given in this chapter.

12.3 This chapter does not apply to the rare use of unsealed alpha-emitting radionuclides for therapeutic purposes. The advice of the RPA and the MPE should be sought on the additional precautions and special procedures needed when handling such materials before any decision concerning their use is taken.

Hazards from unsealed radioactive substances for therapeutic use

12.4 The hazards from unsealed sources and the principles for their control are the same for therapeutic uses as for diagnostic uses (see paragraphs 10.4 to 10.9). However, the radiation emitted, the activities used and the physical half-lives of the radionuclides will be different from those usually encountered in diagnostic work and will require additional radiation protection measures.

12.5 The advice of the RPA should be sought before new therapeutic procedures are introduced. A prior risk assessment must be made and that should also include consideration of the items discussed in 12.10 and 12.17.

Pregnant or breastfeeding staff

12.6 Special care should be taken when involving a pregnant or breastfeeding member of staff in a therapeutic procedure with unsealed sources. A prior risk assessment of likely doses to the fetus or breastfeeding infant should be made [11]. Guidance is given in paragraphs 10.10 and 10.11. Reallocation of some duties may be indicated. For example, the administration of therapeutic amounts of radioiodine in liquid form is likely to be one of the tasks that pregnant or breastfeeding staff should avoid.

Protection of the patient

12.7 The general provisions of paragraphs 10.12 to 10.27 apply and, where diagnostic procedures are referred to, the provisions should generally be taken to include therapeutic procedures as well, except that:

(a) DRLs are not applicable to therapeutic administrations; it has been customary to dispense therapeutic activities to within 5 per cent of that prescribed but this may not be possible (e.g. in the case of ^{131}I capsules) or desirable (if it leads to increased radiation dose to the operator).

(b) all therapeutic administrations must be planned individually

(c) advice to females and males concerning the avoidance of conception after therapeutic administrations is given in the ARSAC *Notes for Guidance* [35]

(d) female patients should be advised as appropriate that breastfeeding is contraindicated (after almost all therapeutic administrations), and

(e) an MPE must be present at all therapeutic administrations of unsealed radioactive sources, other than those for which a standard protocol is followed; in case of standard treatments, the MPE must be available on site or, at least, contactable.

Design of treatment areas and wards

12.8 The design of treatment areas and wards for radionuclide therapy should conform to the relevant requirements for the design of laboratories and nuclear medicine departments for diagnostic uses of unsealed sources (see paragraphs 10.28 to 10.42). The rest of this section stresses particular requirements for therapeutic procedures.

12.9 Patients treated with unsealed radioactive substances may require inpatient facilities. The design of such facilities, whether new-build or adapted from existing accommodation, should be the subject of a prior risk assessment. The RPA and/or MPE, as appropriate, should be contacted for advice on:

(a) whether the treatments to be given will result in the patient being classed as high-activity (see paragraph 12.10)

(b) the appropriate designation of the areas required

(c) precautions for the protection of staff and visitors, including comforters and carers

(d) whether extra shielding is required in the walls, ceiling or floors to protect persons in adjacent rooms from external irradiation

(e) monitoring arrangements

(f) a suitable waste management system, and

(g) any other special precautions or procedures required.

12.10 Patients should be classed as high-activity if a prior risk assessment has shown that special precautions are necessary to ensure that relevant dose constraints are not likely to be exceeded. The constraints should be applied to estimates of exposure (of staff, other patients or visitors) from the patient or from any associated contamination risk. A useful indication of high-activity for gamma emitters used for therapy is where the product of activity present in the patient and total gamma energy per disintegration exceeds 150 MBq.MeV. This corresponds to just over 400 MBq ^{131}I.

12.11 The guidance in paragraphs 12.12 to 12.15 and 12.25 to 12.41 is relevant to the accommodation and care of high-activity patients.

12.12 High-activity patients should be accommodated in single rooms designed or adapted for the purpose, ideally with their own toilet, washing facilities and, perhaps, food preparation area. The need for each of these as dedicated facilities should be assessed against the level of risk. For example, en-suite toilet facilities are essential wherever significant amounts of radioactivity will be excreted in urine or faeces. The design of safe and comfortable accommodation for visitors is important, particularly for paediatric facilities.

12.13 Floors and other surfaces should be covered with smooth, continuous and non-absorbent surfaces that can be easily cleaned and decontaminated. Floor coverings should be coved against walls and removable if necessary. Walls should be finished with a good hard-gloss paint. (For suitable materials for use in radioactive areas, see BS 4247 *Surface Materials for Use in Radioactive Areas* [102]. For further information on decontamination strategies, see paragraph 10.99.)

12.14 Secure areas should be provided for bins for the temporary storage of linen and waste contaminated with radioactive substances. The storage areas and bins should be in or near the treatment area or ward and clearly marked, using the radiation warning sign (Appendix 12).

12.15 Washing and contamination monitoring facilities complying with the requirements of paragraph 10.36 should be provided for the use of staff and visitors.

Equipment and clothing

12.16   Reference should be made to paragraphs 10.44 to 10.55. It is likely that an assessment of risk will lead to the conclusion that staff must wear gowns or overalls in treatment areas and when caring for high-activity patients. These should be removed on leaving the area, stored if appropriate and monitored as necessary.

Administration of therapeutic radioactive substances

12.17   All arrangements should be discussed as fully as possible with the patient prior to the administration, ideally well in advance of the appointment for treatment. If the patient is unable to understand fully, the most appropriate person, acting on his or her behalf, should also be consulted. Issues to be discussed include:

(a) the manner and place of administration

(b) whether an inpatient stay will be required

(c) whether the patient and any necessary visitors while in hospital are willing and able to co-operate with any necessary restrictions on behaviour (e.g. is the patient incontinent or catheterised? is the patient able to follow simple instructions? does the patient have religious views that may conflict with the requirements?)

(d) whether there are particular difficulties in restricting exposure to other persons once the patient leaves hospital (see Chapter 15)

(e) whether the patient is returning to a place where people are employed, such as a hospice and including community nurses visiting the patient's home (see paragraph 15.3 for guidance on whether notification to HSE under IRR99 [1] and/or arrangements to comply with RSA93 [7] will be required), and

(f) the arrangements for transport home or to the receiving institution.

In addition, but exceptionally (see paragraph 16.24), the IR(ME)R practitioner should explain to patients prior to treatment with a high-activity administration, and if appropriate their relatives, the possible need to accept burial rather than cremation in the unlikely event of their death, and should obtain their written consent. In some circumstances the IR(ME)R practitioner may decide it is more appropriate for a relative to give written consent. The precautions necessary in the event of death should be recorded in the patient's notes (also see paragraph 16.11).

12.18   Treatments should be administered in the designated treatment area close to the dispensing area or in the patient's own room on the ward, whichever creates less hazard, as determined by prior risk assessment. The treatment area chosen must be suitable for the purpose and meet the design provisions set out in paragraphs 12.8 to 12.15.

12.19   The identity of the patient must be checked immediately prior to administration, as detailed in the employer's procedures.

12.20   Local shielding should be used as appropriate against external radiation (see paragraphs 10.65 and 10.66). Automated methods of activity administration and vital signs monitoring (e.g. syringe pump and blood pressure monitor) should be used, where possible, when extended administration times are required for therapeutic procedures (e.g. ^{131}I labelled mIBG). Staff should wear protective clothing (see paragraph 12.16).

12.21   The operator administering the treatment must understand the need to deliver the entirety of the radioactivity to the intended site, avoiding, for example, extravasation. He or she must be familiar with all contingency plans designed to cope with such situations should they arise. Some protection from possible external contamination should be provided for patients who receive oral administrations of radioactive liquids for therapy. An absorbent paper or cotton apron/towel with a plastic backing should be sufficient to protect the patient and his or her clothing. If the patient is feeling nauseous prior to an oral administration, the operator should seek advice from the IR(ME)R practitioner (and MPE, if appropriate) as to the advisability of proceeding. Patients who feel nauseous after oral administrations should not be allowed to leave the area until this contamination hazard passes.

12.22   When radioiodinated compounds are to be administered, the use of a thyroid blocking agent should be considered in order to reduce the radiation dose to the patient's thyroid, to comply with the ARSAC *Notes for Guidance* [35].

12.23   The activity administered should be planned for each patient and should be checked before administration (see paragraph 10.72). The radioactive substance should be clearly labelled, indicating the radionuclide, chemical form, and activity at a given date and time, and batch number if appropriate. Detailed records should be kept of all administrations of radioactive substances (see paragraph 10.68).

12.24   Persons receiving treatment with unsealed radioactive substances (and/or their carers, as appropriate) should receive instructions and information on precautions to be taken and any hazards involved (see also Chapter 15). The instructions and information may be given verbally and/or in written form. They must also be described in an employer's procedure.

General procedures in wards

12.25   The advice in paragraphs 10.39, 10.56 to 10.69 and 10.79 to 10.82 is also applicable to wards used by patients treated with unsealed radioactive substances.

12.26   Appropriate local rules and radiation protection training should be made available to all relevant nursing staff. Local rules should include or refer to any specific radiation safety precautions considered necessary for each technique involving radioactive substances. This will include situations where there is a risk of significant contamination from urine, faeces, vomit, etc., or on account of external radiation from a patient. Relevant parts of the local rules should also be communicated to domestic staff and porters. Appropriate staff training should include night staff, porters and escorts.

12.27   In the case of high-activity patients (see paragraph 12.10), only essential nursing procedures should be carried out and these should be done as rapidly as is consistent with good nursing practice. In a medical emergency the care of the patient is the priority. Any nursing or other procedures that are not urgent should be postponed for as long as possible after administration, to take full advantage of the reduction of activity by decay and excretion. During the initial period there should be only the minimum handling of contaminated bed linen, clothing, towels, crockery, etc. The documentation should state for how long the precautions should be maintained.

12.28   Beds or rooms in which there are high-activity patients should have a notice indicating the designation of the area and including a radiation warning sign (see Appendix 12). The nursing staff should be made familiar with the implications of the notice and be given details of the nature and activity of the radioactive substances, the time and date of administration, and any relevant instructions for nurses and visitors.

12.29   The maximum dose rates at suitable distances from high-activity patients should be determined as part of a risk assessment. This information will assist in identifying controlled areas and deriving appropriate arrangements for entry to the areas by visitors and staff. These arrangements should be written into the local rules.

12.30   Family or friends visiting or caring for patients who have received therapeutic administrations of radionuclides may incur a significant radiation dose themselves. Particular efforts should be made to keep all such doses ALARP. Those comforting or caring for the patient are not subject to any dose limit if, and only if, they come within the definition given in paragraph 1.72. All other visitors are regarded as members of the public for radiation protection purposes and subject to the appropriate dose limit of 5 mSv in 5 years for persons exposed resulting from another's medical exposure (IRR99 Schedule 4 paragraph 7 [1]). Procedures for identifying and advising possibly pregnant visitors and carers should be in place following consultation with the RPA.

12.31   All visitors should be informed of any necessary precautions to be taken when entering the room of a patient treated with an unsealed radioactive source. This may include wearing appropriate protective clothing, visiting time restrictions, not using the patient's designated toilet, and not eating or drinking in the room.

12.32   High-activity patients should not leave the ward suite or treatment room without the approval of the RPS and either the appropriate medical officer or senior nursing officer. A person who has been instructed in necessary precautions must escort them within the hospital. Guidance on procedures to be followed when patients leave hospital after administration of radioactive substances is given in Chapter 15.

12.33   Protective gowns and gloves should be worn when there is any direct contact with the patient or contaminated clothing, bed linen or other articles.

12.34   Persons working with unsealed radioactive substances, or those nursing high-activity patients, should wash their hands thoroughly with mild soap and water before leaving work areas. Particular attention should be paid to cleaning fingernails. Hands should be monitored for residual contamination after washing.

12.35   Whenever possible, high-activity patients should use designated toilets (see paragraph 12.12). Simple precautions like laying plastic-backed absorbent paper securely on the floor around the toilet bowl and instructing the patient to flush the toilet twice after each use will help to minimise the external radiation and contamination hazards. Incontinent or catheterised patients will pose additional risks that should have been identified and assessed as in paragraph 12.17(c). Where a bedpan or urine bottle is provided for such a patient, it should be kept for that patient's exclusive use, preferably in the toilet, and should not be used by another patient until it has been checked and decontaminated as appropriate. Disposable bedpans and urine bottles may be preferable. An authorised route must be used to dispose of these.

12.36   Crockery and cutlery may become contaminated by high-activity patients. The local rules (see paragraph 12.26) should specify washing up procedures (e.g. by the patient where possible) and any necessary segregation of utensils for such patients. These precautions are unnecessary when disposable crockery and cutlery are used, although care is still required when handling such items. Any contaminated disposable items should be treated as radioactive waste.

12.37   Particular care to avoid contamination, and to limit its spread, should be taken in the case of an incontinent patient and, following oral administration, if there are clinical reasons for belief that the patient may vomit. Bedding and personal clothing should be changed promptly if contaminated (see paragraphs 10.96 to 10.98) and retained for monitoring.

12.38   If the medical condition of the patient deteriorates such that intensive nursing care becomes necessary, the advice of the RPA should be sought immediately. The advice should include the maximum time that individual healthcare professionals should spend with the patient unless there is a written procedure authorised by the RPA that covers the circumstances. Urgent medical care is the priority, so this should not be delayed while the advice is being sought.

12.39   In the event of the death of the patient, special precautions may need to be taken (see Chapter 16).

12.40   If a patient is returned or transferred to different ward, to another hospital or to a nursing home, any necessary information on appropriate precautions and person(s) to contact in case of difficulty, should accompany the patient (see Chapter 15). The receiving institution may have to notify HSE as discussed in paragraph 15.3. This should be done as soon as the need for notification is identified and certainly before the patient is transferred. Any radioactive waste generated must be disposed of appropriately, either through an existing authorisation if there is one, by invoking an exemption order, or by transferring the waste back to the administering hospital for disposal by an authorised route there.

12.41   See paragraph 10.69, if maintenance work on any equipment that might be contaminated, e.g. sinks and waste pipes, is required.

Procedures in operating theatres

12.42   Before surgery (other than in an emergency) on a high-activity patient (see paragraph 12.10) information should be sought on the activity remaining in the body. Any precautions against external radiation and possible contamination from body fluids should be determined in collaboration with the RPA. If surgery is not urgent, it should be postponed until the radioactivity in the body has fallen to a suitable level.

12.43   The wearing of two pairs of surgical gloves will give some protection to the hands against beta radiation. If the gloves are cut or torn during the operation and the surgeon's hands are injured the advice given in paragraph 10.91 should be followed. After the operation has been completed the operating theatre, surgical instruments and equipment, and protective clothing should be thoroughly checked for contamination and, if necessary, decontaminated (see paragraphs 10.93 to 10.104).

Monitoring of work areas

12.44   The advice concerning monitoring in paragraphs 10.84 to 10.86 should be applied with particular rigour in laboratories and work areas used for therapeutic applications of unsealed radioactive substances.

12.45   Contamination and dose rate monitors appropriate to the type and energy of the radiation concerned should be readily available and used at all stages of the therapy procedure. Monitoring should be carried out at a frequency decided upon with advice from the RPA, to detect changes in radiation and contamination levels and to ensure that these levels are ALARP. Radiation dose levels in adjacent rooms should be monitored at appropriate intervals. The findings should be recorded.

12.46   Prior to the discharge of high-activity patients (see paragraph 12.10) from a ward, clothing and other personal property should be monitored for contamination. If contamination is found, the items must be stored or decontaminated (see paragraph 12.48). In some cases, items of personal property may be sealed and given to the patient to store at home. The RPA should be consulted.

12.47   Subsequent to the discharge of a high-activity patient, the area of the ward used by the patient should be monitored and, if necessary, decontaminated before further use. Monitoring should also include the bedding and any waste (see paragraph 12.48). Where the area was designated as controlled, it cannot be undesignated until monitoring for contamination and any necessary decontamination has taken place.

Decontamination procedures

12.48   Decontamination procedures used for diagnostic uses of unsealed sources are also applicable to therapeutic uses (see paragraphs 10.87 to 10.104).

13 Ionising radiation in general laboratories

Scope

13.1 This chapter applies to the use of unsealed (dispersible) radioactive substances in medical diagnosis or research where the activities of radionuclides employed in the procedure are typically less than those tabulated in paragraph 10.2. This includes, for example, pathology or haematology departments carrying out vitamin B12 absorption studies or blood volume estimations. It includes the use of small quantities of ^{35}S and ^{32}P in cytogenetics and may include work on tissue samples from theatre, such as those from sentinel node localisation procedures (but see paragraph 10.39). Workers using higher activities should refer to Chapter 10. However, specific advice relating to all work with tritium is given here in Chapter 13.

13.2 This chapter does not apply to work with volatile radioactive materials, such as iodination, which is discussed in Chapter 11. Alpha-emitting radionuclides are also excluded (see paragraph 10.3).

13.3 The AURPO produces guidance notes appropriate to work in research and teaching establishments [9].

Blood irradiators and similar devices

13.4 The work of departments and laboratories coming within the scope of this chapter may include the irradiation of clinical samples. Blood irradiators are well-shielded devices incorporating large sealed radioactive sources. Chapter 14 gives further information on similar devices, which may be helpful. Cabinets for X-ray of tissue samples (e.g. Faxitron™ units) may also be in use. If such cabinets are only used for routine investigations, no prior authorisation is necessary (L121 paragraph 19 [2]). However, if they are in use as part of a research project and do not meet the conditions for generic authorisation for the use of X-ray sets laid down by the HSE (Appendix 18), the employer must apply for an individual authorisation under IRR99 (paragraphs 1.21 to 1.25). Advice should be obtained from the RPA on the purchase, installation and maintenance of devices of either kind and on a system of QA, and the need for and content of local rules. The RPA may also advise on the calibration of the devices. The devices must undergo a critical examination before being brought into use (see paragraph 1.30 and following paragraphs, including paragraph 1.113 if the equipment is on loan). Only staff instructed in their safe and proper operation may use them.

Hazards from radioactive substances and principles for their control

13.5 The radiation hazards associated with unsealed radioactive substances and principles for their control are as detailed in paragraphs 10.4 to 10.9.

13.6 Where work with unsealed radioactive materials involves more than one employer, it is the duty of all such employers to liaise and co-operate in order that all legislative requirements are met (see IRR99 regulation 15 [1]).

Protection of the patient

13.7 If the work involves the administration of radioactive materials to humans, the general provisions of paragraphs 10.12 to 10.27 apply. There is no exemption for the small activities involved. The IR(ME)R practitioner must individually justify any radiation exposure of patients. The IR(ME)R practitioner must hold an appropriate certificate from ARSAC [35].

13.8   Staff who carry out such procedures on patients or calibrate or check any of the associated equipment or prepare the radiopharmaceutical to be given must be given suitable training and comply with the responsibilities of operators as defined in the employer's procedures required under IR(ME)R (see Chapter 2).

Design of work areas

13.9   The requirements for work with unsealed radioactive substances vary with the type of procedures being undertaken. An RPA needs to be consulted about the design of laboratories and other work areas, although a formal appointment may not be necessary. Detailed plans should be drawn up in collaboration with the person(s) responsible for the work. Changes that may become necessary from time to time should also be discussed with an RPA.

13.10   Special procedures to restrict radiation exposure are very unlikely to be needed for work coming within the scope of this chapter and hence the work areas will normally only require to be supervised, if designation is required at all. A prior risk assessment should be undertaken to inform the decision. Chapter 10 should be consulted where larger amounts of radionuclides are used.

13.11   The general provisions of paragraphs 10.28 to 10.37 apply to these areas. A risk assessment will normally show that good modern laboratory facilities need little or no upgrading to conform to the requirements of radioactive work coming within the scope of this chapter.

13.12   It may be sufficient and indeed desirable to confine space for work involving radioactive materials to a specified area within a laboratory. Particularly in a research environment, radioactive work may be spasmodic and the area may have to be released for other purposes. This should only be done after all radioactive sources have been removed, monitoring has confirmed that there is no radioactive contamination remaining and, finally, all radioactive warning signs have been concealed or removed.

13.13   Secure (lockable) storage of radioactive materials must be provided. The store should be sited in a suitable place, taking into account the dose rate from it and the convenience and reduced potential for accidents in transit if it is close to the work area. Facilities for the receipt of radioactive materials and the storage and disposal of radioactive waste should be agreed with the RPA. This is discussed further in Chapter 17.

13.14   An area for the preparation and counting of radioactive samples may be required. It may need to be separate from other areas used for radioactive work.

13.15   If radioactive materials are to be administered to patients, then space must be allocated for the taking of biological samples and any clinical measurements involved. Patients receiving the small tracer amounts covered by this chapter may wait in general waiting rooms. Separate toilets are also not required for these patients.

Equipment and clothing

13.16   The general provisions of paragraphs 10.44 to 10.55 apply. Radioactive sources should be kept in suitable shielding, handled with tongs and worked within drip trays to contain spills. Separate laboratory coats should be worn solely for radioactive work and disposable impermeable gloves should be worn whenever unsealed sources are handled. Suitable monitoring equipment should be readily available.

General procedures

13.17   The general provisions of paragraphs 10.56 to 10.69 apply.

Administration of radioactive materials to patients

13.18   The general provisions of paragraphs 10.70 to 10.78 apply.

Monitoring of staff

13.19   The results of film badge, TLD or other common monitoring devices can be misleading for work with radionuclides of very low penetrating power and energy of emission such as ^{3}H and ^{14}C. The advice of the RPA should be sought. Personal extremity monitoring may be appropriate in some circumstances but, in general, rigorous laboratory technique and good housekeeping are the best safeguards for staff working with these levels and types of radioactive materials.

13.20   Contamination monitoring for tritium is particularly difficult and can be expensive because of the very low energy of the emitted beta particles. Wipe testing (to determine the amount of removable contamination on working surfaces) after each use is normally sufficient to confirm that arrangements are adequate. The surfaces should be wiped in suitable sections with wetted filter paper or other suitable material, and then the activity on each swab can be measured by liquid scintillation counting. This will give a qualitative method of confirming whether contamination is occurring and, if so, whether air sampling would be appropriate. Urine analysis may also be indicated to confirm that arrangements are sufficient to ensure that doses are ALARP. In particular, urine analysis should be instituted in addition to wipe testing where quantities greater than 10 GBq of ^{3}H are used.

13.21   It may not be necessary to vary the duties of staff who are pregnant or breastfeeding on radiation protection grounds, as long as procedures to avoid contamination keep doses ALARP.

Monitoring of areas

13.22   Monitoring of surfaces used for radioactive work should be carried out after every procedure or regularly, at a frequency dependent upon use, and with a monitor suitable for the purpose. Advice should be sought from the RPA if necessary.

Decontamination

13.23   Advice on decontamination of persons, equipment and surfaces is given in paragraphs 10.87 to 10.104.

Keeping, using and disposal of radioactive materials

13.24   Employers wishing to use radioactive materials must notify HSE under IRR99 [1], and comply with RSA93 [7]. Exemption from notification under IRR99 is only granted for very small amounts of radioactivity (see paragraph 10.2). Some users will have to be registered under RSA93 but some small users may be able to operate under the provisions of the Radioactive Substances (Hospitals) Exemption Order [17] although they must still follow the requirements of the exemption order and notify the HSE. Records should be kept to demonstrate to the competent authorities how the requirements of the exemption orders are being met. Limits on the permitted amounts for holding or disposal are normally granted to the site as a whole. It may be advantageous to divide the authorisation between the various departments according to requirements. One department (e.g. medical physics) should administer whatever scheme is chosen and ensure that the limits are not exceeded. Chapter 17 gives further details.

Transport of radioactive materials

13.25   Transport of radioactive substances is covered in Chapter 17.

Disposal of radioactive waste

13.26   Chapter 18 details the requirements for disposal of radioactive waste.

14 Diagnostic uses of sealed or other solid radioactive sources

Scope

14.1 This chapter contains guidance on the use of sealed or other solid sources (see paragraph 9.2) for:

(a) transmission scanning or as anatomical markers used in nuclear medicine investigations, or

(b) diagnostic or clinical research purposes in the fields of bone mineral measurements, X-ray fluorescence scanning of the thyroid and neutron activation analysis.

14.2 The guidance in this chapter applies also when the equipment is being used for experimental purposes or is being tested or calibrated at its place of use, and when sources are being changed.

14.3 Guidance on the use of sealed sources for testing and calibration of gamma cameras and radionuclide calibrators is given in Chapter 10. However, guidance on leakage testing of such sources is given in paragraph 14.8.

14.4 Some clinical research projects may require diagnostic reference measurements on healthy subjects, e.g. bone mineral density, using sealed sources. Guidance on the medical exposure of volunteers, who are included in the term 'patients', is given in paragraphs 2.63 to 2.70 and Appendix 10.

Protection of the patient

14.5 If the radioactive source irradiates the patient or causes induced radioactivity within the patient, then the provisions of IR(ME)R [3] apply and the relevant guidance in paragraphs 10.12 to 10.27 should be followed.

Sources and equipment – general

14.6 Whenever reasonably practicable, sources used in diagnostic and analytical equipment should be sealed sources conforming to BS 5288 [72]. Attention should be paid to the supplier's recommendations on working life and environment of use. Sources with the lowest activity consistent with satisfactory clinical results throughout the useful life of the source should be selected for these applications.

14.7 Prior to receipt of the source, consideration must be given as to whether the source requires registration under RSA93 [7]. The type of registration, whether *Closed Source* or *Mobile Source* also needs to be considered.

14.8 No new source should be used until a leakage test has been carried out, unless a leakage test certificate issued by the manufacturer has been obtained. An assessment of the potential ways in which containment could be lost, and their likelihood of occurring, should be carried out initially. Potential radiation exposure to persons carrying out the leak test should also be estimated. The findings should be used to determine a suitable leak test method and the frequency of such testing. Where testing is appropriate under normal operating conditions, the interval between tests should not exceed 2 years. The frequency of the testing should be increased if sources are stored in harsh environments or when the source is used beyond its recommended life. Records should be kept of the results of leakage testing. Fuller guidance is given in L121 [2] concerning IRR99 regulation 27 [1].

14.9 Records of each sealed source must be kept indicating the source details, i.e. radionuclide(s), activity and reference date, source identification number/mark, date of receipt, location, and when appropriate the date and manner of disposal (see paragraph 17.30). The presence of each sealed source should be confirmed on a regular basis dependent on frequency of use. The loss or theft of a registered sealed source must be notified to the EA and may also require notification to HSE depending on the source activity (see Chapter 19). Any theft should also be reported to the police. Fuller information on accounting is given in L121 [2] (IRR99 regulation 28 [1]).

Anatomical marker sources

14.10   Anatomical marker sources used in nuclear medicine investigations should be placed or attached to the patient's skin or clothing for the minimum time necessary. Special care must be exercised to ensure that any such sources are not left attached to the patient. The frequency of audit of these sources should be chosen to reflect this possibility. The rest of this chapter does not apply to anatomical marker sources.

Sources and equipment – diagnostic investigations

14.11   Except where paragraphs 14.16 or 14.17 apply, sources should be mounted, either permanently or when the equipment is in use, in a housing that has an aperture for the radiation beam. The aperture should be such that the radiation beam will not irradiate a greater part of the patient's body than is necessary. A high degree of collimation will be needed for most scanning techniques.

14.12   Shutters should be interlocked and operated, for example, by means of a patient-presence sensor. For a scanning device, the opening and closing of the shutter may be linked with the scanning movement. Equipment with a manually operated shutter, which has to be pressed by the operator throughout the diagnostic test and which closes the shutter when pressure is released, should be provided with a lock so that the shutter cannot be opened accidentally when the equipment is not in use.

14.13   The automatic interlocks/shutters of equipment with such devices must be tested at a suitable frequency dependent on the dose implications of failure of such devices. Records should be kept of these tests.

14.14   The equipment should be clearly marked to indicate:

(a) that it contains a radioactive source, and
(b) whether any shutter or cover is open or shut.

The marking should include a radiation warning sign (see Appendix 12).

14.15   In the case of equipment where the radiation beam is transmitted through the patient, the detection system should fully intercept the emerging beam and be effective as a beam stop. Preferably, the source housing and the detection system should be mechanically linked so that this condition is met whenever the shutter is open.

14.16   A different relationship between source and patient may be needed occasionally, e.g. a technique in which the patient grips a ^{252}Cf source within a moderator for neutron activation studies. Here the source should be in a shielded housing with an aperture large enough only for the hand and there should be a lockable cover for the aperture when the equipment is not in use.

14.17   If the equipment is to be used exclusively for examining pathological specimens, e.g. bones, it should be completely enclosed and provided with a loading drawer mechanism or, if it is a cabinet, it should have an interlocked door and external shutter mechanism.

Operating procedures

14.18   If the source, its bonding or immediate containment will be in contact with the body, or needs to be placed in the mouth or other cavity, the MARS Regulations will apply [5, 6] and ARSAC certification will be required. These Regulations also apply to neutron activation analysis (see paragraphs 10.12 to 10.27).

14.19 The patient should be properly positioned before the shutter is opened, cover removed or the source brought into position, and should not be exposed to the radiation beam for longer than is necessary to carry out the diagnostic test.

14.20 No one other than the patient should be exposed to the radiation beam. Particular care should be taken that the fingers of staff are neither exposed to the beam nor placed close to a fluorescence or back-scattering device. This applies not only during a diagnostic test but also during any calibration or experimental work when no patient is present.

14.21 If the shutter or cover does not operate automatically the aperture should be closed immediately after the test. Complete closure of the shutter should be confirmed, using an appropriate radiation monitor, after each procedure.

14.22 When the equipment is not in use it should be made safe, e.g. by means of a secure locking mechanism, or kept in a suitably shielded and locked room or store.

Source handling

14.23 Where it is necessary to remove or replace sources, e.g. for storage purposes, they should never be handled directly. A handling tool should be used. It may be necessary to use shielded handling tools where dose rates warrant this.

14.24 Close supervision and application of specific systems of work and written arrangements need to be considered during the loading and unloading of highly radioactive sealed sources.

14.25 Storage and movement of sources are dealt with in Chapter 17.

15 Patients leaving hospital after administration of radioactive substances

Scope

15.1 This chapter gives advice on the conditions under which patients may be allowed to leave hospital following the administration of unsealed or sealed radioactive sources. Its purpose is to minimise the risk of radioactive contamination and the risk from external radiation to family and friends (including those who may be classed as comforters and carers under IRR99 [1]), the general public, or workers who may be classed as members of the public for radiation protection purposes.

15.2 If a patient is sent to another hospital, a nursing home or anywhere other than a private dwelling, the relevant advice on procedures in wards and clinics in Chapters 9 (permanent implants), 10 (diagnostic) or 12 (therapeutic) must be provided to the staff. If a patient is discharged to a private dwelling or place of residence where there are employees who may be exposed to ionising radiation because of their work with the patient, similar advice must be provided to those staff.

15.3 The MPE involved in the administration, in consultation with the RPA, should undertake an assessment of the work performed by employees who may care for patients after discharge from the administering hospital. If the employees are 'working with radiation' then their employer must notify the HSE (see paragraph 1.26). Such notification should be given only once per employer. To be considered as 'working with radiation', the employees will be likely to:

   (a) be exposed to external radiation dose rates from the patient in excess of $0.5 \ \mu Sv \ h^{-1}$ averaged over the working day, and/or

   (b) handle items contaminated in excess of the limits given in paragraph 10.2 (e.g. shortly after a bone scan, if the patient is incontinent).

   The MPE, with advice from the RPA in the administering hospital, should also consider suitable arrangements for waste disposal (see Chapter 18). The two employers should consult about all the arrangements and the receiving employer may need to appoint an RPA if one has not already been appointed.

Principles

15.4 Care should be taken to ensure that patients only leave the hospital if they are unlikely to cause a significant radiation or contamination hazard to other people. Appropriate scenarios and dose constraints should be used in planning discharge dates (see paragraph 15.9). Arrangements should be in place to restrict the exposure of those who come into contact with the discharged patient as far as is reasonably practicable.

15.5 Arrangements for giving advice on the radiation protection of patients and their personal contacts after the patient has left hospital must be detailed in an employer's procedure. The ARSAC certificate holder is normally the best person to oversee such arrangements. The form and content of the advice would normally be agreed with the MPE and the task of communicating it to the patient may be delegated as detailed in the employer's procedure.

15.6 Advice should be based on generic and individual risk assessment as discussed in the remainder of this chapter. Specific details given here are based on guidance entitled *Patients Leaving Hospital after Administration of Radioactive Substances* published by a working party of the British Institute of Radiology (BIR) that included representatives from HSE, DoH, EA and NRPB [103]. Conclusions from a comprehensive study of exposure to families of outpatients treated with ^{131}I for hyperthyroidism (Barrington *et al.* [104]) have also been incorporated.

15.7   Advice on patient transport arrangements and the disposal of radioactive samples and waste from the patient are covered later in this chapter.

Potential hazards

15.8   Radioactive substances present an external irradiation hazard and, if unsealed, a contamination hazard as well. The risks posed to others by discharging a radioactive patient from hospital will depend on the personal circumstances of the patient as well as the type, activity and biokinetics of the radioactive substance administered. Advice intended to enable potential exposures to be kept ALARP should be developed for each clinical procedure.

Risk assessment

15.9   Potential risks to other persons should be assessed by reviewing published data or in-house measurements that have been validated by the MPE or RPA. Calculation from first principles, making realistic or, if that is not possible, conservative assumptions about the behaviour of the patient and other persons, may be necessary if no other suitable data are available. Estimates of potential doses to other people should be compared with a relevant dose constraint (e.g. see Table 15.1) set by the employer. If the potential doses are significant compared to the constraint, then the advice (as indicated in 15.6) must reflect this.

15.10   The risk of contamination and any hazard arising from this must also be assessed. For example, the possibility of a patient causing contamination due to incontinence, vomiting or the use of stoma bags should be considered. The risk assessment must include any ongoing medical treatments if they necessitate the storage, handling or disposal of radioactivity (e.g. frequent blood sampling to monitor blood sugars or anti-coagulant therapy; see paragraph 10.39). Risk assessments should also cover transport (see Chapter 17) and the appropriate regulations must be followed [96, 97, 105 and 106].

15.11   Any advice to reduce radiation exposure resulting from the risk assessment should be discussed with the patient (or the patient's representative if the patient is a child or an adult who lacks the capacity to consent) well before the radioactive material is administered (see also paragraphs 10.25, 10.70, 10.76 and 12.17). It is imperative to check with the patient or the patient's representative that the assumptions on which the advice is based are reasonable in the individual circumstances. Any problems should be referred to the ARSAC certificate holder or to the person specified in the employer's procedure.

Departure from hospital and conduct at home

15.12   The radiation doses to members of the patient's household and to other members of the public that result from the discharge of a radioactive patient from hospital must be kept ALARP. They must not exceed the dose limit indicated in Table 15.1 (and see paragraph 12.30).

Table 15.1. Recommended dose constraints and limits for classes of persons exposed as a result of discharge of radioactive patients from hospital

	Constraint per procedure	Dose limit
Comforters and carers (knowingly and willingly exposed, not pregnant)	5 mSv	None
Other members of the household	1 mSv	5 mSv in 5 years
Members of the general public	0.3 mSv	5 mSv in 5 years

15.13   If someone caring for the patient is pregnant, the risks she and her unborn child may incur, as a result of exposure to ionising radiation, must be explained to her. It would be prudent to use a dose constraint of 0.3 mSv per procedure in formulating the advice to her. It is recommended that, where possible, the dose to the unborn child be kept below 1 mSv over the term of the pregnancy.

15.14   Comforters and carers (as defined in IRR99 [1], see paragraphs 1.72 to 1.74) must be capable of giving informed consent to any exposure they may incur. They should be provided with written instructions that specify how doses to them may be restricted as far as reasonably practicable and set out the risks associated with ionising radiation. Advice to them should be based on a recommended dose constraint of 5 mSv per clinical procedure although there is no dose limit (but see paragraph 15.13).

15.15   It is advisable that a constraint of 1 mSv year^{-1} be applied to members of the household as well as the general public. However, in cases of difficulty, the limit of 5 mSv in 5 years is applicable.

15.16   If, on the basis of the assumptions made about the behaviour of the patient and other persons (paragraph 15.9), it is estimated that the doses received by persons with whom the patient comes into contact may exceed the recommended dose constraints, it may be necessary to keep the patient in hospital. Difficulties are most likely if the patient is the sole or main carer of a small child [104]. In this case, the following options are also available:

(a) delay the treatment until the child is older, or
(b) send the child to stay with relatives or friends for a suitable period following the administration.

The likelihood of repeat administrations should be discussed with the ARSAC certificate holder and systems put in place to detect such events and ensure that dose limits are not thereby exceeded.

15.17   Where it is necessary to restrict the extent of contact between the patient and others, verbal and written instructions should be given and discussed with the patient or his or her representative (see paragraph 15.11). An instruction card, to be carried at all times while restrictions apply and giving key information and summarising the advice, is a suitable means of reminding patients and alerting those who may deal with them in the event of unforeseen illness or death (see Chapter 16). The card may need to include the following information:

(a) name and address of the patient
(b) name, address and telephone number of the hospital
(c) contact name in case of difficulty
(d) the name of the ARSAC certificate holder
(e) type and quantity of radionuclide administered
(f) date of administration
(g) restrictions to be followed, especially concerning contact with young children, and
(h) the period of time for which the restrictions apply.

The patient or representative should be asked to sign that he or she has understood the instructions. General measures to restrict doses should have already been explained to the patient or representative and written instructions provided to those who live with them (see paragraph 12.17).

Diagnostic procedures with unsealed sources

15.18   In general, the quantities of radioactivity currently administered for diagnostic procedures [35] do not necessitate any special precautions or restrictions to be placed on the patient [103]. Known exceptions fall into three categories:

(a) patients who provide the majority of close care to babies and have been administered any of the following – at least 10 MBq ^{111}In labelled white blood cells; 120 MBq ^{111}In octreotide; 200 MBq ^{67}Ga citrate (above DRL); 150 MBq ^{201}Tl chloride; or 800 MBq ^{99}Tc^m myocardial perfusion agent [107 to 110]

(b) breastfeeding mothers [35], or

(c) patients administered 30 MBq or more of [131]I (see Table 15.2)

Restrictions may also be necessary after administration of positron-emitting radionuclides. If the patient works with radioactive materials, or his or her work is radiation-sensitive, the caution in paragraph 15.34 may be relevant.

Therapeutic procedures with unsealed sources

15.19   A risk assessment must be carried out prior to any therapeutic administration of radioactivity, with guidance from the RPA or MPE, as described in paragraphs 15.9 to 15.11. For many therapeutic administrations, this may be based directly on a generic risk assessment carried out for the 'typical' patient. However, each patient must be assessed to ensure that the assumptions made are applicable to the individual concerned, as stressed in paragraph 15.11.

Iodine-131 administered for hyperthyroidism

15.20   The restrictions given in Table 15.2 are based on published recommendations that make assumptions about the behaviour of patients and those who live with them. If the validity of these assumptions is in doubt for any particular patient, the original texts should be consulted [103 and 104]. However, the major assumptions are that the patient:

(a) poses no significant risk of causing a contamination hazard

(b) is being discharged to a private dwelling (not a nursing home or hospital)

(c) will not be in prolonged contact with nurses or other persons employed to care for them at the private dwelling

Table 15.2. Total periods of restriction for patients receiving ^{131}I for hyperthyroidism who pose no risk of causing a contamination hazard

| | Activity of ^{131}I administered in MBq | | | | |
	30	200	400	600	800
Behaviour restriction[a]	Period of restriction in days				
Stay at least 1 m away from children under 3 years (see paragraph 15.16) [b]	1	15	21	25	27
Stay at least 1 m away from children between 3 and 5 years of age [b]	0	11	16	20	22
Stay at least 1 m away from children over 5 years of age and adults who are not comforters and carers[b]	0	5	11	14	16
Sleep separately from comforters and carers[c]	–	–	–	4	8
Avoid prolonged close contact (more than 3 h at < 1 m) with other adults (one-off exposure)[c]	–	–	–	–	1

[a]all behaviour restrictions run concurrently
[b]Barrington *et al.* [104]: conclusions
[c]*Patients Leaving Hospital after Administration of Radioactive Substances* [103]

(d) is only given one administration of radioiodine in a year, and

(e) is able to make suitable arrangements for the alternative care of children under 3 years of age.

Under these conditions the restrictions set out in Table 15.2 are sufficient to control the external dose hazard in the majority of cases of treatment with up to 800 MBq of [131]I. Periods of restriction for other administered activities can be estimated by linear interpolation between the tabulated values. Interpolation should only be used within the tabulated range for each row. It will produce a slight discrepancy (less than a day) with the calculated value. Restriction times should not be estimated by extrapolation.

15.21 The decision to discharge a patient who retains more than 800 MBq of ^{131}I should be based on an individual risk assessment taking into account the home circumstances, particularly the ability and willingness of all potentially exposed individuals to comply with the advice given to them to restrict their exposure. It would also be possible to discharge such patients on compassionate grounds, e.g. to visit a dying friend or relative, as long as other potential exposures have been identified and assessed as detailed in paragraphs 15.9 to 15.11.

15.22 In some cases the pattern of close contact with the patient will differ substantially from the norm assumed for Table 15.2. Provided the actual pattern can be reliably and accurately ascertained, the doses to others that will result, and thus appropriate periods of restriction, can be calculated using freely available software [111 and 112].

15.23 Even if a repeat treatment was needed within 12 months, it is unlikely that this would result in others receiving doses of more than 5 mSv averaged over 5 years. However, the RPA or MPE should be consulted in this situation.

Iodine-131 administered for carcinoma of the thyroid

15.24 The time variation of external dose rate following a first ablative administration of ^{131}I for thyroid cancer is known to differ substantially from that associated with subsequent administrations for residual or recurrent disease (Barrington *et al.* [113]). In both cases the dose rate decreases more rapidly than is seen in the treatment of hyperthyroidism. Barrington *et al.* [113] used the dose-modelling methodology, referenced in paragraph 15.22 to derive recommendations for suitable periods of restriction, based on empirical dose rate data and patterns of close contact which were assumed to be typical for this patient group. However, unlike those incorporated into Table 15.2, these have yet to be verified by measurement of doses actually received by persons coming into contact with the patient.

Other therapeutic administrations using unsealed gamma ray emitters

15.25 The time for which a patient receiving a therapeutic dose of radioactivity will pose a radiation hazard will depend on the amount retained at the time of discharge and its effective half-life. These should be determined before discharge, as part of a risk assessment to determine the appropriate restrictions to be applied (see paragraphs 15.9 to 15.11). Where there are sufficient and reliable data concerning dose rates, effective half-life and patterns of close contact with others, the modelling approach described in paragraph 15.19 should be employed. Otherwise, 'equivalent activity of [131]I' may be used to estimate restrictions [103]. However, caution is advised in the use of this method, which may not always be applicable (see Roberts [114] and Waller [115]).

Therapeutic administrations using radionuclides that only emit beta particles

15.26 Up to 200 MBq of ^{32}P, ^{90}Y or ^{89}Sr may generally be administered without placing any restrictions on the patient [35]. However, the possibility of contamination and the generation of radioactive waste must be considered and may require precautions to be taken if the patient is discharged to a nursing home.

15.27   Patients receiving intra-articular, intraperitoneal or intrapleural administrations of radioactive substances should remain at the treatment centre until monitoring has shown that the insertion site is unlikely to leak.

Therapeutic administrations using sealed/closed sources

15.28   Patients should not be discharged from hospital with temporary implants or surface moulds containing sealed or closed sources. Patients receiving permanent implants should remain in hospital long enough to ascertain that the sources are unlikely to migrate from the implant site and be expelled from the body.

15.29   Patients receiving permanent implants of ^{125}I seeds should be advised to avoid prolonged periods of very close contact (<0.1 m) with children and pregnant women for 2 months after treatment.

15.30   The precautions that are necessary following other types of permanent implant should be determined for each individual patient on the basis of the advice of the appropriate MPE and RPA.

Travel

Private transport

15.31   For journeys up to 6 h, the driver of a private vehicle carrying a radioactive patient retaining up to 800 MBq ^{131}I is extremely unlikely to receive more than 0.3 mSv, provided the patient sits in the rear of the vehicle [103].

Public or hospital transport

15.32   It has been estimated that passengers on most forms of public transport, travelling adjacent to a patient containing up to 800 MBq ^{131}I, are extremely unlikely to receive doses that exceed 0.3 mSv during a journey lasting up to 1 h [103]. Therefore there need be no restriction on the mode of transport if the journey time is less than 1 h. One exception may be travelling in crowded underground trains. It may also be difficult to ensure journey time if patients leave by hospital transport: consideration should be given to insisting on single patient transport for high-activity patients (see paragraph 12.10). Patients who have been administered radioactive substances should not be permitted to travel by public transport if there are particular grounds for belief that they may cause a contamination hazard, e.g. by being incontinent of urine or by vomiting if the administration was by the oral route (see paragraph 12.21).

Return to work following therapeutic doses of radioactive substances

15.33   Many patients leaving hospital after receiving treatment with radioactivity may return to work the following day. Restrictions may be necessary if the patient is likely to spend substantial periods at distances of less than 2 m from other workers, or his or her work involves close contact with an individual, particularly a child or pregnant woman, for more than 15 min day^{-1} [103]. The RPA or MPE should then be consulted about appropriate restrictions.

15.34   If radiation-sensitive work is undertaken at the patient's place of work, or the patient works with radioactive materials, practical difficulties may arise. Although the patient's employer may have procedures in place to detect the situation, the patient should be advised to inform his or her employer in order to prevent inconvenience and possible alarm and to discuss whether he or she must remain away from work.

16 Precautions after the death of a patient to whom radioactive substances have been administered

Scope

16.1 This chapter applies to:

(a) the carrying out of post-mortems/autopsies on corpses which contain radioactive substances, and

(b) the preparation of such corpses for burial or cremation.

16.2 For the purposes of this chapter all administrations of ^{131}I greater than 30 MBq should be considered as therapy procedures.

16.3 This chapter does not apply if alpha-emitting radionuclides have been administered. The advice of the RPA at the administering hospital should be sought in such cases.

Principles

16.4 The procedures used when handling or preparing a radioactive corpse must comply with the requirements of IRR99 [1] and RSA93 [7], particularly in relation to dose restriction, the handling of radioactive materials and the disposal of radioactive waste.

General advice

16.5 The administering department should prepare generic radiation risk assessments for each of its clinical procedures to be applied in the event of the death of the patient following the administration of a radioactive substance. This should identify the groups likely to be exposed to any significant risk and the control measures necessary to ensure that exposures to ionising radiation are ALARP. Reference [116] illustrates a practical example. Where precautions are indicated, the period for which they are necessary needs to be determined. Written instructions should be available to send to funeral directors and mortuaries. The means by which they will be informed that the corpse is radioactive should also be considered (see paragraph 15.17). The instructions should encompass all possible work with radioactive corpses and should consider:

(a) precautions necessary to keep doses ALARP

(b) contact telephone numbers for further advice

(c) any need for whole body and/or extremity monitoring of personnel and how this should be arranged

(d) any need for monitoring of the premises and how this should be arranged, and

(e) the requirement for the HSE to be notified by the undertakers and mortuaries that they are working with ionising radiation if they have never previously done so (IRR99 schedule 6, column 3 [1]) and any requirements under RSA93 [7] (see paragraph 13.24).

16.6 The external radiation hazard associated with the handling of a corpse after most diagnostic administrations of radioactive substances will be small and special precautions are unlikely to be required.

16.7 The generic radiation risk assessments for therapy procedures should include a radiological impact assessment for burial and cremation.

16.8 There will be a potential for contamination and the production of radioactive waste if a post-mortem and/or embalming is carried out on any corpse containing radioactive substances. Appropriate precautions on the handling of radioactive materials as detailed in Chapter 10 should be followed. Paragraphs 12.42 and 12.43 on work in operating theatres may be helpful.

16.9 Skin doses may be significant if the hands are likely to come into contact with any body tissues that may have concentrated levels of radioactivity. Finger monitoring may be necessary in such cases.

16.10 For patients in hospitals, nursing homes, hospices, etc., information about any radioactive substances administered, the time for which the patient will be radioactive and who to contact if anything untoward happens to the patient should always be available (see paragraphs 10.79, 15.2 and 15.17). If a radioactive patient dies in such establishments, the corpse should be labelled as being radioactive and anyone who may subsequently come into contact with it notified of any precautions to be taken during autopsy and disposal. Instructions on the precautions to be taken should be obtainable from the department that administered the radioactive substance, as detailed in paragraph 16.5. For hospitals where patients are routinely administered radioactive materials, or premises where patients containing radioactive materials are regularly received, these precautions should be specified in the local rules.

16.11 When a patient is sent home during the precautionary period (see paragraph 16.5), the presence of the card described in paragraph 15.17 should be enough to alert any attending physician to the need to ask for advice from the administering department in the event of the death of the patient. For most diagnostic administrations, the hazards to those coming into contact with the corpse are very low and the risk of contravention of IRR99 [1] or RSA93 [7] is also low. Risk assessments for those returning home after therapeutic administrations should consider the possibility of the death of the patient and suitable systems should be put in place to deal with this situation should it arise. A rota system for the provision of expert advice by telephone may be sufficient.

Death following administration of diagnostic quantities of radioactive substances

16.12 For most diagnostic administrations of radioactive substances, no extra precautions to those normally employed when carrying out post-mortems/embalming will be necessary unless death occurs within the precautionary period determined by the risk assessment (see also paragraph 16.5).

16.13 There is no need to place any restrictions on the method of disposal of the body.

Death following administration of therapeutic quantities of radioactive substances

16.14 The MPE involved in the administration should be contacted for any further information required on the level of hazard remaining, in all cases where the patient dies while still under restrictions applied after a therapeutic administration of a radioactive substance.

16.15 Temporary implants of radionuclides should be removed from corpses as soon as possible after death and before the body is released for post-mortem or disposal.

16.16 Nuclear-powered cardiac pacemakers must never be left in a corpse. At the time these were brought into use, it was arranged for patients fitted with pacemakers of this kind to wear an identity bracelet and carry an identity (ID) card. These patients also agreed at the time of the implant to the removal of their pacemakers on death. RPAs may wish to discuss the following points with local cardiology departments to minimise the likelihood of a potentially serious problem:

(a) check whether there are any unaccounted devices

(b) check whether any patients fitted with such pacemakers are still alive and confirm that they still carry a bracelet and ID card, and

(c) advise cardiac and mortuary services of the potential hazards when removing pacemakers.

Disposal of such pacemakers must be in full compliance with RSA93 [7] (see Chapter 18).

Post-mortem examinations

16.17   If a post-mortem is to be done on a patient who has recently received radioactive substances, the post-mortem room and any equipment used may become contaminated. Radioactive waste, particularly aqueous liquid waste, may be produced.

16.18   Mortuaries in hospitals that have nuclear medicine departments should be provided with written guidance for staff carrying out autopsies on radioactive patients. The guidance should include the information and instructions as described in paragraph 16.5.

16.19   When post-mortem examinations are performed at establishments not covered in paragraph 16.18, written procedures and advice should be requested from the department that administered the radioactive substance. Further advice may be obtained from the RPA for either the administering or receiving establishment.

16.20   The MPE should be consulted about radiation levels likely to be encountered, and the hazards involved, whenever a post-mortem needs to be carried out before the end of the precautionary period (see paragraph 16.5). The appropriate RPA may also need to be contacted for advice.

16.21   If an isolation facility is available, the post-mortem should be conducted there for ease of decontamination afterwards. Similar precautions should be taken to those for operating theatres (see paragraphs 10.83, 12.42 and 12.43). Those carrying out the autopsy should wear heavy-duty gloves, waterproof coveralls and face shields.

16.22   If samples of tissues are required for histology or forensic assessment, the receiving laboratory should be notified if the samples may be radioactive. They should also be told about any precautions that need to be taken, including dealing with any radioactive waste (see paragraph 10.39). Dispatch of the samples should be in accordance with the requirements of IRR99 [1] or road transport regulations [96], as appropriate (see Chapter 17).

Embalming

16.23   Embalming should not be carried out if death occurs within the period covered by an instruction card (see paragraph 15.17), or within 48 h of administration of radioactive substances unless a risk assessment indicates otherwise. The embalmer should be advised by the RPA appointed to the hospital where the radioactive material was administered as to the necessary precautions to ensure that doses are kept ALARP.

Burial

16.24   No special precautions are necessary during the burial of corpses that have residual activities less than those indicated in column 2 of Table 16.1.

16.25   For higher activities, and before the corpse is released, the RPA should be consulted to identify control measures that may need to be applied to those who approach the corpse to ensure that doses are ALARP.

Cremation

16.26   No special precautions need to be taken during cremation where the residual activity is less than that in column 3 of Table 16.1, except where the source is encapsulated or contained, e.g. ^{125}I or ^{103}Pd seeds in prostate brachytherapy, or ^{32}P stents in interventional techniques, see paragraphs 16.29 to 16.31.

16.27   The advice given in paragraph 16.23 is appropriate for the handling of corpses during preparation for cremation.

Table 16.1 Maximum activities of radionuclides for disposal of corpses without special precautions (activities in MBq)

Radionuclide	Burial	Cremation
^{131}I	400[a]	400[a]
^{125}I seeds	4000[b]	see paragraphs 16.29 to 16.31
^{103}Pd seeds	15000[a]	see paragraphs 16.29 to 16.31
^{90}Y colloid	2000[b]	70[c]
^{198}Au seeds	4000[a]	see paragraphs 16.29 to 16.31
^{198}Au colloid	400[a]	100[c]
^{32}P	2000[b]	30[c]
^{89}Sr	2000[b]	200[c, d]

note: the values in columns 2 and 3 relate to the greatest risk to those involved in the procedures.
[a]based on dose rate external to the body.
[b]based on bremsstrahlung dose at 0.5 m.
[c]based on contamination hazard assuming that these radionuclides remain in the ash.
[d]relaxed from earlier guidance, HSE Advice 1989 [117].

16.28   For higher activities, and before the corpse is released, the RPA should be consulted to identify control measures that may need to be applied to ensure that doses are ALARP for those who approach the corpse.

Encapsulated sealed sources

16.29   The generic radiation risk assessment (and environmental impact assessment) for the burial or cremation of a therapy patient where the source is encapsulated or contained (e.g. ^{125}I or ^{103}Pd seeds in prostate brachytherapy, or ^{32}P stents in interventional techniques) should include consideration of the fact that the source is most likely a sealed source manufactured to BS 5288 [72] or ISO 2919:1999 *Sealed Radioactive Sources* [118] and, as such, should not be dispersed by cremation and might not be contained by burial.

16.30   It is recommended that, in the event of death within a given number of half-lives of the radionuclide after the administration (the actual number to be determined by risk assessment and administered activity), cremation be avoided. If this is not possible, excision of the sources should be considered (see paragraph 9.11).

16.31   For the cremation of corpses where the source is encapsulated or contained, the advice and control measures in the generic radiation risk assessment should be communicated to the employer at the crematorium and followed to ensure that doses are ALARP. It is recommended that such generic radiation risk and environmental impact assessments be documented for discussion with the Statutory Inspectors at the next inspection.

17 Keeping, accounting for and moving radioactive substances (including transport)

Introduction

17.1   In addition to the requirements for keeping and accounting for radioactive material in IRR99 [1], employers must be registered under RSA93 [7] or operate under an RSA93 Exemption Order [17]. Employers are legally required to comply with any specific conditions for keeping and accounting of radioactive materials specified in their Certificate of Registration or Exemption Order. Authorisations to dispose of radioactive waste must be obtained prior to keeping, use and disposal (see Chapter 18). The implementation of a single system for keeping and accounting for radioactive materials that satisfies both sets of legal requirements should normally be readily achievable (see IRIS8 Control of Radioactive Substances [119]).

Lost or damaged sources

17.2   Lost or damaged sources will have to be notified to the HSE and the appropriate EA if the quantities exceed those given in IRR99 Schedule 8 Part 1 column 5 [1]. This quantity is generally ten times that listed for notification to HSE of work with the radionuclides. This is the case for all radionuclides listed in paragraph 10.2, except for $^{81}Kr^m$ for which no quantity is specified in IRR99 [1] requiring the notification of an occurrence because of its very short half-life.

Principles

17.3   Radioactive substances that are not in use should be kept in a properly designed store, unless their removal from the work area is likely to result in a greater hazard to the persons concerned. The arrangements made should provide security against loss or theft and damage by fire as well as protection against radiation hazards. Appropriate designation of the store as a controlled or supervised area will depend on the contents, contamination risk and external dose rates (see paragraphs 1.52 to 1.61 and Appendix 11).

17.4   Radioactive substances should not be retained unnecessarily once they are no longer required. They should be declared radioactive waste and arrangements should be made for their disposal (where appropriate, after a period to allow radioactive decay, see Chapter 18). The need to retain substances should be reviewed during the annual audit (see paragraph 17.38).

Responsibility

17.5   A condition of registration and authorisation under RSA93 [7] is that the employer must appoint a competent person to be responsible for the keeping and use of all radioactive substances at the establishment and for all the necessary records [119]. Often, in hospitals, the RPS in the medical physics department will also be the custodian of radioactive substances for the entire site. However, the roles are distinct in law. The RPS supervises the arrangements for work with ionising radiation as set out in the local rules. The custodial duties described in this chapter should be clearly documented, e.g. in the local rules.

17.6   Radioactive substances issued from a store should be in the care of responsible individuals at all times until their return or disposal. The responsibilities of individuals for the care of radioactive substances must be clearly set down in writing.

Design of stores

17.7 A store for radioactive substances may be a room or separate space outside the work area, or it may be a locked cupboard, locked refrigerator, locked freezer or safe, often situated in the work area. The suitability of a store for radioactive materials should be the subject of a prior risk assessment, taking into account the following:

(a) whether unsealed and/or sealed sources are to be stored

(b) the length of storage required

(c) the adequacy of any shielding, given the emission type and activity of the radionuclides, and the security, designation and occupancy of all surrounding areas, including above the ceiling and below the floor

(d) the need for reduced temperatures or other forms of control of the storage environment, and

(e) ease of decontamination of the materials from which the store is made.

17.8 A condition of RSA93 certificates [7] is that radioactive materials are separated from non-radioactive, to avoid cross-contamination and to aid in waste minimisation (but see Chapter 18 when the disposal route is with domestic refuse).

17.9 The store should be sited in a suitable place, taking into account the dose rate from it and the convenience and reduced potential for accidents in transit if it is close to the work area. The store should be designed so that all persons are adequately protected during both storage and transfer of substances to and from the stores.

17.10 Shielding for radioactive substances should take account of scattered radiation and source distribution. For example, it is not sufficient to store large activities behind a thick barrier that protects the torso if the radiation scattered above the barrier presents a significant hazard to the eyes. Advantage can sometimes be taken of self-shielding, e.g. by arranging a group of spent radionuclide generators so that the one with the highest activity is at the centre.

17.11 Unless only a few sealed or solid sources (see paragraph 9.2) are to be stored, or the dose rates in their vicinity are low, a number of separate compartments (e.g. drawers or slides) should be provided in the store so that the total stock can be sub-divided. A separate compartment should normally be provided for each different type of source, while several compartments should be provided for each type when the number of sources is considerable. An individual compartment should not normally contain more than 20 sources, or a total activity exceeding about 10 GBq of ^{137}Cs or its equivalent in MBq.MeV. Each compartment should be so marked as to permit easy identification of the contents.

17.12 The store should be ventilated by mechanical means when radioactive gas, dust or vapour is liable to be present. The mechanical means may be an extractor fan that should operate for a sufficient time to dispel any airborne radioactivity before the room is entered or the cupboard opened and while persons are present in the storeroom or near to an open store cupboard. Stack height and position should be sufficient to ensure adequate dispersal of the extracted air into the environment. Filters are not required for the quantities and types of radioactive materials normally stored in hospitals. If fitted, they cause maintenance and disposal problems.

17.13 The store should be sited and constructed with due regard for the need for security and the radiation hazards that may arise from stored radioactive substances in the event of fire and flood. Advice on these matters may be sought from both the HSE and the Chief Fire Officer.[1] Flammable materials, e.g. solvents, should not be stored near to radioactive substances. However, paraffin wax used as a neutron moderator may be kept in the store provided that it is in a closed metal container.

---

1   In Scotland, the Firemaster.

17.14   A warning notice should be displayed outside the store: a suitable design is shown in Figure A12.4 in Appendix 12. This notice should list the principal contents of the store: this can be of help in cases of emergency. Alternatively, the maximum activity of the principal radionuclides likely to be in the store may be indicated.

17.15   Stores (including refrigerators and freezers) should be kept locked for security.

Keeping of radionuclide generators

17.16   All generators should be kept secure, whether in use or not. While in current use, generators, such as ^{99}Mo/^{99}Tc^m, used in the production of radiopharmaceuticals, should remain in the radiopharmacy and be stored as referenced in paragraph 11.13. Suitable instructions should be made available to assure the adequate security of generators, such as ^{81}Rb/^{81}Kr^m, which must be sited in the imaging room while in use. These instructions should be developed from a risk assessment that takes account of the security considerations such as department layout and availability of staff. The instructions would normally be referred to or included in the local rules. Spent generators awaiting recycling or disposal should be moved to a store. Where the radioactive substances are liable to become airborne, see paragraphs 10.35 and 10.75.

Keeping of mobile and portable equipment

17.17   Mobile and portable equipment containing sealed sources, e.g. low activity after-loading equipment, should be moved to a store or to a secure place when not in use.

Special precautions for keeping unsealed radioactive substances

17.18   Breakable containers, such as glass vials, should be stored inside robust leak-proof containers with absorbent packing. If not for immediate use, the containers should be kept in a store (see paragraph 17.7).

17.19   Some chemically unstable solutions containing radioactive substances can be hazardous and should be stored in vented containers and kept in ventilated storage areas. Examples include solutions that are by-products of HPLC analysis or purification; and nitric acid or other oxidising solutions containing traces of organic material, peroxides and chlorates.

17.20   Special care should be taken when retrieving or opening containers of radioactive substances that have been kept in store for more than a few months and where there may be a risk from bursting or frothing. They should be opened only over a drip tray in a safety cabinet.

17.21   Solutions stored in refrigerators or cold-storage units should be in suitable containers that will not break at low temperatures.

Identification, inspection and leakage testing of radioactive substances

17.22   Every radioactive source or quantity of unsealed radioactive substance should be identified uniquely by number, mark, label or other appropriate method, unless the activity is so low that the source is not considered radioactive. Sources below 0.4 Bq g^{-1} are exempt from the requirements of RSA93 [7] by virtue of the Radioactive Substances (Substances of Low Activity) Exemption Order [120]. For very small sources (i.e. no dimension greater than 5 mm) and dispersible radioactive substances, the identification should be on the container, e.g. source applicator, magazine containing ^{125}I grains, or vial of solution. Identification of the contents should appear on both containers referred to in paragraph 17.18. If lengths of foil or wire, e.g. ^{192}Ir, are cut off for immediate use they need not be identified individually, but a container holding cut lengths should be labelled.

17.23   Labels on containers such as bottles of radioactive solution, or attached to lengths of wire or foil sources, should bear the radiation symbol (Appendix 12).

17.24   Where two or more types of solid source have a similar appearance, a method of discrimination should be adopted; a check should be made at appropriate intervals depending upon the frequency of use to verify that the sources have retained their individual identification.

17.25   Sources should be inspected after use for evidence of damage before being returned to store. A competent person should also examine them with sufficient frequency to permit the early detection of progressive damage that might lead to the leakage of radioactive substances.

17.26   Leakage tests should be made thoroughly but quickly, using forceps, and in a manner that minimises the radiation dose to the operator. Guidance on the determination of methods and frequency of testing is given in paragraph 14.8. Bottles of radiochemicals in store should be closed tightly to prevent leakage and confirmatory leakage tests may be needed. Areas where vials of radiopharmaceuticals are kept should be monitored for contamination.

Maintenance and checking of stores

17.27   The stores should be maintained in an orderly fashion and should be inspected regularly by the custodian (paragraph 17.37) or by some other responsible person (see also paragraph 17.38).

17.28   Monitoring should be undertaken in and around stores to ensure that contamination has not occurred. Monitoring of dose rates in and outside stores to confirm their appropriate designation should also be undertaken. The frequency of the monitoring will depend upon the use, quantity and form of the substances; monthly monitoring should suffice for a typical store (see paragraphs 10.84 to 10.86). Records of the monitoring should be kept.

Stock records and control procedures

17.29   Stock and audit records as described in this section should be kept for at least 2 years under IRR99 [1] and 4 years (5 years in Scotland) after the date of disposal under RSA93 [7].

17.30   A central register of sealed and solid sources should be kept, which gives particulars of all sources that have a half-life greater than a few days. This register should include the following relevant information:

(a)   the radionuclide
(b)   the activity on a given date
(c)   the serial number or other distinguishing mark
(d)   the date of receipt
(e)   the normal location of the source, and
(f)   the date and manner of disposal.

It may be useful to add further information, such as a more detailed description of the source. Entries should be made relating to examinations, leakage tests and repairs; alternatively, leakage test certificates may be attached to the register. Where lengths are cut from a foil or wire source (e.g. of ^{192}Ir) for an individual patient, the total amount should be accounted for, but records of the activity of each individual piece need not be kept for IRR99 (also see paragraphs 17.22 and 9.16).

17.31   Transfers of radioactive substances to and from departments or areas must be recorded (IRR99 regulation 28 [1]).

17.32   Records should be kept in each store of radioactive substances received, issued and returned.

17.33   The records for sealed or other solid sources should contain sufficient detail and be arranged so that information concerning the whereabouts of every solid source is immediately available. This will also provide a means for showing at any time the number of sources of each type actually in each store and available for issue. The records should enable a loss or theft to be detected quickly by the employer (L121 paragraph 493 [2]). The total quantity of each radionuclide held on the premises should also be available.

17.34   Records of the receipt, issue and disposal of unsealed sources should be kept in such a way as to allow stock control, enable loss or theft to be noticed quickly, and estimate the total quantity of each radionuclide at any particular time.

17.35   Where radionuclide generators are used there should be:

(a)   a record showing the receipt of new generators with their activity and reference date and the return or disposal of spent ones, and

(b)   a record of use for each generator showing all relevant information, e.g. the date, time and activity of each elution for a ^{99}Mo/^{99}Tc^m generator, and the date and list of patients administered with activity from a ^{81}Rb/ ^{81}Kr^m generator.

17.36   When radioactive substances are administered to patients, entries should be made in the hospital's stock records and in the patients' individual records (see 10.71). Entries will also be needed when temporary implants are removed.

17.37   The custodian or the person responsible for the store must carry out an audit at regular intervals to account for every solid source in storage or in use. The frequency of the audit should be established in a prior risk assessment. Sources in the store should be counted. Checking of serial numbers must be included if the risk assessment indicated it. Sources that are no longer in the store should be covered by an entry in the record. The stock of unsealed radioactive substances should be inspected to ensure that it agrees with receipts, issues and disposals, taking into account radioactive decay.

17.38   A senior officer nominated by the employer should undertake an annual check audit.

Movement of radioactive substances (in areas wholly within the employer's control)

17.39   Containers used to store radioactive substances may not be suitable for movement and may need additional physical protection when taken outside a building. Consideration should be given to the need for total containment in case of spills and any requirement to reduce the external dose rate. Further advice is provided in L121 for guidance on IRR99 regulation 29(2) [2].

17.40   The container should be marked clearly to indicate that its contents are radioactive and the label should carry the warning sign shown in Appendix 12.

17.41   Only members of staff who are adequately trained should move radioactive substances between rooms or buildings.

Transport of radioactive materials

17.42   Transport by road of radioactive materials occurs when the materials are placed in a vehicle and taken outside the confines of the establishment or on any road running through the establishment to which the public has access. All transport of radioactive materials should conform to the current national and international regulations and codes of practice relating to the various means of transport used, road, rail, sea or air [96, 97, 105, 106, 121 and 122].

17.43   The RPA should be consulted for advice before the establishment first transports any radioactive material, to ensure compliance with IRR99 [1]. The RPA may also be qualified to give advice on the other regulations listed in paragraph 17.42. Exemption from the need to appoint a qualified Transport Safety Adviser under the Transport of Dangerous Goods (Safety Advisers) (TDGSA) Regulations [97] is given if:

(a) only excepted packages[2] are being transported

(b) the only involvement in transport is the unloading of radioactive material at its final destination, or

(c) the transport of radioactive material is not the employer's main or secondary activity and not more than ten type A packages with a total maximum transport index (TI) of 3 are being transported at any one time.

17.44   If radioactive materials are to be transported, other than as the exemptions listed in paragraph 17.43, the employer will need to appoint a safety adviser under TDGSA. The employer should keep all annual reports and accident reports prepared by the safety adviser for a minimum period of 5 years [97].

17.45   When radioactive materials are transported, the consignor should ensure that they are properly packaged and labelled. A transport document must be issued to the carrier or driver (where the consignor acts as carrier). The driver must be given appropriate information and must be adequately trained, as required by the regulations referenced in paragraph 17.42. The consignor must keep a record of all shipments of excepted and type A and B packages for 2 years from the date of shipment [96]. This record may consist of the transport documents themselves or the equivalent information recorded thereon. Adequate security should be ensured wherever vehicles are parked, particularly if this is a place other than that set aside for unloading. The police may be able to advise in cases of particular difficulty.

17.46   Incoming packages of radioactive materials should be opened only by persons having the necessary knowledge and in an area set apart for the purpose. While waiting to be opened, packages should be stored securely. Category II and III packages (yellow labels) may also require additional shielding. The maximum dose rate in millisievert per hour at 1 m can generally be found by dividing the TI marked on the package by 100 (reversing the method by which the TI was found). Category I (white labels) can only be used for packages containing small amounts of radioactive material (e.g. up to 800 MBq ^{99}Tc^m). Category I packages are limited to 5 μSv h^{-1} at the surface and give rise to negligible dose rates at 1 m. Further information on labelling and packaging for road and rail transport is given in [96] and [105].

17.47   New international marking and labelling requirements came into force in January 2002. Any radioactive package that is sent abroad must fulfil these requirements which include the display of the United Nations (UN) number on the external surface of an excepted package. Note that there are differences in the UN numbers for United Kingdom legislation in force at January 2002 although later United Kingdom legislation should be consistent.

Transfrontier shipment of radioactive materials

17.48   For the transfrontier shipment of radioactive materials between European Union (EU) Member States, reference should be made to EU regulation 93/1493/EURATOM [123]. Being an EU regulation it has the same effect in all Member States and there is no specific United Kingdom regulation. This regulation does not apply to shipments to and from the United Kingdom to countries outside the EU.

17.49   For transfrontier shipments of sealed sources within the EU, the holder (supplier) of the sealed sources must obtain a prior written declaration from the consignee (the hospital) to the effect that the consignee has complied with all applicable provisions implementing the basic safety standards directive 80/836/ EURATOM [124]. For the United Kingdom, this declaration should indicate compliance with RSA93 [7] and IRR99 [1] as being the appropriate implementing legislation. The declaration must be noted and stamped by the competent authority (e.g. EA, SEPA or EHSNI) of the EU State to which the shipment is being made prior to the declaration being sent to the holder (supplier) of the sealed source. The declaration may be valid for a single shipment or for several shipments up to 3 years.

---

2   Excepted and type A packages are defined in the road transport regulations [96].

17.50   For radioactive materials other than sealed sources, the situation is simpler and the suppliers are only required to provide the competent authorities of the Member State of destination with a summary of deliveries.

17.51   The definitions of radioactive materials, sealed sources and radioactive waste under the EU regulation [124] and RSA 93 [7] are different. Currently there is not an enforcement regime in place for the former regulations within the United Kingdom, although EA/SEPA/EHSNI act as the competent authority for non-nuclear sites.

18 Disposal of radioactive waste

General requirements

18.1 Accumulation and disposal of radioactive waste is controlled under the Radioactive Substances Act 1993 [7] as amended by the Environment Act 1995 [125]. If the radioactive waste has other properties that, if it were not radioactive, would make it special waste, then the Special Waste Regulations 1996 [126] also have to be complied with when disposing of the waste. The Radioactive Material (Road Transport) (Great Britain) Regulations 1996 [96] or subsequent legislation must be complied with if radioactive material is taken off-site for disposal.

18.2 The following types of radioactive waste may occur in medical practice:

(a) sealed and other solid sources
(b) spent radionuclide generators
(c) excreta from patients treated or tested with unsealed radionuclides
(d) unused solutions of radionuclides originally intended for diagnostic or therapeutic use
(e) very low level liquid waste, e.g. from washing of apparatus
(f) liquids immiscible with water, such as liquid scintillation fluids, counting residues
(g) solid waste in the form of pipettes, syringes, etc., for relatively long-lived radionuclides (e.g. ^{32}P)
(h) very low level solid waste, e.g. paper, glass, syringes, vials, waste from spills and decontamination
(i) gases (including gaseous waste from patients)
(j) animal waste from medical research, and
(k) incinerator ash.

The employer must ensure that appropriate authorised waste disposal routes exist for each type of waste. Radioactive waste should be included in the overall waste management system.

18.3 Appropriate risk assessments including environmental impact assessments for waste disposal should be performed, documented and must be available for inspection and review. These will contribute to the requirements for completion of the RSA93 [7] application form needed for a certificate of authorisation to accumulate and dispose of radioactive waste.

18.4 Disposals of all radioactive waste from medical practices must be in accordance with either:

(a) a 'waste disposal authorisation' granted by the EA, SEPA or EHSNI, or

(b) an appropriate 'RSA exemption order'. These are currently under review but for example could be:
    (i) the Radioactive Substances (Hospitals) Exemption Order 1990 [17]
    (ii) the Radioactive Substances (Waste Closed Sources) Exemption Order 1963 [127]
    (iii) the Radioactive Substances (Testing Instruments) Exemption Order 1985 [128]
    (iv) the Radioactive Substances (Substances of Low Activity) Exemption Order 1986 [120], or
    (v) the Radioactive Substances (Prepared Uranium and Thorium Compounds) Exemption Order 1962 [129].

18.5 Most hospital Trusts fall within the Radioactive Waste Management Advisory Committee (RWMAC) category of 'small users' of radioactive substances. The vast majority of solid radioactive waste (excluding spent sealed sources) is either:

(a) low level waste (LLW), less than 12 GBq beta/gamma activity per tonne, or

(b) very low level waste (VLLW), individual items of less than 40 kBq beta/gamma and containing less than 400 kBq beta/gamma per 0.1 m^3 of non-radioactive waste.

Each of these will need to be covered by an appropriate authorisation or exemption order. The employer must ensure that an appropriate authorisation is obtained for each type of radioactive waste (solid, liquid or gaseous) or that the proposed disposal is within the terms of an exemption order.

18.6 The employer must appoint an appropriate competent person to have overall responsibility for waste disposal. A qualified expert (QE) must also be appointed as a consequence of the Radioactive Substances (Basic Safety Standards) (England and Wales) Direction 2000 [130] and the Radioactive Substances (Basic Safety Standards) (Scotland) Direction 2000 [131]. The names of the persons appointed should be communicated to the relevant statutory authority (EA/SEPA/EHSNI). The QE is required by the basic safety standards directive [124] to advise on the use and disposal of radioactive substances with respect to the protection of the population and the environment. The QE will need to have relevant training, knowledge and experience to ensure all requirements are met under RSA93 [7]. For most uses of radioactive material, an appointed RPA or appropriate MPE will have the required expertise, but this will need to be agreed with the relevant statutory authority (see IRIS8 Control of Radioactive Substances [119]). (It should be noted that the regulators are currently working on the criteria for the recognition of QEs.)

18.7 The employer must ensure that the conditions specified in the authorisation or exemption order are complied with by adherence to a robust waste management system. The advice of the RPA/QE should be sought to this effect.

18.8 Authorised routes for the disposal of each type of waste are specified in the authorisation/exemption order. The conditions listed in the authorisation or exemption order will include specification of:

(a) permitted method(s) of disposal

(b) the maximum activities and activity concentrations of the waste which may be disposed of in a particular period, day/week/month/year

(c) the containment of the waste while awaiting disposal

(d) the limit for accumulation on amount and volume

(e) the maximum time which waste may be stored prior to disposal, and

(f) the records which must be kept.

18.9 Records of the type and amount of activity and the time of disposal should be kept for inspection by regulatory authorities, to show compliance with the disposal authorisation (see also paragraphs 18.28 to 18.33). The records should be submitted to the appropriate regulatory authorities in the prescribed format and at the frequency specified in the authorisation.

18.10 Certificates of Authorisation must be displayed on the premises to which they relate, along with the name(s) of the competent person responsible for demonstrating compliance with RSA93 [7]. For completeness, the name(s) of the department or person(s) keeping the appropriate records and the RPA/QE may also be displayed.

18.11 Radioactive waste disposal is only one component of the clinical waste management process. The employer should ensure that this is:

(a) legal (i.e. authorised or exempt under RSA93)

(b) safe (the waste should be contained, shielded and segregated)

(c) simple (the waste system should be easily understood by all those who are to apply it), and

(d) economical (the final disposal of some radioactive waste can be very expensive, e.g. high activity sealed sources, such as tritium tubes used for generating neutrons, Am/Be neutron sources and redundant ^{60}Co and ^{137}Cs radiotherapy sources).

Types of waste

Solid waste

18.12 Much of the radioactive waste generated in hospitals arises from the preparation and administration of radionuclides to patients, or from *in-vitro* tests in laboratories, and may be considered as solid waste. Other sources of solid waste include patient-generated waste, not disposable via the sewer system, and waste arising from decontamination procedures. Research laboratories are also likely to generate a great deal of solid waste.

18.13 Solid waste may be disposed of by any of the authorised means as follows:

(a) collection by the local authority or their contractor as refuse for co-disposal with large amounts of non-radioactive waste at a landfill site or municipal incinerator (VLLW and some small sealed sources)

(b) transfer to an authorised contractor for incineration at their facilities (LLW)

(c) return to the manufacturer (e.g. sealed sources, spent generators), or

(d) transfer to a contractor as refuse for co-disposal with large amounts of non-radioactive waste at a landfill site.

Liquid waste

18.14 Aqueous liquid waste may be disposed of via the hospital drainage system, either via sinks/sluices for waste arising in laboratories or direct to the main drains via toilets/sluices for patient excreta. Dilution of high activities is recommended. Sinks/toilets/sluices designated for disposal should be clearly marked, as should the waste outlet run. The designated discharge points should afford the highest dilution of the waste, e.g. which drain directly into a sewer or main drain. There should be records of periodic contamination monitoring of the sink and associated nearby pipes and outlets.

18.15 Organic liquid waste includes ^{14}C and tritium and other beta emitters mixed with liquid scintillation fluid. The scintillant material, which is immiscible with water, toxic and/or flammable, should not be disposed of via the drains. The new generation of non-flammable low-toxicity biodegradable scintillants that do not penetrate plastics may be disposed of via the drains, subject to prior permission being obtained from the local sewerage company. The options for disposal of scintillant wastes are:

(a) incineration of the whole vials and contents

(b) separation of the scintillant from the vials followed by incineration of bulked scintillant by a licensed contractor, and

(c) separation of biodegradable scintillant(s) from the vials followed by disposal to drains, with approval from the local sewerage company.

18.16 For some laboratory waste, vial crushers and splitters may be an effective means of rendering solid waste to liquid form, disposing of it to sewer and thereby operating within the terms of an exemption order [17] for liquid waste. Some crushers are effective on both glass and plastic vials, while those for plastic vials usually split them rather than crush them. Some can be effective in achieving separation of the broken vials from the scintillant, but some granulators can reduce plastic vials to such small particles that the large surface area absorbs the scintillant causing problems for subsequent separation. The efficacy of their use for disposal needs to be determined and documented prior to use.

Gaseous or airborne waste

18.17   Gaseous radioactive waste may arise from many different operations, for example:

(a)   patient investigation involving either a radioactive gas or aerosol (^{133}Xe or Technegas) or a radioactive substance (^{14}C Urea)

(b)   research involving animals

(c)   radiochemical operations using gaseous or volatile radioactive substances, e.g. ^{3}H, ^{14}C (dioxide or monoxide), ^{125}I, ^{131}I in a fume cupboard or safety cabinet

(d)   discharges from an incinerator, or

(e)   exhaust from a store for radioactive materials/radioactive waste or fume cupboards.

For some radioactive gases used in diagnostic nuclear medicine (e.g. ^{81}Kr^{m}) and positron emitters such as ^{13}N, ^{15}O and ^{11}C and their derivatives, quantification of their disposal can be difficult and the advice of the RPA/QE should be sought.

18.18   All gaseous radioactive waste should normally be discharged from the building via suitable ducting in such a manner that it cannot easily re-enter other parts of the same building or enter other buildings nearby; some very short half-life gases do not require specific discharge conditions.

18.19   Filters in microbiological safety cabinets should be checked periodically and replaced. Any contaminated filters should be treated as solid waste and disposed of accordingly.

Animal waste products

18.20   Animal waste products (including carcasses, dismembered if necessary) should be incinerated or macerated. The macerator should be plumbed directly into the waste system. Large animals can present particular problems, as there can be high activities in the urine and faeces. These should be collected and disposed of as aqueous radioactive waste to drains or as solid waste by incineration. For small carcasses containing longer half-life radionuclides (e.g. ^{32}P, ^{125}I) some form of segregation and decay storage may be required.

Alpha emitters

18.21   Alpha emitters require special authorisation for disposal and will necessitate extensive consultation with EA/SEPA and the RPA/QE. The services of an authorised contractor will be required.

Special waste

18.22   Some radioactive waste is also special waste and as such needs to conform to the requirement of the Special Waste Regulations 1996 [126]. All radioactive medicinal products are prescription-only medicines (POMS) [18]. Waste POMS are defined as special waste under the Special Waste Regulations [126]. The regulatory authorities have given advice to the effect that they will not normally take enforcement action where small quantities of waste radiopharmaceuticals disposed of under the terms of an authorisation granted under RSA93 [7] are not declared as special waste. They have, however, stated that this will not apply where they consider that the waste is being managed in such a way as to endanger human health or harm the environment.

18.23   The statutory authorities have indicated that, with the exception of small quantities of waste POMS, shipments of radioactive waste that is special waste will be required to be accompanied by consignment notes. These consignment notes, which meet the requirements of the Special Waste Regulations [126] are in addition to those conditions imposed by authorisations issued under RSA93 [7].

Storage of radioactive waste material

18.24   An RSA93 authorisation [7] may allow waste to be accumulated up to a certain activity for a certain period of time, pending disposal subject to certain conditions. This may facilitate the storage of radionuclides, to allow radioactive decay to reduce the activity disposed of and accumulation for final disposal in an economic manner. A clear distinction needs to be made between the short-term storage of short half-life radionuclides and the long-term storage of long half-life radionuclides and likewise those radionuclides with differing permitted routes of disposal.

18.25   A robust management system is required for segregation and storage of radioactive waste. Radioactive waste must not be stored with flammable material. The waste store must be secure and of a design appropriate to the hazards present. It will require surfaces that are easily decontaminated and may require shielding and an appropriate ventilation system. If putrescible waste (such as patient tissue/samples, animal carcasses, etc.) is to be stored, a coldroom or freezer will also be required. Waste stores should be clearly marked with radiation warning signs and suitable information on their contents. The waste management systems and procedures for the waste store should be clearly documented. An auditable accounting system is required for logging-in, checking and logging-out the waste. Clear auditable pathways should be maintained. Management should review the waste storage procedures periodically. The RPA/QE should advise management as to the suitability of their arrangements.

18.26   Waste may be segregated into the following categories, or combinations of these, as follows:

(a) radioactive waste of a range of activities

(b) radioactive waste of half-lives in different ranges

(c) radioactive waste of different physical types, solid, sealed, aqueous, scintillant, organic, and

(d) radioactive waste to be disposed of by different routes, e.g. solid waste to landfill or incineration or return to manufacturer (sealed source).

The categories should reflect those contained in the waste disposal authorisation/exemption order.

18.27   Some RSA93 [7] authorisations allow the decay storage of longer half-life radionuclides, e.g. ^{125}I, ^{35}S, ^{59}Fe, ^{89}Sr, if the employer can demonstrate a well-organised and safe system for the medium term storage of radioactive materials. It should be noted, however, that the waste from some procedures, e.g. ^{125}I iodinations, may require storage for over 2 years before the waste has decayed to a level at which it can be disposed of. Appropriate risk assessments will identify the control measures required, e.g. ventilation systems and the risk of contamination by volatilisation, or penetration or breakdown of the plastic containers. The decay storage system should conform to all conditions specified in the authorisation.

Records

18.28   Certain specified records of radioactive waste disposals must be kept indefinitely. The date, radionuclide(s), type and quantities disposed of and disposal route must be recorded on the date of disposal. A record of all stored waste (solid or liquid) must also be kept. Monthly summaries of all waste from a site should be kept by a designated person/department, particularly if there are multiple users on a site. Records should include disposals of patient excreta via the sewage system. Although there will be time lags in the system, and such monthly waste disposal records will be retrospective, they should be sufficient to show compliance with the conditions of the RSA93 authorisation [7].

18.29   Records relating to the accumulation and disposal of radioactive waste (which could include monitoring of waste pipes and the environment) should be retained for the periods specified by the appropriate authority. Records should not be destroyed without the written agreement of the appropriate regulatory authority (see guidance in Inspectors Technical Note on RSA93 records [132]). This is more restrictive than the requirement in IRR99 [1] to retain records for 2 years from the date of disposal. Generally, records relating to disposals under the terms of an authorisation should be retained for the time indicated

Table 18.1 Retention of disposal records

Type of record	Retention period
Accumulation of waste	4 years from disposal date
Disposal of long-lived radionuclides, except ^{14}C and ^{3}H in liquid waste to drain	Indefinite
Disposal of LLW to landfill for 'burial at a specified location'	Indefinite
Disposal of small quantities and/or disposals of radionuclides of low radiotoxicity or short half-life	4 years from disposal date
All other disposals	4 years from disposal date

in Table 18.1. However, users, should consult their local inspector (HSE/EA/SEPA/EHSNI) on any proposals to destroy records.

18.30   For sealed sources or radioactive material held under certificates of registration but not subject to an authorisation, records should be retained for 4 years after the source(s)/material(s) are removed from the premises or become radioactive waste. Many of the exemption orders [17] also require the keeping of records of disposals made under them. The advice of the appropriate authority should be sought about retention of such records.

18.31   For disposals from laboratories, the amount of activity disposed of via the various routes should be estimated from measurements of the partitioning of the waste for the various procedures carried out. These figures should be verified by periodic check measurements.

18.32   For radioactive materials administered to patients, the fraction recorded as waste should be in accordance with guidelines issued by the appropriate authority, some of which are reproduced in Appendix 17 from the EA *Internal Handbook on Guidance for Inspectors* [133]. Alternatively, an agreement can be made with local regulatory inspectors, who may be flexible in their interpretation if justifiable evidence can be produced for alternative values. For example, measurements at the Cookridge Hospital after ^{131}I-ablation therapy for cancer of the thyroid have indicated that less than 100 per cent of the administered activity was actually discharged. With the agreement of the local EA inspector, a value of 85 per cent is used as the discharged quantity over a 4 day inpatient period for the first treatment. Following subsequent treatments, the discharged activity also amounts to 85 per cent of the newly administered activity (see Driver and Packer [134].

18.33   Various computer packages are available commercially to cover the whole accounting procedure from ordering of radionuclides through their receipt and usage to accumulation and disposal of waste. Their use should be considered, particularly by large NHS Trusts with multiple user departments, as they may lead to standardisation and simplification of record systems.

Transfrontier shipment of radioactive waste

18.34   The shipment of radioactive waste across frontiers is covered by RSA93 [7] and exemption orders and the Transfrontier Shipment of Radioactive Waste Regulations 1993 (TSRWR93) [135]. Unfortunately, radioactive waste is defined differently in both pieces of legislation. TSRWR93 provides for the issue by EA/SEPA of prior authorisations and prior approvals in respect of shipments (imports, exports and transhipments) of radioactive waste into, from and through the United Kingdom. It does not apply to shipments where a sealed source is returned by its user to the supplier of the source in another country nor where the shipment does not exceed an exemption level in the original 1980 basic safety standards directive 80/836/EURATOM [124]. EA/SEPA act as the competent authority.

19 Contingency planning and emergency procedures

Scope

19.1   This chapter gives guidance on the plans needed to deal with accidents and other incidents related to work with radioactive substances: the general guidance in paragraph 19.13 is relevant to the operation of X-ray equipment. The purpose of any plan should be to restrict possible exposures. The plan, or at least a reference to it, should be included in the local rules.

19.2   Detailed advice is given in Chapter 7 regarding preparations for dealing with incidents involving beam therapy or remotely operated after-loading equipment, and in Chapter 9 regarding brachytherapy sources.

19.3   REPPIR [28] complement the requirements of IRR99 [1] for contingency planning. REPPIR apply to premises and to rail transport. There are exemptions in REPPIR for the storage and use of non-dispersible sources (e.g. iridium wire), special-form sealed sources with valid certificates, and radioactive substances in live bodies or corpses of humans and animals. The exemption for sealed sources does not extend to the transport of non-dispersible sources, however in most cases the activities involved will not require action under REPPIR. There are also exemptions for substances of low activity concentration, substances in type B packages, low specific activity materials, and surface contaminated objects (see REPPIR [28] regulation 3). REPPIR will apply where there are centralised radiopharmacies holding activities in excess of 2 TBq ^{99}Mo or 90 GBq ^{131}I, for example, or the equivalent quantity ratio. These Regulations are unlikely to apply to the transportation of radioactive materials between hospitals, or to any other similar transport operations, because of the exemptions provided and because the materials are almost exclusively carried by road. Any contingency plan prepared under the IRR99 [1] may be helpful in preparing the emergency plans needed under REPPIR [28] (see paragraph 19.12). REPPIR are enforced by the HSE, who have a number of important roles to play in relation to the regulations. The EA and SEPA as well as the HSE and a number of other bodies are statutory consultees on the emergency plans. The impact of REPPIR on non-nuclear sites is expected to be minimal. Actions concerning other transport modes do not come within REPPIR and will be implemented and enforced by:

- the Radioactive Materials Transport Division of the DTLR for road transport

- the Civil Aviation Authority for air transport, and

- the Maritime and Coastguard Agency for transport by sea and inland waterways.

Contingency planning for incidents on-site

19.4   Typical incidents which could involve the need for a contingency plan include:

(a) the loss or suspected loss (or theft) of a sealed or solid source (see paragraph 9.2)

(b) the loss or spillage of unsealed radioactive substances (including excreta)

(c) breakage of a sealed or solid source; an accident to a caesium therapy source or an old radium container should be treated as a serious emergency (also see paragraph 9.37)

(d) failure to retract a radioactive source, close a shutter or switch off a radiation beam by normal methods, and

(e) fire or explosion, including such occurrences during transport.

19.5   Experience has shown that most incidents involving spills of unsealed radioactive substances in hospitals or clinics do not warrant any drastic emergency action but, on assessment, require only simple remedial action by local staff, often as part of their routine procedures, for the control of spread of contamination. Nevertheless, more serious incidents are foreseeable and could occur and for such cases a contingency plan must be prepared.

19.6   There should be a readily available up-to-date list of all places in the establishment where there are or may be radiation hazards. This list should show the exact location of, and the means of access to, all rooms likely to contain amounts of radioactive substances in excess of those in column 5 of Schedule 8 of IRR99 [1]. A copy should be available in each place where there is a potential hazard and a copy should be kept by the Fire Officer and by the Emergency Planning Officer, if appointed.

19.7   Notices should be posted at places where foreseeable accidents may occur, and they should show:

(a) how to contact the RPS, or an alternative person, who should be notified immediately of any emergency

(b) how to call the fire brigade and medical services, and

(c) the location of emergency equipment.

19.8   Arrangements should be made with the Chief Fire Officer[1] for the local fire brigade to visit the establishment to obtain information about the layout of the premises, warning notices and signs, and the location and types of radiation sources. Useful information on radioactive releases during a fire engulfment is given in a Health and Safety Laboratory report at http://www.hse.gov.uk/research/hsl_pdf/2002/ fractrad.pdf. The Chief Fire Officer should also be consulted about the suitability of the fire-fighting equipment.

19.9   Equipment should be kept available for use in an emergency wherever unsealed radioactive substances are used. This may need to include some or all of the following items:

(a) overshoes, protective clothing (including gloves and caps) and respirators or breathing apparatus

(b) decontamination materials for the affected area, including absorbent material for wiping up spills

(c) decontamination materials for persons

(d) barriers, or means for roping off affected areas

(e) warning notices

(f) handling tools and receptacles for contaminated articles

(g) portable monitoring equipment, including personal monitoring devices such as electronic dosemeters, pocket dosemeters, TLD and film badges

(h) non-porous floor covering, to be used only after any liquid spill has been cleared up, and

(i) sundry items, such as adhesive tape, labels, torch, notebook and pencils, and simple first-aid equipment.

19.10   An appropriate selection of emergency equipment should be kept in a clearly labelled portable container in a readily accessible place. A list of the emergency equipment should be fixed to the container and checks made periodically and immediately after use to ensure that all items are present or replaced as necessary.

19.11   Practical exercises should be held, at least every 3 years, to test the effectiveness of the arrangements and to ensure that all persons concerned know what action to take in an emergency. Mock or low-activity sources should be used during training exercises.

---

1   In Scotland, the Firemaster.

19.12   If REPPIR [28] apply, the employer must identify the hazards, evaluate the risks, and send a report of the assessment to the HSE. If a radiation emergency is reasonably foreseeable and emergency plans are required, then both the emergency plan prepared by the hospital and an off-site emergency plan prepared by the local authority will be necessary.

Action during an emergency

19.13   The best course of action in an emergency depends very much on local circumstances and the nature of the emergency. If it involves an X-ray generator (other than capacitor discharge type) or accelerator where the exposure controls have all failed, it is necessary only to switch off the main supply in order to remove all radiation hazards (except possibly from induced radioactivity in the case of high energy accelerators). If radioactive substances are present the emergency may involve actual or potential dispersal of activity or an HDR. Occasionally both hazards may be present.

19.14   If an activity greater than that specified in column 5 of Schedule 8 to IRR99 [1] has been dispersed, urgent actions would include:

(a) deciding on the need for the fire services, medical assistance and advice from the RPA

(b) warning persons in the immediate vicinity of the accident or evacuating the area as dictated by circumstances, e.g. those believed to involve activities greater than a hundred times those in column 5 of Schedule 8 to the IRR99 [1]

(c) rendering first aid to any person who may be injured

(d) notifying the RPS, and

(e) dealing with the emergency.

19.15   In the case of solids and liquids, the dispersal of the radioactive substance should be contained as far as possible. In the case of radioactive gases or vapours they should be dispersed as quickly as possible.

19.16   If evacuation is required, and where time permits, all functioning apparatus in the area should be made safe. Ventilation, and all laboratory services except lighting, should be switched off and all doors and windows should be closed. However, when radioactive gas or vapour, e.g. tritiated water vapour, has been released, mechanical ventilation should be left on and, with discretion, doors and windows should be opened.

19.17   The spread of contamination, particularly on shoes or clothing of persons leaving the affected area, should be minimised. Evacuated persons who might be contaminated should be monitored immediately outside the area. Appropriate arrangements should be made for their decontamination.

19.18   Clothing contaminated in an emergency should be removed and left in or near the affected area. Contaminated parts of the body should be washed thoroughly but gently until monitoring shows that contamination will not be significantly reduced further by this method, care being taken not to roughen or break the skin which would allow contamination to enter the blood stream. Any contaminated wound, however trivial, should be irrigated with water or saline solution, care being taken to limit any spread of contamination to or from other parts of the skin. If measurable contamination persists, an assessment of the resulting radiation dose should be obtained from an MPE. If morbidity is likely, specialist medical advice should also be sought. Section 7 of the radiation annex of the document *Planning for Major Incidents: the NHS Guidance* [136] may be helpful.

19.19   Persons entering the affected area to carry out emergency procedures should wear appropriate protective clothing, which they should monitor and remove when they leave the area. In the event of an emergency involving a serious spill, those concerned with the cleaning up procedures should, if necessary, wear properly fitting respirators or breathing apparatus appropriate to the radioactivity being handled, so that even under these conditions air monitoring will rarely be needed.

19.20   A direct radiation hazard may arise through loss of shielding or through failure of a shutter or source transport mechanism. Temporary shielding should be used as necessary and the immediate area should be evacuated and barriers erected to restrict access. Recovery of the source should then be undertaken, in accordance with pre-planned procedures that take into consideration the doses likely to be incurred. Advice on dealing with an emergency which occurs during the treatment of a patient is given in paragraphs 7.38, 7.43 and 7.56 and 9.28.

19.21   If a source of notifiable activity (see column 5 of Schedule 8 to IRR99 [1]) is lost, or thought to be lost or stolen:

(a)   the person responsible for security of sources (see paragraphs 17.5 and 17.6), as well as the RPS, should be informed without delay; the RPS should arrange for a competent person to make an immediate search for the lost source; the possibility that a lost sealed or solid source might have fallen into a gap in protective material should not be overlooked

(b)   all means by which the lost source might be moved further astray should, as far as possible, be eliminated until the search has been carried out; floors should not be swept, furniture should not be moved, and sinks should not be used; incinerators should not be used nor their ashes disturbed

(c)   the possibility of contamination by spilled radioactive substances should be borne in mind if there is any reason to suspect that the lost source might have become damaged, rigorous precautionary measures should be instituted as soon as contamination is detected, and

(d)   a report of the loss should be made to the competent authorities, the HSE in the case of IRR99 and the EA, SEPA or EHNSI under RSA93 registrations.

19.22   Access to an area affected by an emergency should be restricted until radiation surveys show that the area may be reoccupied. Any radiation generator should be examined for defects before it is re-energised. Leakage tests should be carried out if it is suspected that a radioactive substance is leaking from any container.

19.23   In consultation with the RPA, the employer should review all emergencies in order to learn any appropriate lessons from the way they have been managed, and where appropriate to revise the contingency plan in the light of those lessons.

Incidents involving radioactivity which occur off-site

19.24   The Health Departments have issued extensive guidance to health authorities in *Planning for Major Incidents: The NHS Guidance* [136] and, in Scotland, *Manual of Guidance: Responding to Emergencies*. Chapter 9 of the first document covers incidents involving radioactivity, and the radiation annex entitled *Practical guidance on planning for incidents involving radioactivity* details the requirements for health authorities and ambulance services who may need to deal with casualties likely to be contaminated by radioactivity.

19.25   All health authorities need contingency plans to deal with the medical consequences of transport accidents, lost or stolen radioactive material, or the effects of a large-scale incident elsewhere.

19.26   Heath authorities with fixed nuclear sites within their area must be involved in the site operators' emergency planning and response arrangements and in the off-site emergency plan. Carriers who make a carrier's emergency plan under REPPIR [28] may also consult them. There should be liaison between hospitals and local employers who use radioactive substances, so that arrangements for dealing with contaminated casualties can be made.

19.27   All health authorities should designate hospitals prepared to receive radiation casualties. They must have specific plans and resources for dealing with incidents involving radioactivity. The design of decontamination areas in casualty departments for use in major incidents is discussed in the NHS guidance [136].

19.28   The essential features for designation are:

(a) 24-hour A&E cover
(b) ready availability of medical physics facilities to measure contamination, and
(c) simple facilities for decontamination.

19.29   All A&E departments need to ensure that they have access to expert advice on how to manage patients who have been exposed to radioactivity. In the event of a casualty having received a high radiation dose, the first signs of which may be nausea and vomiting, immediate transfer to a designated hospital is imperative.

19.30   The RPA should be consulted if it is known or suspected that a casualty is contaminated, and as much information as possible about the incident and the radionuclide(s) involved should be sought.

19.31   A&E staff should be monitored for external radiation dose while dealing with contaminated casualties, and should also be checked for contamination immediately afterwards. Arrangements must be in place to ensure that the doses received by all members of staff are ALARP. Unless members of staff have been designated as classified persons, the doses received from a combination of such emergency work and their normal duties must be restricted below 6 mSv year^{-1}. Pregnant and breastfeeding staff should not normally be involved in treating casualties contaminated with radioactivity.

19.32   In the case of accidents and situations which are not readily foreseeable, or for which formal plans cannot be made, a scheme exists to support the police, who are usually the first officials on the scene, with expert help and advice. The national arrangements for incidents involving radioactivity (NAIR) [137] are co-ordinated by the NRPB. Help is offered in two stages:

(a) stage 1 is monitoring and advice from a radiation expert on action to take
(b) stage 2 is invoked in more serious cases and when extensive action is needed to protect the public.

Under NAIR, help is provided by major nuclear installations, Ministry of Defence (MOD) and hospitals' medical physics departments nominated under the scheme and listed in *The NAIR Handbook* [137].

Appendix 1   Roles and responsibilities of the employer[1] using ionising radiation

While every attempt has been made to include as many of the employer's responsibilities as possible, the list in this Appendix is not necessarily exhaustive. Guidance has been issued jointly by the HSE and the Health Departments as The Regulatory Requirements for Medical Exposure to Ionising Radiation: An Employer's Overview HSG223 [138].

Before starting work with ionising radiation

1. Make a prior risk assessment[2] before starting a new radiation activity; establish suitable dose constraints for the restriction of exposure of each category of person likely to be exposed.

2. Obtain prior authorisation, either in generic or specific individual form, for the use of X-ray equipment for research or medical treatment and the use of accelerators (except electron microscopes).

3. Notify the HSE before radiation work is undertaken for the first time, or if any material changes are made to a previous notification.

4. Obtain registration and authorisation under RSA93 [7] or an exemption and conform to its conditions, if keeping, using or disposing of radioactive substances.

5. Prepare contingency plans and incorporate them in local rules if the risk assessment shows that an accident is reasonably foreseeable.

On commencing radiation work

6. Consult and appoint one or more suitable radiation protection advisers (RPA), providing adequate information and facilities for this function (Appendix 4).

7. Designate as appropriate the necessary controlled and supervised areas (to be described in local rules) with the necessary monitoring and controls (demarcation, signs, restricted access, systems of work, written arrangements, etc.) to provide adequate protection from external radiation and radioactive contamination, including washing and changing facilities as required.

8. Provide suitable and sufficient monitoring equipment and arrange for its maintenance and testing; ensure records of tests of monitoring equipment made by a qualified person are kept.

9. Ensure records of monitoring of designated areas are kept.

10. Obtain information from the manufacturer and installer about the proper use, testing and maintenance of radiation equipment after its critical examination, and involve the RPA.

11. Ensure the necessary steps are taken to restrict exposures to ionising radiation for staff, patients and others who may be exposed, setting investigation levels and providing written arrangements if necessary.

12. Demonstrate commitment to radiation protection through a written radiation safety policy, the establishment of a radiation protection committee and by clear management lines, clear actions and the involvement of senior staff.

---

1. For example, the NHS Trust, university dental school, private hospital or radiological clinic that is undertaking radiation exposures for diagnosis or treatment of patients.
2. It would be prudent to consult an RPA at this stage.

13   Provide sufficient engineering controls, design features, safety features and warning devices to restrict exposures so far as is reasonably practicable, and ensure that these are properly maintained and tested at suitable intervals.

14   Ensure personal protective equipment is provided, worn and maintained as appropriate, after all other measures have been considered.

15   Provide relevant local rules in compliance with the legislation, appointing radiation protection supervisors (RPS) as necessary to ensure the local rules are implemented.

16   Ensure that all employees (including RPS) are given appropriate radiation protection training sufficient to understand the risks and precautions needed, including female workers who may be pregnant or breastfeeding.

17   Co-operate with other employers concerning exposure of others, as appropriate.

18   Designate classified persons, if necessary, and provide appropriate radiation monitoring and medical surveillance (health record); inform all persons when they are designated as classified persons.

19   Provide personal radiation monitoring and dosimetry records as necessary; ensure that the results of personal monitoring are kept under review (as low as reasonably practical; ALARP) and that any unusual results are investigated.

20   Ensure that dose limits are not exceeded, including those for pregnant and breastfeeding staff.

21   Investigate and notify to the HSE overexposures received by staff, respecting subsequent dose limitations, and medical exposures that are significantly greater than intended resulting from an equipment malfunction or defect.

22   Review procedures periodically, preferably with the support of the radiation protection committee.

On using radioactive substances

23   Ensure radioactive substances in use are sealed wherever practicable to prevent leakage. Where this is impracticable, the substance should be contained to prevent leakage in so far as is practicable, keeping records of appropriate leakage tests in both cases.

24   Account for and keep records of the quantity and location (including ultimate disposal) of all radioactive substances.

25   Ensure radioactive substances are suitably contained and stored when not in use.

26   Ensure radioactive substances are suitably contained and labelled when in transit.

27   Notify the HSE (and EA/SEPA/EHSNI) if a quantity of radioactive substance is released or spilled in excess of that identified for the particular radionuclide resulting in significant contamination, having made an immediate investigation and a report of the incident.

On making medical exposures

28   Determine locally those who are the referrers, IR(ME)R practitioners, operators and medical physics experts (MPE) in diagnostic radiology, diagnostic nuclear medicine, radiotherapy and radiotherapy nuclear medicine.

29   Maintain records (available for inspection) of the training and continuing education of the above practitioners and operators, even when they are practising on contract at a site belonging to another radiation employer.

30   Ensure an MPE is closely involved in every radiotherapeutic medical exposure, except those involving standardised therapeutic nuclear medicine.

31   Ensure an MPE is available in standardised therapeutic nuclear medicine and diagnostic nuclear medicine practices.

32   Ensure an MPE is involved as appropriate for consultation on optimisation, including patient dosimetry and quality assurance (QA) and other radiation protection advice concerning medical exposure, in all other radiological practices not covered in paragraphs 30 and 31.

33   Ensure written protocols are in place for every type of standard radiological practice for each piece of equipment and a current inventory of equipment is kept for and at each radiological installation, ensuring the amount of equipment is limited to that necessary for the proper carrying out of medical exposures.

34   Establish QA programmes for standard operating procedures.

35   Establish recommendations concerning referral criteria for medical exposure, including radiation doses, and ensure these are available to the referrer.

36   Establish local diagnostic reference levels, undertake reviews and ensure corrective action is taken as necessary.

37   Establish dose constraints for research programmes where no direct medical benefit for the individual is expected from the exposure.

38   Ensure a clinical evaluation of the outcome of each medical exposure, including factors relevant to the patient dose, is recorded.

39   Ensure clinical audit is carried out in accordance with national procedures.

40   Implement written procedures (as specified in Schedule 1 of IR(ME)R [3] and reproduced here) and ensure these are complied with by the IR(ME)R practitioners and operators:

(a) to correctly identify the individual to be exposed to ionising radiation

(b) to identify individuals entitled to act as referrer or IR(ME)R practitioner or operator

(c) to be observed in the case of medicolegal exposures

(d) for making enquiries of females of childbearing age, to establish whether the individual is or may be pregnant or breastfeeding

(e) to ensure that QA programmes are followed

(f) for the assessment of patient dose and administered activity

(g) for the use of diagnostic reference levels for radiodiagnostic examinations

(h) for determining that research programmes are conducted on informed volunteers, subject to dose constraints when no direct medical benefit is expected, or subject to individual target levels of dose for patients who are expected to benefit from the exposure

(i) for the giving of information and written instructions to patients undergoing treatment or diagnosis with radioactive medicinal products

(j) for the carrying out and recording of a clinical evaluation for each medical exposure including, where appropriate, factors relevant to the patient dose, and

(k) to ensure that the probability and magnitude of accidental or unintended doses to patients from radiological practices is reduced so far as reasonably practicable.

41   Make an investigation of any incident involving a suspected or actual medical exposure that is significantly greater than intended (other than an incident resulting from an equipment malfunction (see paragraph 21) and notify the appropriate authority if the exposure has indeed occurred, with a detailed investigation.

42   Review procedures periodically, preferably with the support of a medical exposures committee.

On using equipment for medical exposure

43   Ensure that the equipment available for the range of examinations or treatments using ionising radiation is appropriate and is not used for procedures for which it is not suitable.

44   Ensure that the equipment is maintained in a manner consistent with the manufacturer's recommendations, to ensure that medical exposures are ALARP, and compatible with the intended clinical purpose or research objective.

45   Ensure that new or replacement diagnostic X-ray equipment is provided with a suitable means of indicating the quantity of radiation produced during a radiological procedure.

46   Draw up a suitable QA for the radiation equipment, having consulted the RPA and MPE.

47   Identify, provide, maintain and calibrate appropriate test equipment as part of the QA programme.

On investigating radiation incidents

48   Establish a mechanism for reporting, investigating, evaluating and recording incidents (including near misses) which lead to or have the potential for unnecessary or excessive exposure to ionising radiation.

49   Investigate and notify to the HSE overexposures received by staff, respecting subsequent dose limitations, and medical exposures that are significantly greater than intended resulting from an equipment malfunction or defect (copy of paragraph 21).

50   Notify the HSE (and EA/SEPA/EHSNI) if a quantity of radioactive substance is released or spilled in excess of that identified for the particular radionuclide resulting in significant contamination, having made an immediate investigation and a report of the incident (copy of paragraph 27).

51   Make an investigation of any incident involving a suspected or actual medical exposure that is significantly greater than intended (other than an incident resulting from an equipment malfunction (see paragraph 21) and notify the appropriate authority if the exposure has indeed occurred, with a detailed investigation (copy of paragraph 41).

Appendix 2 Example of radiation safety policy for NHS Trusts

For the generic purpose of this policy, non-ionising radiation has been included.

... NHS Trust will ensure, as far as reasonably practicable, the health and safety of its employees, of contractors working on the premises and of members of the public who may be exposed to the hazards arising from the use of ionising radiations, *lasers, ultra-violet and other non-ionising radiations.*

... NHS Trust will ensure that all diagnostic examinations involving medical exposures are performed with the radiation dose to the patient being as low as reasonably practicable (ALARP) to achieve the required clinical purpose, consistent with the employer's written procedures and protocols.

... NHS Trust will ensure that all exposures of target volumes for therapeutic radiology are individually planned, taking into account that doses of non-target volumes and tissues shall be ALARP, consistent with the intended radiotherapeutic purpose and the employer's written procedures and protocols.

... NHS Trust is committed to a policy of restricting exposures to ionising radiation in accordance with the ALARP principle and will effect this through the following organisational arrangements, through clear actions and through the involvement of senior staff.

Overall responsibility for ensuring that a radiation protection programme is implemented and reviewed will lie with ... through a Radiation Protection Committee, as part of the management and communication framework for Health and Safety.

Responsibility for the task of supervising the work with radiation, and ensuring that it is carried out in accordance with 'local rules', will lie with the Radiation Protection Supervisors (RPS) *and Laser Protection Supervisors.* The Director of Personnel/Human Resources has appointed these persons in writing and allocated the appropriate resources for them to carry out their functions.

Responsibility for the task of advising managers, departmental heads and staff, and the public on radiation matters will lie with ... a Radiation Protection Adviser appointed by the Trust, following consultation.

Responsibility for the task of medical supervision of employees designated as classified persons will lie with ... the Appointed Doctor.

Responsibility for the task of ensuring that radiation risk assessments are performed and reviewed, and the findings implemented, will lie with ...

Responsibility for the task of ensuring that all radiation equipment is installed, critically examined, commissioned and maintained to satisfy radiation safety requirement, and included in the equipment replacement programme of the appropriate Directorate, will lie with the relevant Clinical Director.

Responsibility for the task of maintaining a record of training of duty holders under IR(ME)R 2000 [3] (including other staff carrying out procedures on Trust premises) will lie with the relevant Clinical Directors and the Medical Director.

Responsibility for the justification and optimisation of each medical exposure will lie with the individual duty holder clearly identified in the employer's procedures.

Responsibility for maintaining a Trust inventory of radiation equipment, and ensuring that requests for radiation equipment are considered within the Trust's overall replacement programme, will lie with ...

Responsibility for ensuring that systems are in place for the safeguarding of radioactive materials, for the safe disposal of radioactive waste and ensuring that all requirements of the relevant regulations are satisfied will lie with ... The appointed Qualified Expert(s) are ... Responsibility for drawing up such systems and ensuring their implementation will lie with the relevant Clinical Directors.

Specific responsibility for laser advice will lie with ... a Laser Protection Adviser appointed by the Trust, and responsibility for advice on ultraviolet or other non-ionising radiation will lie with any of the appointed protection advisers.

... NHS Trust will establish good communication and co-operation between managers and advisers, and will give each adviser:

(a) the power to inspect and perform such tests as they consider appropriate, and

(b) sufficient resources to carry out their duties and any supporting work,

and will give each line manager the responsibility for the task of managing the radiation protection of all their members of staff in their area.

... NHS Trust will establish good communication and co-operation with those employers whose staff may be occupationally exposed by the Trust's radiation work.

Individual workers are required to work with radiation in such a way that they:

(a) exercise reasonable care and follow any relevant local rules

(b) use, as instructed, any protective equipment and personal dosemeters provided by the employer

(c) report to their line manager and RPS any defect in such equipment and dosemeters

(d) undertake any training deemed necessary

(e) comply with the employer's procedures and protocols for medical exposures

(f) report immediately to their RPS if any incident occurs in which a patient may have received a radiation exposure significantly greater than intended or any other incident in which a person is exposed to radiation, and

(g) do not recklessly endanger the safety of others.

Appendix 3   Role of the radiation protection supervisor

All the following items listed are the employer's legal responsibility, but the employer (e.g. the Trust Chief Executive or designated senior manager) may allocate the functions to a suitably trained radiation protection supervisor (RPS) or another appropriate person. Those functions shown in italics are unlikely to be within the scope of the RPS. The employer may find it helpful to copy the information mentioned in the list to the radiation protection adviser (RPA), or indeed request the RPS or other person to do this, so that the appropriate advice regarding subsequent actions can be given without undue delay.

General functions of the radiation protection supervisor

1   To oversee the work performed in the department for which the RPS is appointed so that it may be carried out in accordance with the local rules for that department.

2   To supervise the issue and collection of personal monitoring dosemeters at the appropriate times.

3   To keep copies of all results of dose monitoring for the current and at least four preceding years, noting that the approved dosimetry service maintains the dose records for classified persons for 50 years or to age 75 years.

4   To investigate and report to the Head of Department and the employer (e.g. the Trust Chief Executive or designated senior manager) any single dose reading exceeding 1 mSv, or the locally agreed investigation level.

5   To investigate and report to the Head of Department and the employer, without delay, incidents that may have exposed any person(s) to an unforeseen radiation exposure or any patient to an exposure significantly greater than that intended.

6   To observe, from time to time, all procedures involving ionising radiations carried on within the areas for which the RPS is responsible, and issue any instructions necessary to maintain doses to persons as low as reasonably practicable (ALARP).

7   To notify the employer of any changes in procedure or technique that might affect the designation of areas or of staff.

8   To assist in performing risk assessments, including those for pregnant and breastfeeding staff, as appropriate.

9   To ensure that all radiation monitors in the department's care are regularly checked, and are calibrated annually under the guidance of a qualified person (QP).

10   To supply the employer, on request and at least annually, with a summary of the personal monitoring results.

11   *To ensure that any necessary action is taken as advised by reports of the RPA.*

12   *To ensure that the employer appoints a deputy to act on behalf of the RPS during any extended period of absence from the department.*

13   *To undertake an annual review of radiation safety and submit an annual report to the Radiation Protection Committee.*

14   To ensure that local rules and amendments are read and understood by all relevant staff and that a record of such occasions is kept.

15   *To ensure that any contingency plans are reviewed on a regular basis.*

16   *To ensure that, after maintenance or repair, any equipment affecting radiation exposure of patients is checked for correct performance before being put back into clinical use.*

17   To make arrangements for the medical supervision of any classified persons working in the designated areas.

18   To make appropriate arrangements for outside workers working in controlled areas.

19   To act as the first point of reference on questions of practical radiation protection.

20   To assist in the derivation of local rules and schemes of work to ensure that they are practicable and usable.

21   *To ensure that staff are adequately trained and instructed before carrying out new techniques or using new equipment.*

In addition, for work with diagnostic and dental X-ray machines

22   To ensure that all protective lead aprons and gloves associated with the department are examined at least annually, and to keep a record of the results.

23   To arrange for appropriate dosimetric measurements to be made, and records kept, when staff are required to support patients undergoing a radiodiagnostic examination.

24   *To ensure that an effective quality assurance (QA) programme is maintained for all radiological equipment in the department and that records of QA, including equipment faults and actions, are available for inspection by the Health and Safety Inspectors and IR(ME)R Inspectors.*

In addition, for work in nuclear medicine and the therapeutic use of radionuclides

25   To supervise the carrying out of contamination monitoring on a regular basis and the recording of the results thereof.

26   *To ensure that staff are adequately trained and instructed before carrying out new radionuclide procedures.*

27   To arrange for the monitoring of controlled areas before allowing cleaners or tradesmen to enter in accordance with a system of work.

28   *To supply the employer (competent person) and qualified expert (RPA), on request and at least annually, with a record of radionuclide use and waste disposal, in accordance with IRR99 [1] and the conditions of an authorisation certificate under RSA93 [7].*

29   To ensure that appropriate action is taken following any contamination by radioactive material of the workplace or person. To record the results thereof and to report to the employer when contamination cannot be reduced below 40 Bq cm^{-2}.

30   *To ensure that an effective QA programme is maintained for all counting and imaging equipment and that records of QA are available for inspection by the Health and Safety Inspectors and the IR(ME)R Inspectors.*

In addition, for work with radionuclides

31   To supervise the carrying out of contamination monitoring on a regular basis, and the recording of the results thereof.

32   *To ensure that staff are adequately trained and instructed before carrying out new radionuclide procedures.*

33   To arrange for the monitoring of controlled areas before allowing cleaners or tradesmen to enter in accordance with a system of work.

34   *To supply the employer (competent person) and qualified expert (RPA/QE), on request and at least annually, with a record of radionuclide use and waste disposal, in accordance with IRR99 and the conditions of an authorisation certificate under RSA93.*

35   To ensure that appropriate action is taken following any contamination by radioactive material of the workplace or person. To record the results thereof and to report to the employer when contamination cannot be reduced below the appropriate derived level.

36   *To ensure that an effective QA programme is maintained for dose measuring equipment and procedures and that records of QA including equipment faults and actions are available for inspection by the Health and Safety Inspectors and IR(ME)R Inspectors.*

In addition, for work in radiotherapy

37   *To investigate and report to the Head of Department and the employer, without delay, incidents (in addition to item 5) that may have exposed any patient to a medical exposure significantly less than that intended.*

38   *To ensure that an effective QA programme is maintained for all radiotherapy equipment in the department and that records of QA, including equipment faults and actions, are available for inspection by the Health and Safety Inspectors and IR(ME)R Inspectors.*

In addition, for work with sealed sources

39   *To supply the employer (competent person) and qualified expert (RPA/QE), on request and at least annually, with a record of radionuclide use and waste disposal, in accordance with IRR99 and the conditions of an authorisation certificate under RSA93.*

40   *To supply the employer (competent person) and qualified expert (RPA/QE), on request and at least annually, with a record of leakage testing, in accordance with IRR99 and the conditions of an authorisation certificate under RSA93.*

Appendix 4   Role of the radiation protection adviser

The radiation protection adviser (RPA) is an individual or corporate body that meets the criteria of competence specified by the HSE and, for ongoing consultation, is appointed in writing by a radiation employer. The appointment includes the scope of the advice that is required as appropriate on the following matters (IRR99 Schedule 5 [1])

1   The implementation of requirements as to controlled and supervised areas.

2   The prior examination of plans for installations and the acceptance into service of new or modified sources of ionising radiation in relation to any engineering controls, design features, safety features and warning devices provided to restrict exposure to ionising radiation.

3   The regular calibration of equipment provided for monitoring levels of ionising radiation and the regular checking that such equipment is serviceable and correctly used.

4   The periodic examination and testing of engineering controls, design features, safety features and warning devices and regular checking of systems of work, including any written arrangements provided to restrict exposure to ionising radiation.

In addition, the employer and the radiation employer should consult an RPA on the following matters

5   Risk assessments, and contingency plans if necessary.

6   The form and content of local rules for each designated controlled or supervised area.

7   The conduct of investigations and subsequent reports as necessary.

8   Dose assessment and recording, including personal and area monitoring.

9   The selection and use of appropriate personal protective equipment.

10   Critical examinations of newly installed or repaired equipment and articles for work with ionising radiation.

11   Quality assurance programmes for medical radiation equipment.

12   Arrangements for outside workers.

13   Staff training as appropriate for classified persons, outside workers, those who enter controlled areas under written arrangements, other staff as necessary, safety representatives, radiation protection supervisors, staff undertaking monitoring, supervisors and managers with specific radiation responsibilities.

14   Information and instructions for pregnant and breastfeeding employees.

15   Radiopharmacy design and associated protocols in conjunction with the radiopharmacist.

16   Training for emergencies.

The employer will also need advice on any other matters as listed in Appendix 1, although items 28 to 45 may lie in the domain of the medical physics expert.

The HSE Criteria of Competence are detailed on their web site and require that, to meet the definition of an RPA in IRR99 [1] an individual must hold either a National or Scottish Vocational qualification in radiation protection at level 4 or a certificate issued by an assessing body recognised by HSE for that purpose, e.g. RPA2000.[1] Persons who were previously appointed as RPAs under previous regulations will need to comply with this requirement not later than 31 December 2004 to remain eligible under IRR99 [1].

---

1   RPA2000 was set up by the Society for Radiological Protection, the Institute of Physics and Engineering in Medicine, the Institute of Radiation Protection and the Association of University Radiation Protection Officers. Details about making an application are available from http://www.srp-uk.org/

Appendix 5   Role of the medical physics expert

General

In this appendix the role of the medical physics expert (MPE) is detailed. An MPE is defined as a state registered clinical scientist with MIPEM or equivalent and at least six years of appropriate experience in the clinical specialty.

The involvement of an MPE, and the need for close collaboration with professional colleagues, is clearly indicated for every aspect leading to a medical exposure and is essential where therapeutic exposures are concerned. The involvement will include: advice on patient doses which will help in the risk assessment and so the justification process; measurement of patient doses and equipment performance which will enable optimisation of exposures; advice on medical exposures required for research proposals; and advice on radiation protection concerning medical exposures. The extent of the involvement of the MPE in research will vary with the modality and the project.

It should be recognised that some of the duties and responsibilities identified here may not necessarily be the sole preserve of the MPE. However, at least some input, lead or advice from an MPE will be necessary on all medical exposure issues which might impinge on radiation safety, radiation dose measurement or optimisation.

The medical physicist working in the clinical environment can have many roles in addition to the MPE role. These roles are detailed elsewhere in the relevant IPEM role documents available from the IPEM web site at http://www.ipem.org.uk.

1   Medical physics expert in diagnostic radiology

The MPE in diagnostic radiology will be actively involved in, or available for consultation on, all matters concerning diagnostic and interventional radiology exposures, including research applications. Their involvement will be especially warranted where doses are known to be high, e.g. computed tomography (CT) and interventional radiology, for optimisation of doses for high risk groups such as infants, for dose constraints in health screening and for risk assessment in research proposals. The various matters are listed here.

1.1   Role in justification:

  (a) generic risk assessment, especially for new equipment or techniques
  (b) communication with practitioner
  (c) risk assessment for research proposals, and
  (d) dose constraints in research.

1.2   Optimisation, including dosimetry and equipment quality assurance (QA)

  (a) systems for dose calibration and quantification
  (b) diagnostic reference levels and review
  (c) patient dose monitoring programme and review, including dose reduction strategy
  (d) image quality evaluation and outcome performance indicators
  (e) QA, advice on quality control, communication and review
  (f) selection of equipment to include purchase and specification of radiology equipment
  (g) commissioning of new equipment and communication with applications specialist
  (h) advice on suspension of existing equipment
  (i) maintenance of equipment inventory
  (j) imaging equipment replacement policy review
  (k) audit and development of audit for medical exposures
  (l) operator functions as identified for the MPE in the employer's procedures, and
  (m) communication with other employees and with maintenance engineers on practical aspects.

1.3   Other radiation protection matters concerning medical exposures:

    (a) incident investigation including patient dose assessment

    (b) radiation protection of comforters and carers

    (c) communication role during inspection by the relevant statutory authorities

    (d) communication with other employers

    (e) advice on the implementation of the employer's procedures

    (f) training

    (g) role in multidisciplinary medical audit and review, and

    (h) clarifying overlaps with other radiation protection and exposure legislation.

2   Medical physics expert in nuclear medicine

The role of the medical physicist in nuclear medicine has been described in detail by a joint working group of the BIR, BNMS and IPEM, *Guidelines for the Provision of Physics Support to Nuclear Medicine* [139]. This report emphasises the need for every department undertaking nuclear medicine to have the support of at least one MPE in nuclear medicine. The report also recommends suitable staffing levels, depending on the number and type of procedures undertaken and the type of institution.

It is essential that the MPE is closely involved in all non-standard nuclear medicine therapy administrations and is available for the following activities, either personally or by directing local medical physics support.

2.1   Role in justification:

    (a) involvement in all applications for ARSAC certification [7], to be able to sign that the staff and facilities available are sufficient to undertake all procedures for which certification is sought

    (b) agreement on protocols for all therapeutic administrations

    (c) advice regarding dosimetry for pregnant and breastfeeding patients

    (d) dose constraints for research proposals, and

    (e) introduction and validation of new procedures and protocols.

2.2   Optimisation, including patient dosimetry and equipment QA:

    (a) advice on all scientific and technical aspects for diagnostic procedures, including patient dosimetry and the establishment and review of diagnostic reference levels

    (b) advice on dosimetry for radionuclide therapy (also see item 3.2 (c))

    (c) continuous monitoring of all QA aspects of the service, including calibration of radionuclide dose calibrators

    (d) involvement in the provision and assessment of dedicated nuclear medicine software

    (e) equipment management and equipment quality control (QC), including the inventory

    (f) involvement in the specification, choice and acceptance testing of new equipment

    (g) agreement regarding the form of all QC procedures on equipment, and

    (h) advice on suitability of equipment for specific tasks and need for maintenance, repair or replacement.

2.3   Other radiation protection matters concerning medical exposures:

    (a) presence at all therapeutic administrations that are non-standard or being undertaken for the first time

    (b) involvement in the design of all nuclear medicine facilities in collaboration with the radiation protection adviser (RPA)

(c) involvement in radiation protection, in collaboration with the RPA and radiation protection supervisor (RPS); this will include the assessment of risk, provision of local rules, stock control and transport of radioactive materials, management and responsibility for radioactive waste, advice to staff who nurse or come into contact with nuclear medicine patients, advice to patients leaving hospital and to their comforters and carers, the investigation of incidents and response to radioactive contamination emergencies, and

(d) involvement in multidisciplinary clinical audit and external audit (e.g. by HSE or EA (SEPA in Scotland or EHSNI in Northern Ireland)).

3 Medical physics expert in radiotherapy

The MPE in radiotherapy must be closely involved in and have the responsibility, where indicated, for the following.

3.1 Role in justification:

(a) consultation on the suitability of treatment techniques, with involvement at a level commensurate with the responsibility for the dosimetry and accuracy of treatment.

3.2 Optimisation including patient dosimetry and equipment QA:

(a) responsibility for management of the QC programme

(b) responsibility for the technical management of clinical computer software and computer systems

(c) available to give advice on the dosimetry of radionuclide therapy and, in co-operation with the RPA and RPS, on the radiation safety of these procedures; being present at all administrations not covered by a protocol (see also items 2.2(b) and 2.3(a))

(d) management of all decommissioning of radiotherapy or brachytherapy equipment, in co-operation with the RPA and RPS as appropriate

(e) consultation on, and responsibility for, the suitability and accuracy of the methods used to calculate dose distributions in radiotherapy and in brachytherapy procedures, and in particular the optimisation of complex treatment plans

(f) responsibility for management of the patient dosimetry programme

(g) responsibility for the definitive calibration of radiotherapy equipment and dosemeters (see Appendix 15)

(h) responsibility for all aspects of the management of secondary standard dosemeters

(i) responsibility for management of the routine dosimetry programme

(j) advice on specification and selection of all radiotherapy and brachytherapy equipment

(k) oversight of the installation and responsibility for all acceptance testing and commissioning, and

(l) collaboration with the RPA concerning the critical examination of all new and upgraded equipment.

3.3 Other radiation protection matters concerning medical exposures:

(a) consultation on all strategic planning issues which involve possible changes to the radiotherapy and brachytherapy service, including decisions on therapy equipment, treatment modalities and techniques, and changes to the design and layout of the building where radiation protection considerations may apply

(b) co-operation with the RPA over treatment room design

(c) advice and involvement as appropriate, in co-operation with the RPA and RPS, regarding all aspects of the safety of radiotherapy and brachytherapy equipment

(d) investigation of any radiation incidents, including dose reconstruction, in co-operation with the RPA and RPS

(e) consultation on the radiation safety aspects of all research projects in radiotherapy or brachytherapy, with an RPA as appropriate, and

(f) management and co-ordination of the response to radiation emergencies, in co-operation with the RPA and RPS.

Appendix 6 Example of a pro-forma risk assessment for the Ionising Radiations Regulations 1999

Location of work
Date of commencement
Description of work
Source of radiation
Hazards (radiation accident)
Staff involved
Other persons involved

Exposed groups and dose constraints

ALARP assessment

Hazard assessment

Control measures

Action to be taken

Signature: .... Date: ....

Designation: .... Date to be reviewed: ....

c.c. *Line Manager, RPS, Head of Department, RPA, and H&S Adviser*

Appendix 7 Example of a radiation incident report

1 What happened?

2 When did it occur?

3 Where did it happen?

4 Who was involved?

5 Assessment of doses received by people exposed or injured?

6 Who was notified? When?

7 What action was taken?

8 Any further action required?

Date: .... Signature: ....

Position: ....

Please return to:

Appendix 8   Ionising Radiation Incident Database

1 Introduction

In the United Kingdom in 1996, the National Radiological Protection Board (NRPB), the Health and Safety Executive (HSE) and the Environment Agency (the Agency) jointly established the Ionising Radiations Incident Database (IRID) and published its specifications [26]. This Appendix provides an overview of the database and its operation. Details of the first 100 cases reported have been published [27]. These relate mainly to the industrial and research and teaching sectors, but IRID was designed to encompass occupational exposure in the medical sector and the purpose of this Appendix is to encourage reporting of such incidents. More details can be obtained from the IRID co-ordinator at NRPB, Chilton, Didcot, Oxon, OX11 0RQ, Tel/Fax: 01235 822781.

2 Objectives

The objectives of the database are:

(a)   to act as a national focus on ionising radiation incidents, primarily in the non-nuclear sector

(b)   through appropriate publications to provide feedback and guidance to users on preventing, or limiting the consequences of, radiation accidents, and

(c)   to provide regulatory bodies, and others with advisory responsibilities, with analyses of data that help in assessing priorities in resource allocation.

3 Scope

The database is designed to cover radiological accidents and incidents involving actual or potential occupational and public exposure. It specifically includes near misses as there are often valuable lessons to be learned from such occurrences. Therefore in developing the database, it was felt more appropriate to use the word 'incident', as this has a wider meaning than 'accident'. The definition used for IRID is:

An ionising radiation incident is any unintended or ill-advised event, including events resulting from operator error, equipment failure, or the failure of management systems that warranted investigation.

The database deals primarily with the non-nuclear sector, i.e. industry, research, teaching and medicine. It specifically excludes nuclear, transport and patient exposure incidents, as there are existing mechanisms for recording these sorts of event.

4 Confidentiality

Many organisations see the value of sharing information and learning the lesson, but if this is likely to bring them adverse publicity or increased scrutiny by the regulators, then they might be very cautious about contributing to the database. Therefore it was clear from the beginning that the confidentiality of information would be a major issue.

To address this problem, all information contained in the database is unattributable and confidential. Only the originator of the incident entry will know the names of the organisations or individuals concerned and all data are presented to NRPB in a format that provides anonymity. There will be some instances where, because of the affiliation of the contributor, NRPB may be aware of the organisation involved (but not the names of the persons). For its part, NRPB undertakes not to divulge any such privileged information to a third party. HSE and the Agency are well aware of the natural wariness that potential contributors may have in respect of the involvement of regulatory bodies. Therefore they have given assurances that they will not seek to obtain further information from the other partners (or the contributing organisation if different) about any incident recorded on the database that was not reported to the regulators. This would not prevent HSE and the Agency following up incidents that are notified to them by other means, e.g. through statutory reporting requirements or complaints from employees or members of the public.

5 Format

The database consists of 24 fields, including a text field as summarised in Table A8.1 below. Each non-text field contains either numerical data (e.g. dose in millisieverts) or one or more codes that categorise the incident.

Table A8.1 IRID fields

Field	Title	Field	Title
1	Case number	13	Occupation of worker(s)
2	Area	14	Type of equipment
3	Incident date	15	Nuclide(s) involved
4	Incident category	16	Activity
5	Exposure level	17	Kilovoltage of radiation generator
6	Site level	18	Cause of incident
7	Nature of incident	19	Contingency plans
8	Number exposed: occupational	20	RPA involvement
9	Number exposed: public	21	RPS involvement
10	Whole body dose(s)	22	Follow-up action (e.g. improvements)
11	Extremity dose(s)	23	Date of entry in database
12	Internal organ dose(s)	24	Description: text field

Each field has a range of options to choose from that allow incidents to be categorised and so facilitate searching and analysis of the database. For example, Table A8.2 shows the top level coding for types of equipment involved, while Table A8.3 shows the subsidiary coding for the main types of medical equipment.

Table A8.2 Type of equipment involved

01	Diagnostic X-ray	15	Analytical equipment
02	Veterinary X-ray	16	X-ray optics
03	Teletherapy	17	Electron beam equipment
04	Brachytherapy	18	Unsealed radioactive materials (not covered
05	Nuclear medicine (therapy and diagnostic)		elsewhere)
06	Baggage inspection/security	19	Smoke detectors
07	Gamma radiography site	20	Consumer products
08	Gamma radiography facility (permanent)	21	Static eliminators
09	X-ray radiography site	22	Laboratory/calibration sealed sources
10	X-ray radiography facility (permanent)	23	Yield monitors on agricultural equipment
11	Irradiation facilities (X, gamma, electron)	24	Radioactive waste treatment plant
12	Thickness gauges	25	Environmental tracer work
13	Level gauges	26	Processing of ore and scrap materials
14	Density/moisture gauges	27	Other (specify in text description)

Table A8.3

01 Diagnostic X-ray	03 Teletherapy	04 Brachytherapy
01 = Dental intra-oral (standard)	01 = Gamma	01 = Interstitial implants
02 = Dental OPG	02 = Megavoltage	02 = Applicators
03 = Dental cephalostat	03 = Orthovoltage	03 = Remote after loading
04 = Mobile radiography	04 = Superficial voltage	04 = Intracavity implants
05 = Mobile image intensifier	05 = Electron	
06 = General radiography	06 = Neutron	
07 = Installed image intensifier	07 = Therapy simulator	
08 = Mammography		05 Nuclear medicine
09 = Computed tomography		01 = Therapy
10 = X-ray bone mineralisation		02 = Diagnostic
11 = Gamma bone mineralisation		

6 Feedback

Field 24 is a text field that follows the general format of description of incident, doses received, other actual or potential consequences, e.g. environmental or health, and lesson learned. The format was designed to be readily reproducible in reports and for subsequent use as training material. The first review of cases reported and operation of the database was published in 1999 [27]. It covered 100 cases and, for a number of the cases, artists' drawings of the circumstances of the incident were produced. The descriptions of the incidents and the drawings may be freely copied for use as training material or in published documents, providing an appropriate acknowledgement of IRID is included.

Appendix 9   Record keeping

The following records (**in bold type**), which should be kept for the time stated, are required either by the Ionising Radiations Regulations 1999 (IRR99 with regulation number or schedule) and L121 (paragraph number) [1, 2], the Ionising Radiation (Medical Exposures) Regulations 2000 (IR(ME)R with regulation number) and regulatory guidance (RG with paragraph number) [3, 4], the Radioactive Substances Act (RSA93) [7], the Radiation (Emergency Preparedness and Public Information) Regulations [28], the Health and Safety at Work Act (HSWA) [21] or by the Management of Health and Safety at Work Regulations 1999 (MHSWR with regulation number) [16] or as otherwise indicated. Other records or documents recommended to be kept to demonstrate regulatory compliance (in plain text) should be kept up to date. The list is not necessarily exhaustive.

Record or documentation	Number of years	Regulation	MDGN paragraph
Radiation protection policy		HSWA 2(3)	1.5
Health and safety arrangements including periodic reviews of protection measures		HSWA 5 MHSWR 4	1.4,16.18
Authorisations		IRR99 5	1.21, Appendix 18
Notifications and any subsequent changes		IRR99 6, Sch.2 and Sch.3	1.26, 8.16
Risk assessments and their review		IRR99 7, MHSWR 3(6)	1.16, 1.18, 2.72, 8.14, 9.51, 16.5
Local rules, systems of work and written arrangements		IRR99 8, 17	1.59, 1.61, 1.65, 8.46, 8.57, 9.52, 11.21, 12.29, 14.24
Investigation report for doses over the investigation level	at least 2 years	IRR99 8(7), L121 paragraphs 158 and 162	1.97
Examination of engineering controls etc to restrict exposures	until next test	IRR99 10(1), L121 paragraph 175	14.13
Inspection and verification of protective clothing including respiratory equipment	**at least 2 years**	**IRR99 10(2)**	**3.122, 10.55**
Personal dose records for classified staff, including outside workers	**to age 75 years but at least 50 years from last entry**	**IRR99 11 and 21**	**1.8, 1.78**
Contingency plans		IRR99 12	8.48, 14.24
Details of incidents involving the possibility of radioactive contamination			1.100, 10.91 Appendix 7
Appointment of RPAs		IRR99 13	7.9
Radiation protection training of all staff		IRR99 14	1.4, 12.26, Appendix 1 item 16
Appointment of RPSs and their duties		IRR99 17(4)	1.69
Personal monitoring	**2 years**	**IRR99 18(5)**	**1.83, 5.35**

continued

Record or documentation	Number of years	Regulation	MDGN paragraph
Monitoring measurements of controlled and supervised areas	**at least 2 years**	IRR99 16, **IRR99 19(4)**	1.61, 1.96, 10.32, 10.84, 11.25, 12.45, 17.28, 18.14
Monitoring equipment annual tests	**at least 2 years**	**IRR99 19(4)**	**1.64**
QP appointment and training			1.63
Health record for classified staff (details in IRR99 Schedule 7)	**to age 75 years but at least 50 years**	**IRR99 20(2), 24(3)**	**1.76, Appendix 1 item 18**
Outside worker's passbook		IRR99 21(5), Sch.6	1.82
Dose record summary	**at least 2 years from end of year to which summary relates**	**IRR99 21(7)**	**1.78**
ADS issue of radiation passbooks – retention of record required by the now revoked IR(OW)R 5 [140]	**at least 5 years after the passbook ceases to be used**	**IRR99 41(4)**	**1.82**
Record of those supporting diagnostic X-ray patients			3.42
Estimated exposure investigation	**at least 2 years**	**IRR99 22(4)**	**1.78**
Dosimetry assessment after an accident	**to age 75 years but at least 50 years from the date of the accident**	**IRR99 23(2)**	**1.90**
Report of immediate investigation of an overexposure	**at least 2 years**	**IRR99 25(2)**	**1.99**
Report of full investigation of a notifiable overexposure	**to age 75 years but at least 50 years from the overexposure**	**IRR99 25(2)**	**1.99**
Leakage tests for radioactive substances (at least every 2 years)	**at least 2 years or until a further test record is made**	**IRR99 27(3)**	**8.36, 14.8, 17.30**
Stock and audit records re quantity and location of radioactive substances, as received, issued and returned, or administered to patients	**at least 2 years from date of last entry (with annual verification)**	**IRR99 28 RSA93**	**8.6, 9.53, 10.68, 10.71, 11.25, 12.23, 13.24, 14.9, 17.5, 17.29, 17.30**
Radioactive shipments (e.g. transport documents)	**at least 2 years**	**[96]**	**17.45**
Safety adviser's annual and accident reports	**at least 5 years**	**[97]**	**17.44**
Disposal of radioactive substances	**at least 2 years from disposal**	**IRR99 28**	**13.24, 17.29, 17.37, 18.8, 18.9, 18.28**
Report of immediate investigation following an occurrence of radioactive release, loss or theft	**at least 2 years from the date of the investigation**	**IRR99 30(5)**	**14.9, 17.34**

continued overleaf

Record or documentation	Number of years	Regulation	MDGN paragraph
Report of full investigation following a notifiable occurrence of radioactive release, loss or theft	**at least 50 years**	**IRR99 30(5)**	**14.9**
Critical examination	from acceptance for the working life of the equipment	IRR99 31	1.30, 8.22
Incident report following a medical exposure significantly greater than intended due to equipment malfunction	**at least 2 years for the immediate report and at least 50 years for the detailed report**	**IRR99 32(7)**	**1.101, Appendices 7 and 8**
Maintenance and defects record for radiation equipment, including QA measurements and calibrations		IRR99 32, HSG226 [10]	1.51, 2.54, 3.32, 3.80, 5.26, 8.21, 8.24, 8.26, 8.32, 8.39, 10.50, 11.25
Emergency exposures	**to age 75 years but at least 50 years**	**REPPIR 14(8)**	**19.12**
Referrers, practitioners and operators	*** up to date**	**IR(ME)R 11(4)**	**2.6, 7.5, 7.7, 7.10**
Training and continuing education for practitioners and operators whether directly employed or subcontracted	*** up to date**	**IR(ME)R 4(4), 11(4), RG37, RG85 to RG87**	**2.6, 2.13, 2.75, 2.76**
Employer's standard operating procedures	**regular (annual) review**	**IR(ME)R 4(1), Sch. 1, RG14, RG33**	**2.6, 2.45, Appendix 1**
Written protocols for equipment	**up to date**	**IR(ME)R 4(2), RG29**	**Appendix 1 item 33**
QA programmes		IR(ME)R 4(3)	2.13, 2.57, 3.9, 3.32, 8.23, 8.2, 11.25
Diagnostic reference levels	**regular review**	**IR(ME)R 4(3)**	**2.48**
Patient dose over the DRL		IR(ME)R 4(6)	2.58
Research projects		IR(ME)R 4(3), 7(4c), RG65	2.64, 2.68, Appendix 10
Justification of medical exposures		**IR(ME)R 6(1), RG50**	**3.7, 3.9, 5.43, 7.6, 9.3, 9.9, 10.19**
Generic risk assessments for patient exposures			2.66, 2.72
Pregnant or breastfeeding patients		IR(ME)R 6(1e), 6(3c), 7(7e), RG71, RG71, RG92	2.33, 3.9, 3.56, 10.19, 10.26
Written instructions to patients	review at least every 3 years	IR(ME)R 7(5), 7(6)	2.72, 7.10, 10.69, 15.17
Clinical evaluation report and patient dose factors	*****	**IR(ME)R 7(8)**	**2.55, 2.56, 2.57**
Administrations of radioactive substances recorded in patients' records	*	IR(ME)R 7(8)	10.71, 12.23, 17.36

continued

Record or documentation	Number of years	Regulation	MDGN paragraph
Treatment records including doses	at least 8 years after the end of treatment*#	IR(ME)R 7(8)	2.25, 7.6, 8.65
Record of administration of radioactive sources and of the removal of temporary implants		IR(ME)R 7(8)	9.50, 9.53, 14.9, 17.31, 17.36
Patient diagnostic X-ray dose	*	IR(ME)R 7(8)	2.33, 2.57, 3.63, 3.77, 3.91, 5.43
Record of completion of patient examination		RG72	2.33
Incident report following a medical exposure significantly greater than intended due to human error	*** at least 2 years for the immediate report and at least 50 years for the detailed report**	**IR(ME)R 4(5)**	**2.58, 2.60**
Decisions regarding notification of patient exposures significantly greater than intended	*	IR(ME)R 4(5), RG68	2.62
Medical physics experts		IR(ME)R 9	2.6, 7.8
Radiation equipment inventory	*** up to date**	**IR(ME)R 10, RG82**	**8.5, 8.6, 8.7**
Alteration of output or quality of radiation as a result of modification or maintenance of apparatus		RG16, HSG226	1.32, 2.39, 3.32, 3.33, 5.26, 8.21, 8.43, 10.51
Patient dosimetry equipment		HSG226	8.26, 10.48

* See Health Services Circular HSC 1999/053 *For the Record* [141] for guidance on retention of records; available at http://www.doh.gov.uk/nhsexec/manrec.htm

The RCR recommends radiotherapy records are kept as a permanent record on a computer database. Where this is not possible hard-copy records and simulator films should be kept for the patient's lifetime plus 5 years [142].

Appendix 10 Guidance on medical research exposures

1 Regulatory aspects

1.1   Practitioners, operators and employers who expose human subjects to ionising radiation for the purpose of medical research have statutory duties under IR(ME)R 2000 [3] in addition to the radiation protection requirements of the IRR99 [1] for medical exposures.

1.2   Every individual medical exposure shall take place under the responsibility of an IR(ME)R practitioner who justifies the exposure. Such a person has to be adequately trained with respect to IR(ME)R Schedule 2 [3]. If this training is not obtained through a formal educational route then the regulations recognise a certificate obtained from an institute that is entitled to award degrees or diplomas, that attests to the person being adequately trained, as proof of training.

1.3   The IR(ME)R practitioner may delegate, to the operator (see paragraph 1.4 below) who directly exposes the individual to ionising radiation, the authorisation of exposures in accordance with written guidelines issued by the IR(ME)R practitioner and conforming with the employer's procedure for authorisation.

1.4   The operator is the person responsible for carrying out any practical aspects of the exposures (e.g. pressing the exposure button, injecting the radionuclide). The operator must be adequately trained and be able to provide proof of training.

1.5   There is evidence that young persons have a significantly greater than average risk of radiation-induced cancer. Consequently, individuals over 50 years of age should be selected for recruitment into research studies where practicable. Ionising radiation should not be used on children and young persons (under 18 years of age) unless the area of research is directly aimed at this age group. When children are entered into the research study, special justification is required if the effective dose exceeds 0.1 mSv.

1.6   Pregnant or potentially pregnant subjects (both volunteers and patients) should be excluded, unless their participation is essential to the research study.

1.7   In the case of studies involving the administration of radioactive substances, subjects who are breastfeeding should be excluded unless their participation is essential.

1.8   Radiation from clinical exposures otherwise normally indicated for the patient should be excluded from the risk assessment of the research proposal.

1.9   Procedures should be selected such as to ensure a dose of ionising radiation to the patient as low as reasonably practicable (ALARP), consistent with the intended purpose.

1.10 Dose constraints should be set down and adhered to for individuals for whom no direct benefit is expected. Target doses for patients who can expect some individual benefit should be identified and not exceeded, to ensure the ratio of benefit to risk remains greater than one.

1.11 The information for patients must be honest without causing concern. The involvement of ionising radiation should be made clear. Many patients are not aware that, say, mammography, a computed tomography (CT) scan or bone densitometry involves the use of X-rays.

2 Levels of risk

2.1   The general guidelines that are used in looking at a research proposal appear in ICRP Publication 62, *Radiological Protection in Biomedical Research* [31], which contains the following Table A10.1.

Table A10.1 Levels of risk

Level of risk	Total risk of detrimental radiation effect	Effective dose for adults (mSv)	Level of societal benefit needed
I Trivial	~10^{-6} or less	<0.1	Minor
IIa Minor	~10^{-5}	0.1 to 1	Intermediate
IIb Intermediate	~10^{-4}	1 to 10	Moderate
III Moderate	~10^{-3} or more	>10	Substantial

2.2   It should be noted that the risk is the total detriment from the exposure; namely the sum of the probability of fatal cancers, the weighted probability of non-fatal cancers and the probability over all succeeding generations of serious hereditary disease, resulting from the dose. For investigations involving children, the detriment per unit dose is 2 to 3 times larger than for young adults; for people aged 50 years or over it is only about 1/5 of that for young adults.

2.3   As a rough guide, for studies where the benefit will be related to increases in knowledge leading to a general benefit but are of no direct benefit to the irradiated individual, the effective dose should be no higher than that in IIa. These figures could be used to give a guide to values of dose constraints. Higher dose constraints may be acceptable if the benefit is more directly aimed at the cure or prevention of disease.

2.4   An important task for the Local Research Ethics Committee (LREC) is to satisfy itself that the extra clinical information to be gained from the study warrants the risk involved. This is not possible unless the risk can be estimated, which is only possible if the radiation dose the subjects are likely to receive is known.

Where there is benefit to the individual volunteer

2.5   The risks at levels I, IIa and IIb are quite small compared with risks inherent in many of the diseases studied. It is possible that, if the risk of the research exposure is accepted, some risk of comparable magnitude may be avoided. If so, this benefit should be argued in the proposal.

Where there is no benefit to the individual volunteer

2.6   Where there is no particular benefit to the individual, it must be recognised by the researcher that the risk is one that the individual does not need to take. It is therefore essential to tell potential volunteers about the radiation risk in ways that enable them to give informed consent. For this purpose, it is equally undesirable to leave them with too high or too low a perception of risk. Guidance on the significance of the risk in each category, and on its presentation to potential volunteers, is given in Table A10.2.

3   Communication of risk

3.1   The communication and explanation of risk is very difficult, due to the facts that the public's perception of risk is often poor and that their responses to risk are bound up with their own self-perception, their values and their social and cultural background. Risk assessments should be performed to help inform the LREC and the volunteers, well in advance, about the risks of the exposure. This must be communicated to the volunteers by the referrer or research co-ordinator and confirmed by the operator.

3.2   Risk comparisons may be communicated using:

(a) dose comparison (either natural background, other examination or other activity)

(b) lifetime risk of death comparison (e.g. cancer, ischaemic heart disease, struck by lightning), and

(c) annual risk of death comparison (e.g. smoking 10 cigarettes per day, accident on road or at work, work in construction industry).

The form of the comparison will depend on the nature of the study and the health of the volunteers.

Table A10.2 Levels of risk, significance and presentation

Level of risk	Dose and risk perspective	Information to potential volunteers
Trivial (10^{-6} or less) 1 in a million {<0.1 mSv}	The radiation dose is less than the variation in annual dose from natural sources between different locations in the UK. For example, a greater dose increase would arise if someone, normally resident in York, took a hotel holiday in Cornwall for 2 weeks. The annual risk of homicide (1 in 100,000) is more than ten times greater than the risk (less than 1 in 1,000,000) from the research exposure.	At the **Trivial** level of risk, it is not helpful to quote numbers to potential volunteers who are unfamiliar with very low risks. They are far more likely to appreciate comparisons with risks of everyday activities.
Minor (10^{-5}) 1 in a hundred thousand {0.1 mSv to 1 mSv}	The radiation dose is less than the annual dose from natural sources in the UK. The risk is similar to the annual risk of homicide (1 in 100,000); 5 times less than the annual risk of a fatal road accident (1 in 17,000); and at least 250 times less than the natural annual cancer risk (1 in 400).	At the **Minor** level of risk, it may be helpful (but is not essential) to quote numerical risks. However, the protocol should require risk information to be given to volunteers in writing at the time of obtaining consent and a copy of that information should be included in the LREC submission.
Intermediate (10^{-4}) 1 in ten thousand {1 mSv to 10 mSv}	The radiation dose may exceed the classification level for occupational exposure or equivalent to at most 4 years natural background radiation. The risk (1 in 10,000) is similar to the annual risk of death in coal mining, at least 10 times less than the average annual risk of death from all causes at age 40 years (1 in 700) and at least 20 times less than the natural annual cancer risk (1 in 400).	At the **Intermediate** level of risk, the protocol must require risk information to be given to volunteers in writing at the time of obtaining consent and a copy of that information should be included in the LREC submission. It will be important to make comparisons with the risk arising from the doses proposed and subjects to be recruited (the examples opposite relate to the highest dose in the category, applied to a population of all ages). The nature of the comparisons is likely to raise doubts, which may only be resolved by quoting numerical risks.
Moderate (10^{-3} or more) 1 in a thousand {>10 mSv}	The radiation dose in some cases exceeds the annual dose limit for occupational exposure and significantly increases the annual risk of death from cancer (1 in 400). The risk (1 in 1000) is similar to the average annual risk of death from all causes at age 40 years (1 in 700) and some 15 times greater than the annual risk of a fatal accident at home.	At the **Moderate** level of risk, it is likely that only exceptional circumstances would lead a properly informed individual to volunteer for the risk in the absence of a balancing individual benefit. Informed consent must be demonstrated. Therefore, any research programmes proposed in this category must include the best possible estimates of numerical risks as well as the clearest valid risk comparisons for the patients.

4 Project details for dose assessment

The information necessary for the LREC in conjunction with a research application is indicated in this and the following section. The Department of Health is producing application forms to be applied nationally and the information recommended here is currently supplementary to any national requirements. Submission of the completed information to the radiation protection adviser/medical physics expert (RPA/MPE) at least 4 weeks before next LREC deadline is suggested so that it can be submitted together with the full research application, to avoid delays in the LREC decision process.

**Information to support a research application
for procedures which involve medical exposure to ionising radiation in excess
of normally indicated clinical needs**

4.1 Project

Title of project
Name of Principal Investigator/Research Co-ordinator
Name of IR(ME)R Practitioner justifying the exposure

(A list of consultant medical staff qualified to act as IR(ME)R practitioners should be available from the employer.)

4.2 Radioactive substances

(i) **Details of substances to be administered** (to be completed by the IR(ME)R practitioner, i.e. Administration of Radioactive Substances Advisory Committee (ARSAC) Certificate holder)

Radionuclide	Chemical form	Route of administration	DRL (MBq)	Proposed activity (MBq)	Number of administrations per subject	Effective dose per administration

(ii) **Total estimated effective dose** (please supply source of reference or attach calculation) … **(mSv)**

(iii) **Administration of Radioactive Substances Advisory Committee Certificate Holder**

All administrations of radioactive materials to persons require a valid Certificate from the ARSAC [35]. Studies that are submitted to the LREC, which involve the administration of radioactive substances, require a specific research application to ARSAC. The only exception is the case of a radionuclide administration that would occur in any case during the routine management of a patient, in which case the administration is not included in the risk assessment for the study (see paragraph 1.8 above).

ARSAC Certificates for research are normally valid for 2 years and a separate application must be made for each new project. If an application is in process, please attach a copy of the ARSAC application.

If the ARSAC Certificate holder or ARSAC applicant is not the principal investigator named on this form, an additional declaration must be signed to identify the principal investigator as a 'person acting in accordance with their directions in writing' (MARS95 [6]) in Section 5.3.

4.3 X-rays

(i) **Details of radiographic procedures (to be completed by the IR(ME)R practitioner)**

Radiographic procedure	DRL (DAP* units, kV, mAs, etc.)	Exposure factors (kV, mAs, etc.)	Number of exposures	Effective dose per exposure

* DAP, dose–area product in $cGy.cm^2$

Each type of radiographic procedure that is necessary for the examination should be listed; the total number and frequency of the examinations needed for the study (also see paragraph 1.8 above) should be given in Section 4.4. It is important to include exposure factors. These may be obtained from the radiation protection supervisor (RPS). The RPA or MPE can advise about effective dose.

4.4 Details of patients / normal control subjects to be studied

To be completed by the Principal Investigator				RPA	Principal Investigator	RPA
Number of subjects	Age range	Sex	Clinical condition	Estimate of effective dose per examination (mSv)	Number and frequency of examinations	Estimate of total effective dose per subject (mSv)
Patients						
Controls						

5 Risk assessment and declarations

5.1 General questions

5.1.1	Have pregnant patients/volunteers (except in specified exceptional circumstances) been excluded?	Yes/No
5.1.2	Have breastfeeding volunteers (for radionuclide studies only) been excluded?	Yes/No
5.1.3	For patients, are there any radiation exposures specific for the project over and above those required for normal clinical management?	Yes/No
5.1.4	Does the project involve individual medical benefit for the participant? – If **NO**, what is the dose constraint (see Sections 3 and 4 above)? – If **YES**, what is the target dose (see Sections 3 and 4 above)?	Yes/No
5.1.5	Does the information to patients/volunteers make clear that some additional exposure to ionising radiation is involved and the consequent risk?	Yes/No
5.1.6	Could the clinical information be obtained by an alternative method involving less dose? – If **YES**, attach details describing reasons for choosing the proposed examination.	Yes/No

5.2 Risk assessment

Comparison of risk and dose constraint

To be completed by the RPA		One category to be assigned[#]	
Lifetime risk from exposure to total effective dose for study for a 40 year old person*	**Equivalent number of days exposure to natural background radiation**	**Target dose** (applies only to subjects receiving some benefit from the study) Study must aim not to exceed this dose	**Dose constraint** (applies only to subjects not receiving any benefit from the study) If the constraint is exceeded a report to LREC must be made immediately.
1 in			

*Note that the risks presented in the table above assume the subjects are from a normal population group in normal health. The RPA can advise on risk estimates for other groups.

A dose greater than that estimated for the study may be permitted by the LREC to allow for patient variations, clinical difficulties and multiple examinations. The constraint or target dose would normally be set close to the estimated effective dose and may be 'AS STATED' in the details of the examination indicated above in Section 4.4.

The following risk category is assigned by the RPA:
See risk category as per the attached table (Table A10.2)

Full name of the RPA:

5.3 Declarations

DECLARATION BY IR(ME)R PRACTITIONER (see paragraph 4.1 above):

(If the study involves the administration of radioactive substances this declaration must be made by the ARSAC licence holder for the proposed study and a copy of the ARSAC licence must be attached. See also last declaration if necessary.)

I am satisfied that the legal requirements of the Ionising Radiation (Medical Exposure) Regulations 2000 will be fulfilled.

Signature	Date

DECLARATION BY RADIATION PROTECTION ADVISER:

I am satisfied that the value indicated above (see paragraph 4.4 above) is a reasonable estimate of the radiation dose to which subjects will be exposed.

Signature	Date

DECLARATION BY PRINCIPAL INVESTIGATOR/RESEARCH CO-ORDINATOR:

(If the study involves an intermediate or moderate risk, a copy of the risk information for volunteers must be attached, see Table A10.2.)

I will communicate the risk to the volunteers as a condition of the project and a legal requirement of IR(ME)R 2000.

Signature	Date

DECLARATION BY ARSAC CERTIFICATE HOLDER (see paragraph 4.2 above):

I agree that the Principal Investigator named above (see paragraph 4.1 above) may administer the radioactive substance(s) under the ARSAC Certificate for this study and I approve the arrangements that have been made to comply with the Medicines (Administration of Radioactive Substances) Regulations 1978 and the Medicines (Administration of Radioactive Substances) Amendment Regulations 1995.

Signature	Date

Appendix 11 Designation of controlled and supervised areas

The following guidance and the flow charts should be read in conjunction with paragraphs 1.54 to 1.57 of the main text and the values indicated in Table 1.2 (reproduced below).

Table 1.2 Guideline dose rates (μSv h^{-1}) used to designate areas

	Controlled areas	Supervised areas	Unsupervised public areas
IDR	>2000	>7.5	<7.5
TADR	>7.5	>2.5	<0.5
TADR2000	> 3	>0.5	<0.15*

* 0.15 μSv h^{-1} is 3/10 of 0.5 μSv h^{-1} or 300 μSv year^{-1} – this is an appropriate dose constraint for an office worker, assuming an occupancy of 2000 h year^{-1}.

1   The instantaneous dose rate (IDR) is used as the starting point for designation, as it is easily measurable and not dependent on workload. In the flow diagrams, a staged structured assessment of IDR has been used first, then workload and use (to estimate the time-averaged dose rate (TADR), and finally occupancy to estimate the time-averaged dose rate over the working year (TADR2000), to determine the need for designation. This sequence forms the basis for the risk assessments for these areas.

2   The IDR should be measured, ideally by integrating the dose over the duration of the exposure (highest exposure used clinically but within the ratings of the unit) and time-averaging over 1 min, to avoid potentially erroneous results due to:

(a) the pulsed nature of many radiation sources
(b) their possible short duration, and
(c) the slow response time of many dosemeters at low dose rates.

Calculated IDRs should be confirmed by measurement.

3   For existing installations it will normally be sufficient to work to the TADR in designating areas, except for areas of high public occupancy (busy thoroughfares, offices, etc.) when it is recommended to use also the TADR2000.

4   Areas where the TADR exceeds 7.5 μSv h^{-1} should normally be designated as controlled, with appropriate controls to ensure ALARP below the individual dose limit.

5   Areas where the TADR exceeds 2.5 μSv h^{-1} (but less than 7.5 μSv h^{-1}) can normally be designated as supervised, provided the TADR2000 is less than 3 μSv h^{-1} (otherwise it will need to be designated as controlled). This will be satisfied in all cases where the occupancy factor is less than 0.4 for a TADR up to 7.5 μSv h^{-1} (800 hours or 100 days a year).

6   By default, non-public areas[1] where the TADR is not more than 2.5 μSv h^{-1} are non-designated. However, appropriate consideration of occupancy should be made to ensure that persons present in these areas would not exceed 1mSv year^{-1} (see IRR99 regulation 16(3)(b) [1]). This requires the TADR2000 to be less than 0.5 μSv h^{-1}, a condition which will be satisfied if the occupancy factor is less than 0.2 (400 hours or 50 days a year) for a TADR up to 2.5 μSv h^{-1}. If this is not satisfied, the area may need to be supervised.

7   Non-designated areas, which do not need to be supervised and to which the general public have free access (unsupervised public areas), should normally have a TADR less than 0.5 μSv h^{-1}. However, the

---

1   Non-public areas are defined as those areas where only occupationally exposed workers are normally present.

area can be non-designated for a TADR up to 2.5 μSv h⁻¹ provided that the TADR2000 is less than 0.15 μSv h⁻¹ (occupancy factor is less than 0.06 or 120 hours (15 days) per year).

8   Any area into which members of the public or employees untrained in radiological protection are likely to enter, and where the IDR exceeds 7.5 μSv h⁻¹, should normally be considered for designation as a controlled area (L121 paragraph 249 [2]). The controls should ensure that no member of the public is likely to exceed a dose of 0.3 μSv year⁻¹. However, if the IDR is intermittent and a risk assessment identifies that the TADR value complies with another designation indicated in Table 1.2, designation as a controlled area may not be necessary.

9   New installations should normally be designed to satisfy both the TADR and TADR2000 values given in Table 1.2 (or pre-determined values similarly based on an appropriate dose constraint). Wherever practicable, a dose constraint of 0.3 μSv year⁻¹ should be applied (0.15 μSv h⁻¹ TADR2000) at the design stage so that no designation is needed for adjacent areas.

10   If the TADR2000 is more than 3 μSv h⁻¹ the area will need to be designated as controlled.

11   This appendix and the flow charts indicate a prudent approach to designation on the basis of ambient dose equivalent rates. If in spite of normally low ambient dose rates, there is a potential for contamination, or for accidental exposure, the area should be designated as controlled or supervised, as appropriate, on the basis of the potential exposures.

Figure A11.1 Designation of controlled and supervised areas (numbers in μSv h⁻¹): non-public areas

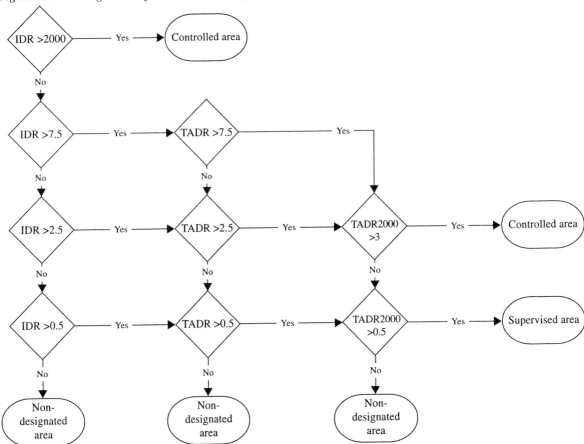

Figure A11.2 Designation of controlled and supervised areas (numbers in µSv h⁻¹): public areas

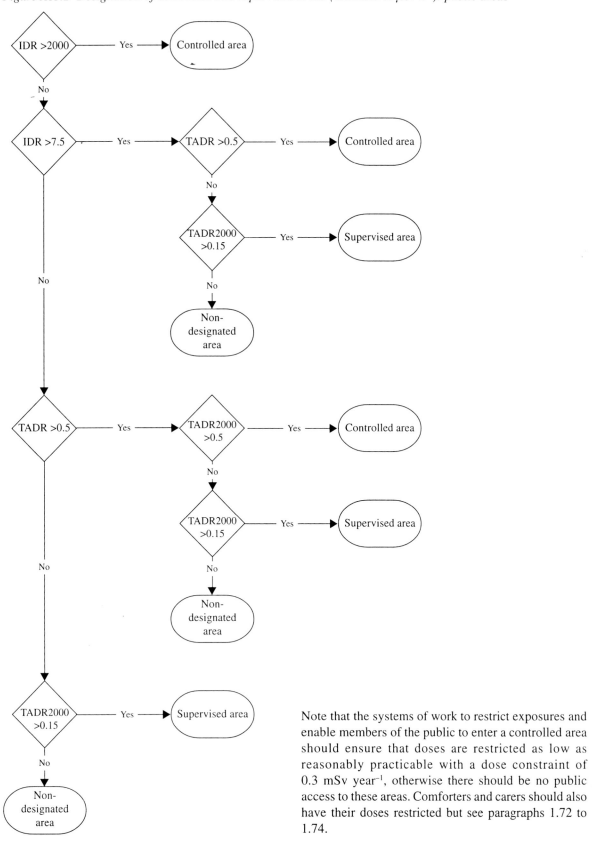

Note that the systems of work to restrict exposures and enable members of the public to enter a controlled area should ensure that doses are restricted as low as reasonably practicable with a dose constraint of 0.3 mSv year⁻¹, otherwise there should be no public access to these areas. Comforters and carers should also have their doses restricted but see paragraphs 1.72 to 1.74.

Appendix 12 Warning signs and notices

1   All safety signs giving health or safety information or instruction to persons at work (apart from the exceptions referred to in paragraphs 10 and 11 below) should comply with the Health and Safety (Safety Signs and Signals) Regulations 1996 [143] and BS 5378, *Safety Signs and Colours* Part 1 [144]. These apply to all workplaces and activities where people are employed in Great Britain. Separate regulations apply in Northern Ireland. However, they exclude signs used in connection with transport, which are separately covered under other regulations.

2   BS 3510 *Specification for a Basic Symbol to Denote the Actual or Potential Presence of Ionizing Radiation* [145] specifies the basic symbol (see Figure A12.1) to denote the actual or potential presence of ionising radiation and to identify objects, devices or substances which emit ionising radiation. The standard does not specify any radiation levels at which the symbol is to be used.

3   Both the safety signs and signals regulations [143] and BS 5378 Part 1 [144] specify various types of safety sign including a warning sign indicating 'Caution, risk of ionising radiation'. This warning sign (see Figure A12.2) is triangular in shape, has a yellow background (of a colour approximating to colour No. 309 of BS 381C *Specification for Colours for Identification, Coding and Special Purposes*) [146] and a black border, and the radiation symbol is placed centrally on the background. It is specified that at least 50 per cent of the area of the safety sign shall be yellow; consequently, the relative sizes of the triangle and of the symbol have to satisfy the following conditions:

$$\ell \geq 27R$$

The warning sign and radiation symbol should be sufficiently large to be distinctive and the sign should be fixed in a prominent position, which is well lit and easily visible.

Figure A12.1 Basic ionising radiation warning symbol   *Figure A12.2 Warning sign – ionising radiation*

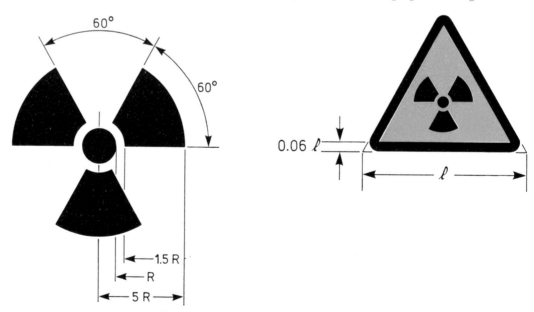

4   Explanatory wording may be needed. This should be put on a supplementary sign. BS 5378 [144] specifies that supplementary signs shall be oblong or square with the text in black on a background which is either white or of the same colour as the safety sign (i.e. yellow in the case of a warning sign).

The wording might be used to identify a controlled or supervised area, to give information about access, to indicate the nature of the source of radiation or the type of radiation, to draw attention to special precautions, etc. The number of words should be kept to the minimum necessary

5   A warning sign and its supplementary sign may, if desired, be mounted on a common, white background. Examples of warning and supplementary signs are given in Figures A12.3, A12.4 and A12.5. The preferred sizes for the overall height of safety signs and letter sizes on signs are given in BS 5378, *Safety Signs and Colours* Part 2 [147].

Figure A12.3 Sign at the entry to a controlled area

Figure A12.4 Sign on a storage cabinet for radioactive materials

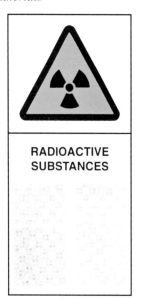

Figure A12.5 Sign on the door of an X-ray room

6   A warning sign may have been attached to a piece of equipment by its manufacturer but it is the employer's responsibility to ensure compliance with the safety signs and signals regulations [143].

7   Safety signs may be displayed only to provide the health or safety information or instruction indicated by that sign. They should therefore be taken down when not required. To ensure the effectiveness of signs, the placing of too many signs too close together should be avoided.

8   Illuminated warning signs are essential for radiotherapy rooms (see paragraphs 7.29 and 7.30 of the main text). An example is given in Figure A12.6. Illuminated warning signals are essential for fixed diagnostic installations (see paragraphs 3.23 and 3.24 of the main text). It should be noted that two illuminated signs that are likely to be confused are not to be used at the same time.

Figure A12.6 Safety signs and notices (in two languages) at the entrance to a radiotherapy bunker; the illuminated interlocked warning signals are shown in use in the lower image

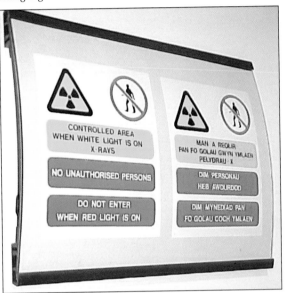

9   Labels, if required, on pipework can be self-adhesive or in painted form and should contain sufficient supplementary wording to indicate the hazard, e.g. 'before dismantling this radioactive waste pipe, contact the RPA'.

10   Labels or markings on a package or container to be transported are excluded from the safety signs and signals regulations [143]. This allows the use of the labels and placards when transporting radioactive materials as specified in the Carriage of Dangerous Goods (Classification, Packaging and Labelling), etc. Regulations 1996 [148] (and in other documents). Such labels include the radiation symbol on a white or yellow background but not the radiation warning sign.

11   This exclusion is not restricted to transport and it is acceptable to label a bottle in a laboratory, as in figure A12.7. However, the door of a cupboard in which the bottle is kept should be labelled with the triangular radiation warning sign as in Figure A12.4.

12   Apart from the radiation warning sign, other safety signs may be needed for protection against ionising radiation, e.g. a sign requiring gloves to be worn in a laboratory using unsealed radioactive materials or a sign to indicate the location of emergency equipment. These signs should also conform to BS 5378 Part 1 [144]. Signs specifically relating to fire fighting or rescue equipment or emergency exits are also covered in BS 5378 [144] and their specifications are in BS 5499, *Fire Safety Signs, Notices and Graphic Symbols* Parts 1 to 3 [149 to 151].

Figure A12.7 Label on a bottle containing radioactive solution

Appendix 13 British Standards for radiotherapy equipment

Note that details concerning British Standards and related international standards may be obtained from British Standards Online at http://bsonline.techindex.co.uk

Accelerators	
Medical electrical equipment Particular requirements for safety Specification for electron accelerators in the range 1 MeV to 50 MeV	BS EN 60601-2-1: 1998 (BS 5724-2-1:1998, IEC 60601-2-1: 1998)
Medical electrical equipment Particular requirements for performance Methods of declaring functional performance characteristics of medical electron accelerators in the range 1 MeV to 50 MeV	BS 5724-3-1:1990 (IEC 60976:1989)
Medical electrical equipment Particular requirements for performance Methods of declaring functional performance characteristics of medical electron accelerators in the range 1 MeV to 50 MeV Guide to functional performance values	BS 5724-3-1: Supplement No. 1: 1990 (IEC 60977: 1989)
Kilovoltage equipment	
Medical electrical equipment Particular requirements for safety Specification for therapeutic X-ray equipment operating in the range 10 kV to 1 MV	BS EN 60601-2- 8: 1998 (BS 5724-2-8:1998, IEC 60601-2-8: 1987)
Gamma-beam teletherapy equipment	
Medical electrical equipment Particular requirements for safety Specification for gamma beam therapy equipment	BS EN 60601-2-11: 1998 (BS 5724-2-11: 1998, IEC 60601-2-11: 1997)

Remotely controlled after-loading equipment	
Medical electrical equipment Particular requirements for safety Specification for remote-controlled automatically driven gamma-ray afterloading equipment	BS EN 60601-2-17: 1996 (BS 5724-2-17: 1990, IEC 60601-2-17:1989)
Medical electrical equipment Particular requirements for safety Specification for remote-controlled automatically driven Revised and additional text	BS EN 60601-2-17/ A1:1996 (BS 5724-2-17: Supplement 1:1996, IEC 60601-2-17: Amendment 1: 1996)
Radiotherapy simulators	
Medical electrical equipment Particular requirements for the safety of radiotherapy simulators	BS EN 60601-2-29: 1999 (BS 5724-2-129: 1999, IEC 60601-2-29: 1999)
Medical electrical equipment Particular requirements for performance Methods of declaring functional performance characteristics of radiotherapy simulators	BS EN 61168:1994 (BS 5724-3-129: 1994, IEC 61168:1993)
Medical electrical equipment Particular requirements for performance Methods of declaring functional performance characteristics of radiotherapy simulators Guide to functional performance values	BS 5724-3-129: Supplement No. 1: 1994 (IEC 61170:1993)
Medical electrical equipment Particular requirements for safety Specification for high voltage generators of diagnostic X-ray generators	BS EN 60601-2-7: 1998 (IEC 60601-2-7: 1998)
Radiotherapy treatment planning	
Medical electrical equipment Requirements for the safety of radiotherapy treatment planning systems	BS EN 62083:2001 (IEC 62083:2000)
Guide to co-ordinates, movements and scales used for radiotherapy equipment	BS EN 61217: 1997 (IEC 61217:1996)

Appendix 14 United Kingdom radiotherapy dosimetry protocols

The IPEM Codes of Practice for Radiotherapy Dosimetry

Radiation	Code of Practice	Reference
Megavoltage X-rays	The IPSM Code of Practice for high energy photon therapy dosimetry based on the NPL absorbed dose calibration service	PMB 35 (1990) 1355–1360
Kilovoltage X-rays	The IPEMB Code of Practice for the determination of absorbed dose for X-rays below 300 kV generating potential (0.035 mm Al – 4 mm Cu HVL; 10–300 kV generating potential)	PMB 41 (1996) 2605–2625
Electrons	The IPEMB Code of Practice for electron dosimetry for radiotherapy beams of initial energy from 2 to 50 MeV based on the air kerma calibration	PMB 41 (1996) 2257–2603
Dosimeter systems	IPEM guidelines on dosimeter systems for use as transfer instruments between the UK primary dosimetry standards laboratory (NPL) and radiotherapy centres	PMB 45 (2000) 2445–2457

Appendix 15 Procedures for the definitive calibration of radiotherapy equipment

Introduction

In order to establish good working practice for definitive calibration of new radiotherapy equipment or following a major modification of existing radiotherapy equipment, the IPEM issues this guidance. The guidance incorporates that issued by IPSM in 1988, but extends the scope to include both external-beam radiotherapy treatment machines and radiation dose measuring equipment. It is assumed that current dosimetry protocols will be followed (see Appendix 14) with adherence to a full quality assurance programme.

A definitive calibration of radiotherapy equipment is one that forms a baseline for subsequent confirmatory measurements. Disagreement between subsequent measurements and the definitive calibration may be an indication for a new definitive calibration as described in recommendations 2.7 and 3.3 below.

Definitive calibrations of external-beam radiotherapy treatment machines or of radiation dose measuring equipment must be carried out in the following circumstances.

External-beam radiotherapy treatment machines

To determine the radiation output per monitor unit or per unit time:

(a) as part of the commissioning procedure of a new linear accelerator, cobalt machine or other external-beam radiotherapy treatment machine

(b) following major repair or modification to external-beam radiotherapy equipment which might reasonably be expected to affect its calibration, e.g. when a new dose monitor is installed in a treatment machine in which dose delivery is controlled by the monitor, or

(c) following the replacement of radioactive sources in cobalt or similar teletherapy equipment.

Radiation dose measuring equipment

To derive a calibration factor:

(a) for new dose measuring equipment which is to be used in the definitive calibration of radiotherapy treatment machines, or

(b) following major repair (e.g. thimble replacement) of dose measuring equipment used in the definitive calibration of radiotherapy treatment machines.

Recommendations

1   General

1.1   The fundamental principle behind these recommendations is that any definitive measurement should be subjected to an independent check and that procedures should incorporate specific cross-checks. Written procedures should be reviewed to ensure that this fundamental principle is adhered to.

1.2   Responsibility for definitive calibration must be vested in a medical physics expert with a minimum of 6 years relevant experience in radiotherapy.

1.3   Written procedures must be drawn up as part of the quality assurance programme and followed. Measurements and observations must be fully documented.

1.4   Any parameters upon which the calibration depends, such as distance measurement and timer operation in cobalt treatment machines, must be checked according to the procedures in the quality assurance programme.

1.5   All factors and quantities in any calculations must be written down even if they are unity.

2   External-beam radiotherapy treatment machines

2.1   The definitive calibration must be derived from two independent sets of measurements using different dosemeters made by two physicists with at least 4 years relevant experience in radiotherapy. The equipment must be removed and all the relevant treatment machine parameters (e.g. TSD and field size) must be changed and reset between these measurements.

2.2   Each of the two dosemeters used in the definitive calibration must have been calibrated according to recommendations 3.1 and 3.2, although each dosemeter calibration may be referred to the same secondary standard dosemeter.

2.3   For teletherapy equipment employing a radioactive source, the definitive calibration measurement must be compared with the supplier's certificate of calibration. Data derived from the certificate of calibration should not be regarded as a substitute for other recommended measurements, but any difference between these data and the definitive calibration must be reconciled.

2.4   Using the data to be supplied for clinical use, the response of a suitable dosemeter in a phantom must be calculated for a different treatment time or number of monitor units from that used in the calibration. The definitive calibration is confirmed if the predicted reading is obtained within the limits of experimental uncertainty.

2.5   Subsequent confirmatory measurements may use simplified measurement procedures. These procedures and the ratios of measurements under the two sets of conditions must be established at the time of the definitive calibration. Comparisons with any previous similar ratios must be made, and if the ratios differ by more than the limits of experimental uncertainty, the difference must be reconciled.

2.6   Confirmatory measurements, according to recommendation 2.1, 2.4 or 2.5 must be made at regular intervals not greater than 1 week for linear accelerators and 1 month for cobalt units, by physics operators under the supervision of a medical physics expert as defined in recommendation 1.2.

2.7   When a confirmatory measurement of the output of a linear accelerator or other X-ray therapy unit is found to differ by 3 per cent or more from the expected value, the possibility of a contributory machine fault or of a measurement error must be considered. The appropriate action will depend upon circumstances in the individual department, but may include carrying out a definitive calibration. The action taken must in all cases be the responsibility of the medical physics expert as defined in recommendation 1.2. Each department should have a written protocol, as part of its quality assurance programme, defining the procedure to be followed.

3   Radiation dose measuring equipment

3.1   A definitive calibration of radiation dose measuring equipment must be derived by a comparison between the field instrument and a reference dosemeter. The reference dosemeter should normally be a secondary standard with a calibration traceable to the National Physical Laboratory. Exceptionally, a tertiary standard may be used, in which case these guidelines must be rigorously followed at each comparison.

3.2   In establishing the procedure for cross-calibration of dosemeters, consideration must be given to the principle described in Section 1.1 above. The following guidelines should be observed.

       (a) Two (or more) independent measurements must be carried out.

(b) Where the chamber is to be calibrated at more than one beam quality and the relative calibration factors are known for chambers of that construction, requirement (a) can be met by demonstrating that the calibrations at the different qualities are consistent within 1.5 per cent of the expected value.

(c) If only one beam is available, a repeat calibration should be carried out in that beam. However, constancy of the readings made with a ^{90}Sr source at the previous definitive calibration may also be regarded as an independent measurement in some circumstances.

(d) Two medical physics experts as defined in recommendation 1.2 must be involved in the measurements. Ideally, the calibrations should be carried out independently by different physicists, but it is sufficient that the second physicist should check the results.

(e) If a repair has been carried out, it is sufficient to show that no change in the calibration factor has occurred at the extremes of beam quality to be used.

(f) For an entirely new dosemeter, calibrations must be carried out for each beam quality. If the expected variation of calibration factors with beam quality is not known, the calibrations must be repeated by an independent medical physics expert as defined in recommendation 1.2.

3.3   A check on the constancy of calibration of all instruments must be made using a ^{90}Sr check source before and after the definitive measurement. An agreement within 1 per cent is necessary.

3.4   Where possible, the calibration factors obtained should be compared with the supplier's certificate of calibration. Data derived from the certificate of calibration should not be regarded as a substitute for other recommended measurements, but any difference between these data and the user's calibration must be reconciled.

3.5   If practicable, the calibrated chamber should be used for the routine calibration of a teletherapy source, and the consistency of the results with previous calibrations confirmed before it is used for other calibrations.

3.6   Paragraph 8.30 of these guidance notes (MDGN) requires that a calibration traceable to the National Physical Laboratory (the national primary standard) should be carried out at least annually. To comply with that requirement, this annual calibration should cover a representative subset of the radiation qualities in use. If a change greater than 1 per cent is observed, a new definitive calibration should be undertaken.

Appendix 16 Addresses of authorities and organisations

The following details were correct as at April 2002.

Authorities

Health and Safety Executive Rose Court 2 Southwark Bridge Road London SE1 9HS Tel: 020 7717 6000 InfoLine: 08701 545500 http://www.hse.gov.uk	Ionising Radiations Regulations and Approved Code of Practice (communications should normally be made through the local area office); guidance leaflets also available
Health and Safety Executive, Northern Ireland 83 Ladas Drive Belfast BT6 9FR Tel: Belfast 028 90 243249 http://www.hseni.gov.uk	Ionising Radiations Regulations and Approved Code of Practice in Northern Ireland
Department of Health Health Services Division Area 402, Wellington House 133–155 Waterloo Road London SE1 8UG Tel: 020 7972 4801 http://www.doh.gov.uk	Scientific services within hospitals in England. Administration of radioactive substances in UK (to be addressed to Secretary of ARSAC)
Medical Devices Agency Hannibal House Elephant and Castle London SE1 6TQ Tel: 020 7972 8000 E-mail: mail@medical-devices.gov.uk http://www.medical-devices.gov.uk	Responsible for ensuring that medical devices and equipment on sale/in use in the UK comply with relevant Directives of the European Council and meet acceptable standards of safety, quality and effectiveness, for evaluation of medical devices and for the investigation of incidents (**Incident Reporting and Investigation Centre**) and the dissemination of safety information
NHS Purchasing and Supplies Agency Premier House 60 Caversham Road Reading Berkshire RG1 7EB Tel: 0118 9808841	Medical equipment procurement (NB central purchasing initiatives are normally run by the **Department of Health** with the operational elements provided by PASA)
Scottish Executive Health Department St Andrew's House Regent Road Edinburgh EH1 3DG Tel: 0131 244 2440 (acc.to web page) E-mail: ceu@scotland.gov.uk http://www.scotland.gov.uk/who/dept_health.asp	Scientific services within hospitals in Scotland

Scottish Healthcare Supplies Common Services Agency Scientific and Technical Branch Trinity Park House South Trinity Road Edinburgh EH5 3SH Tel: 0131 552 6255 http://www.show.scot.nhs.uk/shs/	Radiological equipment in Scotland and for radiation incidents; the Incident Reporting and Investigation Centre at the same address
Scientific Adviser Health Professional Group Welsh Assembly Crown Building Cathays Park Cardiff CF10 3NQ Tel: 02920 825111 http://www.wales.gov.uk	Scientific services within hospitals in Wales
Department of Health, Social Services and Public Safety Castle Building Stormont Belfast BT4 3RA Tel: Belfast 028 90 520000	Scientific services within hospitals in Northern Ireland
Department for Environment, Food and Rural Affairs **Radioactive Substances Division** Ashdown House 123 Victoria Street London SW1E 6DE Tel: 020 7944 6000 http://www.defra.gov.uk	Environment interests in nuclear and radioactive matters encompassing radioactive waste management policy and legislation; environmental radioactivity, including radioactive discharges, contaminated land and radon in the home; response to overseas radiological emergencies; and research
Department for Transport, Local Government and the Regions **Radioactive Materials Transport Division** Zone 2/33 Great Minster House 76 Marsham Street London SW1P 4DR Tel: 020 7890 5768 Fax: 020 7944 2187 http://www.dtlr.gov.uk	Transport of radioactive materials; national and international regulations and advisory material
The Environment Agency Rio House Waterside Drive Aztec West Almondsbury Bristol BS32 4UD Tel: 01454 624400 http://www.environment-agency.gov.uk	Storage of radioactive materials and disposal of radioactive waste in England and Wales (communications should normally be through the local office)

Scottish Environment Protection Agency Erskine Court Castle Business Park Stirling FK9 4TR Tel: 01786 457700 http://www.sepa.org.uk	Storage of radioactive materials and disposal of radioactive waste in Scotland
Northern Ireland, Environment & Heritage Service Calvert House Castle Place Belfast BT1 lFY Tel: Belfast 028 90 251477 http://www.ehsni.gov.uk	Storage, transport and disposal of radioactive substances in Northern Ireland
Post Office Headquarters 148 Old Street London EC1V 9HQ Tel: 020 7490 2888	Transport of radioactive materials by post (communications should normally be made through Customer Services at local letter district offices)
Civil Aviation Authority Aviation House Gatwick Airport South Gatwick West Sussex RH6 0YR Telephone: 01293 567171 Fax: 01293 573999 http://www.caa.co.uk	Air transport safety regulation
Maritime and Coastguard Agency Spring Place 105 Commercial Road Southampton SO15 1EG Tel: 02380 329100 Fax: 02380 329298 http://www.mcga.gov.uk/	Developing, promoting and enforcing high standards of marine safety, including safe transport of dangerous goods
National Radiological Protection Board Chilton Didcot Oxfordshire OX11 0RQ Tel: 01235 831600 E-mail: nrpb@nrpb.org,uk http://www.nrpb.org.uk	Headquarters; general advice and services in the South of England and in South Wales
National Radiological Protection Board Hospital Lane Cookridge Leeds LS16 6RW Tel: 0113 267 9041 E-mail: northern@nrpb.org.uk	General advice and services in the North of England and North Wales

National Radiological Protection Board 155 Hardgate Road Glasgow G51 4LS Tel: 0141 440 2201 E-mail: scotland@nrpb.org.uk	NRPB Scotland; general advice and services in Scotland
Northern Ireland Regional Medical Physics Agency Forster Green Hospital 110 Saintfield Road Belfast BT8 6HD Tel: 028 90 793681	General advice and services in Northern Ireland
National Physical Laboratory Centre for Ionising Radiation Metrology Teddington Middlesex TW11 0LW Tel: 020 8943 6708 Fax: 020 8943 6161 http://www.npl.co.uk/	Responsible for developing and providing the National Measurement System in the fields of ionising radiation, radioactivity and neutron measurement; including the calibration of dosimetry instruments and radionuclide calibrators

Professional organisations

AURPO Association of University Radiation Protection Officers c/o Mrs C. M. Edwards Faculty of Science University of Central Lancashire Preston Lancashire PR1 2HE Tel: 01772 893488 http://www.shef.ac.uk/~aurpo/index.html	**AXREM** Association of X-ray Engineering Manufacturers St George's House 195–203 Waterloo Road London SE1 8WB Tel: 020 7642 8080 Fax: 020 7642 8096
BDA British Dental Association 64 Wimpole Street London W1G 8YF Tel: 020 7935 0875 http://www.bda-dentistry.org.uk/	**BIR** British Institute of Radiology 36 Portland Place London W1B 1AT Tel: 020 7307 1400 http://www.bir.org.uk
BNMS British Nuclear Medicine Society Regent House, 291 Kirkdale London SE26 4QD Tel: 020 8676 7864 Fax: 020 8676 8417 http://www.bnms.org.uk/	**BOHS** British Occupational Hygiene Society Suite 2 Georgian House Great Northern Road Derby DE1 1LT Tel: 01332 298101
CoR The College of Radiographers 207 Providence Square Mill Street London SE1 2EW Tel: 020 7740 7200 http://www.sor.org/	**IPEM** Institute of Physics and Engineering in Medicine Fairmount House 230 Tadcaster Road York YO24 1ES Tel: 01904 610821 http://www.ipem.org.uk/
IRP Institute of Radiation Protection 64 Dalkeith Road Harpenden Herts AL5 5PW Tel: 01582 715026	**RCN** Royal College of Nursing 20 Cavendish Square London W1G 0RN Tel: 020 7647 3861 Fax: 020 7647 3441 http://www.rcn.org.uk
RCR Royal College of Radiologists 38 Portland Place London W1N 4JQ Tel: 020 7636 4432 http://www.rcr.ac.uk/	**SRP** Society for Radiological Protection 76 Portland Place London W1B 1NT Tel: 01364 644487 Fax: 01364 644492 E-mail: admin@srp-uk.org http://www.srp-uk.org

Appendix 17 Environment Agency internal handbook – guidance for inspectors

The following paragraphs are extracted from the Environment Agency (EA) internal handbook [133], with permission; some references have been added and the table numbers have been altered for consistency with the rest of these guidance notes (MDGN), otherwise the text is the same as in the reference.

3.9 Liquid discharges from hospitals via patients

1. When a radiopharmaceutical is administered to a patient, a percentage of the administered dose is excreted in the patient's urine and faeces, and is thus discharged to drain. The percentage varies between different radiopharmaceuticals. Guideline percentage values, providing a reasonably pessimistic but practicable basis for calculating the activity discharged in this liquid waste from hospital premises, were first issued to Inspectors in July 1985. These have been kept under review in the light of available data.

2. Authorised discharge limits set by the Agency, and disposers' systems for accounting for liquid waste disposals, have generally had regard to these best estimate percentage figures. But it has been accepted that, in specific cases, users may propose and officers may agree alternative arrangements if the disposer can provide information to justify departing from the guidelines. (For example, hospitals often assess the proportion of an ^{131}I administration for thyroid ablation therapy which is taken up by each individual patient.) It is advised that this is a sound approach which should continue.

3. The International Commission on Radiological Protection, in ICRP Publication 53 [152], has published biokinetic data for radiopharmaceutical compounds which warrant the following amendments to the previously issued guidelines:

   ^{67}Ga, ^{201}Tl: 30% (previously 100%)

   ^{123}I as meta iodobenzyl guanidine (mIBG): 60% (previously 100%).

4. Medical physicists at Sheffield have undertaken an extensive investigation of the uptake of ^{131}I **administered to inpatients for the treatment of thyrotoxicosis**. This shows that the relevant guideline figure should be amended to 50 per cent (previously 100 per cent).

5. **The full list of figures for administered dose appearing in liquid waste is now as given in Table A17.1.**

6. Where patients have ^{99}Tc^{m} administered in one hospital and return to another, 30 per cent of the administered dose is to be ascribed to the administering hospital and 10 per cent to the hospital to which the patient returns. For other radionuclides the pessimistic '100 per cent (or 30 per cent or 50 per cent or 60 per cent if appropriate) at each' assumption should be made in the absence of evidence to the contrary.

7. **The above amendments should *not* trigger any revisions to existing authorisations**. But Inspectors should refer to them when revising authorisations for other reasons or when considering applications for new authorisations, and may discuss them with site operators.

8. The reasoning behind the amendments was provided to the Agency by Birmingham Medical Physics Services (Queen Elizabeth Medical Centre) and the Royal Hallamshire Hospital, Sheffield, and is included at Annexes 1 and 2 (reproduced here in A17 Annexes 1 and 2).

9. In the case of administrations whose objective is complete long-term retention within the body (such as ^{90}Y silicate injected into arthritic joints), the percentage of administered activity appearing in liquid waste should normally be assumed to be zero.

Table A17.1 Radiopharmaceuticals: percentage of administered dose appearing in liquid waste

Radiopharmaceutical	Administration	Liquid waste
^{131}I	Ablation therapy	100%
	Thyrotoxicosis treatment	50% for inpatients
		30% for outpatients
$^{99}Tc^m$	(Overall figure for the usual broad range of scans)	30% see paragraph 6 of this text
^{32}P		30%
^{67}Ga		30%
^{201}Tl		30%
^{123}I	as mIBG	60%
	as any other compound	100%
Others (e.g. ^{111}In, ^{75}Se, ^{51}Cr)		100%

3.10   Accumulation of technetium-99m waste

Introduction

This guidance represents good practice which *users* of technetium-99m would be expected to observe, and was produced by a user organisation (the Institute of Physics and Engineering in Medicine, IPEM) and endorsed by the joint Liaison Group operated by the Agency and 'Small Users' of Radioactive Materials.

It is issued within the Agency to promote an awareness of accepted good practice which Agency Inspectors may refer to when inspecting relevant premises.

Good practice for users accumulating technetium-99m waste

This procedure applies *only* to technetium-99m waste which will normally be in the form of sharps in a cin-bin or similar container. There is no reason why this procedure cannot equally apply to other forms of technetium waste.

1   Waste containers should not be overfilled. Normally they should be sealed when two-thirds full.

2   There is no need to record the activity of individual items (i.e. hypodermic needles) disposed of into the waste container.

3   When containers are sealed, their total activity should be determined using a suitably calibrated monitor. Normally this will be a contamination monitor fitted with a scintillation probe. The monitor should be regularly tested under the responsibility of the Qualified Person.

4   The container(s) should then be placed in a suitable locked store. Stores suitable for the accumulation of radioactive waste have been described in a number of publications (e.g. IPSM Report 63 *Radiation Protection in Nuclear Medicine and Pathology* [153]).

5   The container should remain in the store for a period of at least 1 week (7 days).

6   On removal from the store the container(s) should be checked with a contamination monitor to ensure that there is no residual activity which would indicate the presence of isotopes other than technetium-99.

7   If activity is detected, the container should be returned to the store and thereafter considered as other radioactive waste to be disposed of accordingly through an approved route. An attempt should be made to determine the isotope present.

8   Containers verified as technetium waste should be disposed of **promptly** as **non-active** waste (clinical or domestic, according to type).

9   A record should be made of each container placed in the store. This should record the date that the container entered the store, the activity on that date and the date of disposal (i.e. removal from the store).

10   If the accumulation of technetium-99m waste is undertaken in a store used for the accumulation of other radioactive waste it must be segregated.

A17 Annex 1: calculations of excreted activity for various radiopharmaceuticals

Relevant data available in ICRP 53 [152]

This ICRP report includes data on radiopharmaceuticals that are or may be coming into common use in human patients, provided that acceptable and sufficient metabolic data are available (for making the absorbed dose calculations). For each compound, a biokinetic model is used to give quantitative estimates for the distribution and metabolism of the radiopharmaceutical in the body, based on results available in the literature. Where appropriate, a range of pathological variation is given.

Data on the time–activity curves and the mechanisms by which the body handles radiopharmaceuticals are used to derive mathematical models, consisting of differential and/or integral equations which describe the variation with time of the activity in the various organs of the body (or the whole body).

The biokinetic model for a radiopharmaceutical is presented in terms of fractions of administered activity that enter the various organs and the associated biological half-time for clearance (assuming an exponential form) for each fraction. This can be used to calculate the activity in each relevant organ or (more usefully for disposal figures) in the whole body as a function of time following administration.

For patient dosimetry, the relevant activity function is integrated from the time of administration to infinite time to determine the *cumulative activity* (A_s) in the body. This has units of activity × time (e.g. MBq.hour). The cumulative activity for each radiopharmaceutical quoted in ICRP 53 takes into account biological clearance and physical radioactive decay of the radionuclide.

Use of ICRP 53 data to estimate the excretion of activity

If a radiopharmaceutical were not cleared biologically from the body (i.e. there is no excretion) then there would be only one exponential term in the activity–time function (for the whole body) and that would describe the physical decay of the radionuclide. Integrating such a function to infinite time would always yield a cumulative activity (A_{ne}) equal to the administered activity (A_0) multiplied by the physical half-life and divided by 0.693.

The difference in the cumulative activity in the absence of biological clearance (A_{ne}) and the cumulative activity quoted in ICRP 53 (A_s) is due to the activity that is excreted from the body. The proportional decrease in the cumulative activity due to excretion is equal to the proportion of the administered activity that is excreted (and the decay of activity prior to excretion is already accounted for). The values for ^{201}Tl, ^{67}Ga and ^{123}I as MIBG are listed below in Table A17.A1.

The proportional decrease in the cumulative activity in the whole body may be used as a basis for estimating the amount of activity that is excreted and discharged to drain. This has been done in the main text of this Note – the values have been rounded up to provide a reasonable degree of pessimism.

Uncertainties in ICRP absorbed dose estimates, and consequences for excretion figures

ICRP 53 states that experimental validation with calculated doses have shown agreement to within 20–60 per cent, the upper bound being for patients who differ considerably from the assumed body size or shape. These anatomical differences affect the distances between source and target organs but should have smaller effects on excretion. Functional impairment may reduce uptake by specific organs but for the radiopharmaceuticals discussed, there would be very little effect upon the whole body retention (the exception would be renal impairment which would act to decrease the activity excreted).

Variation in the body's retention of these radiopharmaceuticals is limited by the short radioactive half-life of the radionuclides. Generally, biological clearance is faster in children and so in some cases the activity excreted may be higher.

Table A17.A1 Estimates of the activity excreted following administration of various radiopharmaceuticals (base on biokinetic data from ICRP 53)

Radiopharmaceutical	Radioactive half-life	ICRP 53 cumulative activity A_s/A_0	Cumulative activity if no excretion A_{ne}/A_0	Proportional decrease in cumulative activity*
^{201}Tl as ion	3.044 d	3.39 d	4.392 d	0.23
^{67}Ga citrate	3.26 d	3.69 d	4.704 d	0.22
^{123}I mIBG	13.2 h	9.97 h	19.05 h	0.48

the cumulative activities have been divided by the administered activity A_0 and so are in units of time rather than activity × time.

* the proportional decrease in the cumulative activity $(A_{ne} - A_s)/A_{ne}$ is equal to the proportion of administered activity that is excreted.

A17 Annex 2: a waste excretion factor for ^{131}I thyrotoxicosis patients staying in hospital for 7 days

In Sheffield the practice is to administer the ^{131}I activity orally and measure percentage uptakes of this activity at 48 hours and 7 days post-administration having corrected for the physical decay of the radionuclide. Pre-therapy uptake measurements are also carried out with a tracer amount of ^{131}I in order to calculate the activity to be administered.

To calculate a percentage activity excreted by these patients over a 7-day period, the results of uptake measurements from a group of 50 consecutive patients were taken and averaged. These average values were then used to calculate the activity excreted by a patient using a two-stage calculation:

Stage 1 the percentage activity excreted in the first 2 days is the activity administered less the percentage of it remaining in the thyroid without any decay correction,

$$= 100 - U_2, \text{ where } U_2 \text{ is the 48 hour or 2 day uptake.}$$

Stage 2 a decay correction is made for the amount excreted between 2 and 7 days by multiplying the difference in the 2 day and 7 day uptakes by the average decay correction factor over this period obtained by simple integration,

$$= (U_2 - U_7) \times CF, \text{ where } U_7 \text{ is the 7 day percentage uptake and CF is the average decay factor between 2 and 7 days.}$$

Thus the percentage excretion, E, is given by:

$$E = 100 - U_2 + CF(U_2 - U_7) \%$$

Since the half-life of ^{131}I is 8.02 days, CF = 0.68.

From measurements on the series of 50 patients: average value for $U_2 = 56.6 \pm 13\%$
average value for $U_7 = 47.5 \pm 13\%$

Hence $E = 43.4\% + 6.2\%$
i.e. $E = 49.6\%$

Therefore, on average and to a good approximation, 50 per cent of the activity administered to these patients is excreted on the first 7 days and will appear in the drains.

Appendix 18 Generic authorisations under the Ionising Radiations Regulations 1999 [1]

The wording of these two Prior Authorisation Certificates is copied directly from the HSE web site at http://www.hse.gov.uk/hthdir/noframes/iradiat.htm#10 (with permission).

Ionising Radiations Regulations 1999

Prior authorisation for the use of electrical equipment intended to produce X-rays

1　　　For the purposes of regulation 5(2) of the Ionising Radiations Regulations 1999, the Health and Safety Executive (HSE) hereby authorises the type of practice referred to in paragraph 3 subject to any such practice being carried out in accordance with the conditions hereby approved by HSE as set out in paragraph 4.

2　　　Notwithstanding the prior authorisation given in paragraph 1, radiation employers must comply with all other relevant requirements of these Regulations, including notifying HSE of their intention to work with radiation in accordance with regulation 6.

3　　　The type of practice referred to in paragraph 1 is:

The use of electrical equipment intended to produce X-rays ('X-ray sets') for: industrial radiography; processing of products; research; or exposure of persons for medical treatment.

4　　　The conditions referred to in paragraph 1 are as follows. The radiation employer shall:

4.1　　as part of satisfying the general requirement in regulation 8 of the Ionising Radiations Regulations 1999 to keep exposure as low as reasonably practicable, take specific steps before starting the work to provide engineering controls, design features, safety devices and warning devices which include at least the following:

(a) where the work is to be carried out in a room, purpose made structure, other enclosure or a cabinet,
    (i) adequate shielding as far as reasonably practicable; and
    (ii) except in the use of X-ray sets for radiotherapy at or below 50 kV, interlocks or trapped key systems or other appropriate safety devices in order to prevent access to high dose rate areas (e.g. in which employed persons could receive an effective dose greater than 20 mSv or an equivalent dose in excess of a dose limit within several minutes when radiation emission is underway). The control system for such safety devices should comply with paragraphs 4.4 or 4.5;

(b) in other cases, adequate local shielding as far as reasonably practicable and, in the case of site radiography, a suitable system for ensuring that:
    (i) persons other than those directly involved in the exposure are excluded from the area by means of a barrier or other suitable means;
    (ii) where employees of another employer may be present in the same workplace, there is co-operation and co-ordination with the other employer(s) for the purposes of restricting access to the controlled area;
    (iii) warning notices displayed at the perimeter of the controlled area; and
    (iv) monitoring of radiation levels to establish that controlled areas have been properly designated;

(c) where there is a risk of significant exposure arising from unauthorised or malicious operation, equipment which has been fitted with locking-off arrangements to prevent its uncontrolled use;

(d) initiation of exposures under key control, or some equally effective means, so as to prevent unintended or accidental emission of a radiation beam; and

(e) suitable warning devices which indicate when the tube is in a state of readiness to emit radiation and, except for diagnostic radiology equipment, give a signal when the useful beam is about to be emitted and a distinguishable signal when the emission is underway, unless this is impracticable;

4.2 arrange for adequate and suitable personal protective equipment to be provided where appropriate;

4.3 arrange for suitable maintenance and testing schedules for the control measures selected; and

4.4 provide safety devices, as referred to in 4.1(a), which for routine operations should be configured so that the control system will ensure that an exposure:

(a) cannot commence while any relevant access door, access hatch, cover or appropriate barrier is open, or safety device is triggered;

(b) is interrupted if the access door, access hatch, cover or barrier is opened; and

(c) does not re-commence on the mere act of closing a door, access hatch, cover or barrier; or

4.5 for non-routine operations such as setting up or aligning equipment, where the safeguards for routine operation are not in use, provide a procedure for an alternative method of working that affords equivalent protection from the risk of exposure which should be documented and incorporated into the local rules.

Notes:

(a) Work referred to in paragraph 3 when carried out in accordance with the conditions in paragraph 4 is not subject to the requirement for individual prior authorisation pursuant to regulation 5(1) of the Ionising Radiations Regulations 1999.

(b) This authorisation is without prejudice to the requirements or prohibitions imposed by any other enactment, in particular, the Health and Safety at Work, etc. Act 1974 and the Ionising Radiations Regulations 1999, and to the provisions of the Approved Code of Practice on the Ionising Radiations Regulations 1999.

Ionising Radiations Regulations 1999

Prior authorisation for the use of accelerators (other than electron microscopes)

1   For the purposes of regulation 5(2) of the Ionising Radiations Regulations 1999, the Health and Safety Executive (HSE) hereby authorises the type of practice referred to in paragraph 3 subject to any such practice being carried out in accordance with the conditions hereby approved by HSE as set out in paragraph 4.

2   Notwithstanding the prior authorisation given in paragraph 1, radiation employers must comply with all other relevant requirements of these Regulations, including notifying HSE of their intention to work with radiation in accordance with regulation 6.

3   The type of practice referred to in paragraph 1 is:

The use of accelerators (other than electron microscopes).

NB: The scope covers all uses of accelerators (other than electron microscopes), including medical and veterinary purposes (an accelerator is an apparatus or installation in which particles are accelerated and which emits ionising radiation with an energy higher than 1 MeV).

4   The conditions referred to in paragraph 1 are as follows. The radiation employer shall:

4.1   as part of satisfying the general requirement in regulation 8 of the Ionising Radiations Regulations 1999 to keep exposure as low as reasonably practicable, take specific steps before starting the work to provide engineering controls, design features, safety devices and warning devices which include at least the following:

    (a) where the work is to be carried out in a room, purpose made structure, other enclosure or a cabinet:
        (i)   adequate shielding as far as reasonably practicable; and
        (ii) interlocks or trapped key systems or other appropriate safety devices in order to prevent access to high dose rate areas (e.g. in which employed persons could receive an effective dose greater than 20 mSv or an equivalent dose in excess of a dose limit within several minutes when radiation emission is underway). The control system for such safety devices should comply with paragraph 4.4;

    (b) in other cases, adequate local shielding as far as reasonably practicable and, in the case of site radiography, a suitable system for ensuring that:
        (i)   persons other than those directly involved in the exposure are excluded from the area by means of a barrier or other suitable means;
        (ii) where employees of another employer may be present in the same workplace, there is co-operation and co-ordination with the other employer(s) for the purposes of restricting access to the controlled area;
        (iii) warning notices are displayed at the perimeter of the controlled area; and
        (iv) radiation levels are monitored to establish that controlled areas have been properly designated;

    (c) suitable means to minimise exposure so far as is reasonably practicable from substances that have been activated by the accelerator;

    (d) a suitable assessment of the hazards arising from the production of adventitious radiation;

    (e) where there is a risk of significant exposure arising from unauthorised or malicious operation, equipment which has been fitted with locking-off arrangements to prevent its uncontrolled use;

    (f) initiation of exposures under key control, or some equally effective means, so as to prevent unintended or accidental emission of a radiation beam; and

    (g) suitable warning devices which indicate when the accelerator is preparing to produce radiation and give a signal when the radiation is about to be produced and a distinguishable signal when the emission is underway, unless this is impracticable;

4.2   arrange for adequate and suitable personal protective equipment to be provided where appropriate;

4.3   arrange for suitable maintenance and testing schedules for the control measures selected; and

4.4   provide safety devices, as referred to in 4.1(a), which should be configured so that the control system will ensure that an exposure:

    (a) cannot commence while any relevant access door, access hatch, cover or appropriate barrier is open, or safety device is triggered;

    (b) is interrupted if the access door, access hatch, cover or barrier is opened; and

    (c) does not re-commence on the mere act of closing a door, access hatch, cover or barrier.

Notes:

(a)   Work referred to in paragraph 3 when carried out in accordance with the conditions in paragraph 4 is not subject to the requirement for individual prior authorisation pursuant to regulation 5(1) of the Ionising Radiations Regulations 1999.

(b)   This authorisation is without prejudice to the requirements or prohibitions imposed by any other enactment, in particular, the Health and Safety at Work, etc. Act 1974 and the Ionising Radiations Regulations 1999, and to the provisions of the Approved Code of Practice supporting the Ionising Radiations Regulations 1999.

(c)   Electron microscopes are not covered by the authorisation as they do not need to be authorised under the Ionising Radiations Regulations 1999.

Appendix 19　List of acronyms

A&E	accident and emergency department
AC	alternating current
ACoP	Approved Code of Practice
ADS	approved dosimetry service
AEC	automatic exposure control
ALARP	as low as reasonably practicable
AP	anteroposterior
ARSAC	Administration of Radioactive Substances Advisory Committee
AURPO	Association of University Radiation Protection Officers
BIR	British Institute of Radiology
BNMS	British Nuclear Medicine Society
BS	British Standard
BSI	British Standards Institution
CE	Communautè Europèen/European Community
CEC	Commission of the European Communities
COSHH	Control of Substances Hazardous to Health
CT	computed tomography
$CTDI_w$	weighted CT dose index
DAP	dose–area product
DC	direct current
DEFRA	Department for Environment, Food and Rural Affairs
DEXA	dual energy X-ray absorptiometry
DLP	dose–length product
DoH	Department of Health
DRL	diagnostic reference level
DTLR	Department for Transport, Local Government and the Regions
EA	Environment Agency
EANM	European Association of Nuclear Medicine
EHSNI	Environment and Heritage Service of Northern Ireland
EPD	electronic personal dosemeter
EU	European Union
FFD	focus to film distance
FGDP-RCS	Faculty of General Dental Practitioners – Royal College of Surgeons
FSD	focus to skin distance

GCAT	Gamma Camera Assessment Team
GP	general practitioner
H&S	Health and Safety
HBN	Health Building Note
HDR	high dose rate
HIV	human immunodeficiency virus
HMSO	Her Majesty's Stationery Office (now known as The Stationery Office)
HPLC	high performance liquid chromatography
HSC	Health and Safety Commission
HSE	Health and Safety Executive
HSG	Health and Safety Guidance documents
HSWA	Health and Safety at Work Act
ICRP	International Commission on Radiological Protection
IDR	instantaneous dose rate
IEC	International Electrotechnical Commission
IEE	Institution of Electrical Engineers
IPEM	Institute of Physics and Engineering in Medicine (previously known as IPSM and IPEMB)
IPEMB	see IPEM
IPSM	see IPEM
IR(ME)R	Ionising Radiation (Medical Exposure) Regulations
IR(OW)R	Ionising Radiation (Outside Workers) Regulations
IRIC	Incident Reporting and Investigation Centre (MDA)
IRID	Ionising Radiation Incident Database
IRIS	Ionising Radiation Information Sheet
IRR99	Ionising Radiations Regulations 1999
ISO	International Organisation for Standardisation
IVP	intravenous pyelography
kVp	peak kilovoltage
L121	ACoP and specific guidance on the Ionising Radiations Regulations 1999
LBD	light beam diaphragm
LDR	low dose rate
LLW	low level (radioactive) waste
LREC	Local Research Ethics Committee
MARS	Medicines (Administration of Radioactive Substances) Regulations
mAs	milli ampere second
MCA	Medicines Control Agency (UK)

MDA	Medical Devices Agency
MDGN	Medical and Dental Guidance Notes (this publication)
MEC	Medical Exposures Committee
MeV	mega electron volts
MHSWR	Management of Health and Safety at Work Regulations
mIBG	meta iodo benzyl guanidine (iobenguane)
MIPEM	corporate member of the IPEM
MOD	Ministry of Defence
MPE	medical physics expert
MRI	magnetic resonance imaging
MV	mega voltage
NAIR	national arrangements for incidents involving radioactivity
NEMA	National Electrical Manufacturers' Association (US)
NHS	National Health Service
NMS	National Measurement System
NPL	National Physical Laboratory
NRPB	National Radiological Protection Board
OPG	orthopantomography
OPT	orthopantography
PA	posteroanterior
PASA	Purchasing and Supplies Agency (NHS)
PCD	profession complementary to dentistry
PDR	pulsed dose rate
PM77	see HSG226 [10]
PMB	Physics in Medicine and Biology
PMMA	polymethylmethacrylate
POMS	'prescription-only' medicines
PPE	personal protective equipment
QA	quality assurance
QC	quality control
QE	qualified expert (for radioactive substances)
QP	qualified person (for instrumentation)
RCR	Royal College of Radiologists
REPPIR	Radiation (Emergency Preparedness and Public Information) Regulations
RIS	radiology information system
RPA	radiation protection adviser

RPS	radiation protection supervisor
RSA	Radioactive Substances Act
RWMAC	Radioactive Waste Management Advisory Committee
SEPA	Scottish Environment Protection Agency
SNM	Society of Nuclear Medicine
TADR	time-averaged dose rate
TADR2000	time-averaged dose rate over 2000 h
TDGSA	Transport of Dangerous Goods (Safety Advisers)
TI	transport index
TLD	thermoluminescent dosemeter
TMJ	temporomandibular joint
TSD	target to skin distance
TSRWR	Transfrontier Shipment of Radioactive Waste Regulations
UK	United Kingdom of Great Britain and Northern Ireland
UN	United Nations
VLLW	very low level (radioactive) waste
WHO	World Health Organization

Appendix 20 Acts and regulations in the United Kingdom

Normally published by the HMSO, London and available from the HMSO, the HSE or the Department of Health: http://www.legislation.hmso.gov.uk/; http://www.hse.gov.uk/; http://www.doh.gov.uk/. **Acts of the UK Parliament since 1988 are available to download directly from the HMSO web site**.

Legal document (in order of appearance)	Acronym (if any)	Ref.
Ionising Radiations Regulations 1999 (SI 1999 No 3232) London, HMSO	IRR99	[1]
Ionising Radiations Regulations (Northern Ireland) 2000 (SR 2000 No 375) London, HMSO	IRR99	[1]
Ionising Radiation (Medical Exposure) Regulations 2000 (SI 2000 No 1059) London, HMSO	IR(ME)R	[3]
Medicines (Administration of Radioactive Substances) Regulations 1978 (SI 1978 No 1006) London, HMSO	MARS78	[5]
Medicines (Administration of Radioactive Substances) Amendment Regulations 1995 (SI 1995 No 2147) London, HMSO	MARS95	[6]
Radioactive Substances Act 1993 (chapter 12) London, HMSO	RSA93	[7]
Safety Representatives and Safety Committees Regulations 1977 (SI 1977 No 500) London, HMSO		[13]
Health and Safety (Consultation with Employees) Regulations 1996 (SI 1996 No 1513) London, HMSO		[14]
Management of Health and Safety at Work Regulations 1999 (SI 1999 No 3242) London, HMSO	MHSWR	[16]
Radioactive Substances (Hospitals) Exemptions Order 1990 (SI 1990 No 2512) and Amendment Order 1995 (SI 1995 No 2395) London, HMSO		[17]
Medicines Act 1968, London, HMSO		[18]
Health and Safety at Work etc. Act 1974, London, HMSO	HSWA	[21]
Radiation (Emergency Preparedness and Public Information) Regulations 2001 (SI 2001 No 2975) London, HMSO	REPPIR	[28]
Medical Devices Regulations 1994 (SI 1994 No 3017) London, HMSO		[45]
Electricity at Work Regulations 1989 (SI 1989 No 635) London, HMSO		[46]
Provision and Use of Work Equipment Regulations 1998 (SI 1998 No 2306, as amended by 1999/860 and 1999/2001) London, HMSO		[47]
Radioactive Substances (Testing Instruments) Exemption Order 1985 (SI 1985 No 1049) London, HMSO		[71]

Legal document (in order of appearance)	Acronym (if any)	Ref.
Manual Handling Operations Regulations 1992 (SI 1992 No 2793) London, HMSO		[80]
Lifting Operations and Lifting Equipment Regulations 1998 (SI 1998 No 2307) London, HMSO		[81]
Radioactive Material (Road Transport) (Great Britain) Regulations 1996 (SI 1996 No 1350) London, HMSO	RAMROAD	[96]
Transport of Dangerous Goods (Safety Advisers) Regulations 1999 (SI 1999 No 257) London, HMSO	TDGSA	[97]
Control of Substances Hazardous to Health (COSHH) Regulations 1999 (SI 1999 No 437) London, HMSO	COSHH	[101]
Packaging, Labelling and Carriage of Radioactive Material by Rail Regulations 1996 (SI 1996 No 2090) London, HMSO		[105]
Carriage of Dangerous Goods by Road (Driver Training) Regulations 1996 (SI 1996 No 2094) London, HMSO		[106]
Radioactive Substances (Substances of Low Activity) Exemption Order 1986 (SI 1986 No 1002) London, HMSO		[120]
Merchant Shipping (Dangerous Goods and Marine Pollutants) Regulations 1997 (SI 1997 No 2367) London, HMSO		[121]
Air Navigation Order 2000 (SI 2000 No 1562) London, HMSO		[122]
Environment Act 1995 (chapter 25) London, HMSO		[125]
Special Waste Regulations 1996 (SI 1996 No 972) London, HMSO		[126]
Radioactive Substances (Waste Closed Sources) Exemption Order 1963 (SI 1963 No 1831) London, HMSO		[127]
Radioactive Substances (Testing Instruments) Exemption Order 1985 (SI 1985 No 1049) London, HMSO		[128]
Radioactive Substances (Prepared Uranium and Thorium Compounds) Exemption Order 1962 (SI 1962 No 2711) London, HMSO		[129]
Radioactive Substances (Basic Safety Standards) (England and Wales) Direction 2000, London, London Gazette		[130]
Radioactive Substances (Basic Safety Standards) (Scotland) Direction 2000, Edinburgh, Scottish Executive		[131]
Transfrontier Shipment of Radioactive Waste Regulations 1993 (SI 1993 No 3031) London, HMSO		[135]

Legal document (in order of appearance)	Acronym (if any)	Ref.
Ionising Radiations (Outside Workers) Regulations 1993 (SI 1993 No 2379) London, HMSO		[140]
Health and Safety (Safety Signs and Signals) Regulations 1996 and Guidance (SI 1996 No 341) London, HMSO		[143]
Carriage of Dangerous Goods (Classification, Packaging and Labelling) and Use of Transportable Pressure Receptacles Regulations 1996 (SI 1996 No 2092) London, HMSO		[148]

Appendix 21 References

[1] **IRR99** Ionising Radiations Regulations 1999 (SI 1999 No 3232) London, HMSO.

[2] **L121** HSE. Work with ionising radiation. Approved code of practice and practical guidance on the Ionising Radiations Regulations 1999, London, HSE (2000).

[3] **IR(ME)R** Ionising Radiation (Medical Exposure) Regulations 2000 (SI 2000 No 1059) London, HMSO.

[4] DoH. The Ionising Radiation (Medical Exposure) Regulations 2000 (together with notes on good practice). London, DoH (2001) http://www.doh.gov.uk/irmer.htm

[5] **MARS78** Medicines (Administration of Radioactive Substances) Regulations 1978 (SI 1978 No 1006) London, HMSO.

[6] **MARS95** Medicines (Administration of Radioactive Substances) Amendment Regulations 1995 (SI 1995 No 2147) London, HMSO.

[7] **RSA93** Radioactive Substances Act 1993 (chapter 12) London, HMSO.

[8] NRPB. Guidance notes for dental practitioners on the safe use of X-ray equipment. Chilton, NRPB (2001) http://www.nrpb.org/publications/misc_publications/dental_guidance_notes.htm

[9] AURPO. Guidance notes on working with ionising radiations in research and teaching (to be published) (draft of May 2001 at http://www.shef.ac.uk/~aurpo/irrgn99.pdf)

[10] **HSG226** Radiation equipment used for medical exposure. Health and Safety Guidance Note 226, London, HSE (2002) (replaces PM77 Fitness of equipment used for medical exposure to ionising radiation 1998).

[11] HSE. Working safely with ionising radiation: guidelines for expectant or breastfeeding mothers. Sudbury, HSE Books (2001).

[12] **HSG65** Successful health and safety management (revised). Health and Safety Guidance Note 65, Sudbury, HSE Books (1997).

[13] Safety Representatives and Safety Committees Regulations 1977 (SI 1977 No 500) London, HMSO.

[14] Health and Safety (Consultation with Employees) Regulations 1996 (SI 1996 No 1513) London, HMSO.

[15] **HSG163** 5 steps to risk assessment. Health and Safety Guidance Note 163, Sudbury, HSE Books (1998).

[16] **MHSWR** Management of Health and Safety at Work Regulations 1999 (SI 1999 No 3242) London, HMSO.

[17] Radioactive Substances (Hospitals) Exemptions Order 1990 (SI 1990 No 2512) and Amendment Order 1995 (SI 1995 No 2395) London, HMSO.

[18] Medicines Act 1968, London, HMSO.

[19] **IPEM79** The critical examination of X-ray generating equipment in diagnostic radiology. IPEM Report No 79, York, IPEM (1998).

[20] **IPEM77** Recommended standards for the routine performance testing of diagnostic X-ray imaging systems. IPEM Report No 77, York, IPEM (1997).

[21] **HSWA** Health and Safety at Work etc. Act 1974, London, HMSO.

[22] MDA. Medical device and equipment management for hospital and community-based organisations. Device Bulletin MDA DB 9801, London, MDA (1998).

[23] IPSM NRPB CoR. National protocol for patient dose measurements in diagnostic radiology. Chilton, NRPB (1992).

[24]   **NPL Guide 14** The examination, testing and calibration of portable radiation protection instruments. Measurement Good Practice Guide No 14, Teddington, NPL (1999).

[25]   Shaw PV, Hudson AP and Grindod EL. Guidance on monitoring and dose assessment for internal exposure of workers. NRPB Memorandum M900, Chilton, NRPB (1998).

[26]   Thomas GO, Croft JR, Williams MK and McHugh JO. IRID: specifications for the ionising radiations incident database. Chilton, NRPB/HSE/EA (1996).

[27]   Croft JR, Thomas GO, Walker S and Williams CR. IRID: ionising radiations incident database: first review of cases reported and operation of the database. Chilton NRPB/HSE/EA (1999) http://www.nrpb.org/publications/misc_publications/irid.htm

[28]   **REPPIR** Radiation (Emergency Preparedness and Public Information) Regulations 2001 (SI 2001 No 2975) London, HMSO

[29]   RCR. Making best use of a department of clinical radiology. Guidelines for doctors, 4th ed, London, RCR (1998).

[30]   RCR. A guide to justification for clinical radiologists. BFCR(00)5, London, RCR (2000).

[31]   ICRP. Radiological protection in biomedical research. ICRP Publication 62, *Ann. ICRP* 22 No 3 (1991).

[32]   Sutton DG and Williams JR (eds). Radiation shielding for diagnostic X-rays. London, BIR (2000).

[33]   **IPEM32** Measurement of the performance characteristics of diagnostic X-Ray systems. IPEM Report No 32 Series 1–6, York, IPEM (1996 and 1997)

[34]   Nicholson RA, Thornton A and Sukumar VP. Awareness by radiology staff of the difference in radiation risk from two opposing lateral lumbar spine examinations. *British Journal of Radiology* 72 221 (1999).

[35]   **ARSAC** Administration of Radioactive Substances Advisory Committee; notes for guidance. London, DoH (1998).

[36]   NRPB CoR RCR. Diagnostic medical exposures: advice on exposure to ionising radiation during pregnancy. Chilton, NRPB (1998) http://www.nrpb.org/publications/misc_publications/advice_during_pregnancy.htm

[37]   Martin CJ, Sutton DG, Workman A, Shaw, AJ and Temperton D. Protocol for measurement of patient entrance surface dose rates for fluoroscopic X-ray equipment. *British Journal of Radiology* 71 1283–1287 (1998).

[38]   ICRP. Avoidance of radiation injuries from interventional procedures. ICRP Publication 85, *Ann. ICRP* 30 No 2 (2000).

[39]   Nicholson R, Tuffee F and Uthappa MC. Skin sparing in interventional radiology: the effect of copper filtration. *British Journal of Radiology* 73 36–42 (2000).

[40]   ICRP. Managing patient dose in CT. ICRP Publication 87, *Ann. ICRP* 30 No 4 (2000).

[41]   CEC. Quality criteria for computed tomography: European guidelines. EUR 16262, Luxembourg, CEC (1999).

[42]   BSI. Protective devices against diagnostic medical X-radiation. Protective clothing and protective devices for gonads. BS EN 61331-3:1999, London, BSI (1999).

[43]   BSI. Medical electrical equipment. Part 1. General requirements for safety. Section 1.3 collateral standard: general requirements for radiation protection in diagnostic X-ray equipment. BS EN 60601-1-3, London, BSI (1995).

[44]   Medical Devices Directive. Council Directive 93/42/EEC *Off. Journal* L169 (1993).

[45]   Medical Devices Regulations 1994 (SI 1994 No 3017) London, HMSO.

[46]   Electricity at Work Regulations 1989 (SI 1989 No 635) London, HMSO.

[47]   Provision and Use of Work Equipment Regulations 1998 (SI 1998 No 2306, as amended by 1999/860 and 1999/2001) London, HMSO.

[48]   BSI. Requirements for Electrical Installations, IEE Wiring Regulations, 16th ed. BS 7671:1992 and Amendments. London, IEE and BSI (1992).

[49]   DoH. Technical requirements for the supply and installation of equipment for diagnostic imaging and radiotherapy. TRS89 NHS Procurement Directorate, London, DoH (1989).

[50]   BSI. Medical electrical equipment. Particular requirements for safety. Specification for X-ray source assemblies and X-ray tube assemblies for medical diagnosis. BS EN 60601-2-28, London, BSI (1993).

[51]   **ICRP33** Protection against ionizing radiation from external sources used in medicine. ICRP Publication 33, *Ann. ICRP* 9 No 1 (1982).

[52]   BSI. Medical electrical equipment. Particular requirements for safety. Particular requirements for the safety of X-ray equipment for computed tomography. BS EN 60601-2-44, London, BSI (1999).

[53]   BSI. Medical electrical equipment. Particular requirements for safety. Specification for high voltage generators of diagnostic X-ray generators. BS EN 60601-2-7, London BSI (1998).

[54]   FGDP (UK). Selection criteria for dental radiography. London, Royal College of Surgeons of England (1998).

[55]   British Orthodontic Society. Guidelines for the use of radiographs in clinical orthodontics. 2nd ed. London, British Orthodontic Society (2001).

[56]   Napier ID. Reference doses for dental radiography. *British Dental Journal* 186 No 8 392-396 (1999).

[57]   **L22** Safe use of work equipment. Approved code of practice and guidance for the Provision and Use of Work Equipment Regulations. London, HSE (1998).

[58]   British Society for the Study of Orthodontics and the British Society of Dental and Maxillofacial Radiology. Reduction of the dose to patients during lateral cephalometric radiography. Working Party Report, *British Dental Journal* 158 415 (1985).

[59]   NRPB. Guidelines on radiology standards for primary dental care. *Docs. NRPB* 5 No 3 (1994).

[60]   **IPEM75** The design of radiotherapy treatment room facilities. IPEM Report No 75, York, IPEM (1997).

[61]   BSI. Code of practice for safety of machinery. BS 5304, London, BSI (1988) (now replaced by Safe use of machinery, PD5304 (2000)).

[62]   HSE. Occupational exposure limits. EH40/2000, London, HSE (2000).

[63]   HSE. Ozone: health hazards and precautionary measures. EH38/96, London, HSE (1996).

[64]   HSC. Management of health and safety at work: Approved code of Practice, Sudbury, HSE Books (2000).

[65]   **IPEM54** Commissioning and quality assurance of linear accelerators. IPEM Report No 54, York, IPEM (1988).

[66]   **IPEM81** Physics aspects of quality control in radiotherapy. IPEM Report No 81, York, IPEM (1999).

[67]   CEC. Criteria for acceptability of radiological (including radiotherapy) and nuclear medicine installations. Radiation Protection 91, Luxembourg, CEC (1997) http://europa.eu.int/comm/environment/radprot/91/91.htm

[68]   WHO. Quality assurance in radiotherapy. Geneva, WHO (1988) http://www.who.int/home-page/

[69]   BSI. Functional safety of electrical/electronic/programmable electronic safety-related systems. BS IEC 61508-1:1998, London, BSI (1998).

[70] **IPEM68** A guide to the commissioning and quality control of treatment planning systems. IPEM Report No 68, York, IPEM (1994).

[71] Radioactive Substances (Testing Instruments) Exemption Order 1985 (SI 1985 No 1049) London, HMSO.

[72] BSI. Specification. Sealed radioactive sources. BS 5288, London, BSI (1976).

[73] ISO. Radiation protection. Sealed radioactive sources. Leakage. ISO 9978:1992, Geneva, International Organization for Standardization (1992).

[74] Mountford PJ. Risk assessment of the nuclear medicine patient. *British Journal of Radiology* 70 671–684 (1997).

[75] Phipps AW, Smith TJ, Tell TP and Harrison JD. Doses to the embryo/foetus and neonate from intakes of radionuclides by the mother – part 1: doses received in utero and from activity present at birth. CRR397/ 2001, London, HSE (2001) http://www.hse.gov.uk/research/crr_htm/2001/crr01397.htm

[76] Williams NR, Tindale WB, Lewington VJ, Nunan TO, Shields RA and Thorley PJ. Guidelines for the provision of physics support to nuclear medicine. *Nuclear Medicine Communications* 20, No 9, 781–787 (1999).

[77] **ICRP52** Protection of the patient in nuclear medicine. ICRP Publication 52, *Ann. ICRP* 17 No 4 (1987).

[78] **ICRP57** Radiological protection of the worker in medicine and dentistry. ICRP Publication 57, *Ann. ICRP* 20 No 3 (1989).

[79] **HBN6** NHS Estates. Facilities for diagnostic imaging and interventional radiology. Health Building Note 6, London, HMSO (2001) http://www.nhsestates.gov.uk/

[80] Manual Handling Operations Regulations 1992 (SI 1992 No 2793) London, HMSO.

[81] Lifting Operations and Lifting Equipment Regulations 1998 (SI 1998 No 2307) London, HMSO.

[82] Waddington WA, Keshtgar MRS, Taylor I, Lakhani SR, Short MD and Ell PJ. Radiation safety of the sentinel lymph node technique in breast cancer. *European Journal of Nuclear Medicine* 27 377–391 (2000).

[83] BSI. Methods of test for Anger type gamma cameras. BS EN 60789, London, BSI (1994).

[84] **IPSM66** Quality control of gamma cameras and associated computer systems. IPSM Report No 66, York, IPSM (1992) (under revision by IPEM).

[85] **IPSM65** Quality standards in nuclear medicine. IPSM Report No 65, York, IPSM (1992).

[86] NRPB, HSE, Department of Health and Social Security, Department of Health and Social Security Northern Ireland, Scottish Home and Health Department and Welsh Office. Guidance notes for the protection of persons against ionising radiations arising from medical and dental use. Chilton, NRPB (1988).

[87] Medicines Control Agency. Rules and guidance for pharmaceutical manufacturers and distributors: the orange guide. London, HMSO (1997).

[88] **HBN29** NHS Estates. Accommodation for pharmaceutical services. Health Building Note 29, EL(97)52, London, HMSO (1997).

[89] **QAAPS** Beaney AM (ed). The quality assurance of aseptic preparation services, 3rd ed, London, Pharmaceutical Press (2001).

[90] **QARP** UK Radiopharmacy Group and the NHS Pharmaceutical Quality Control Committee. Quality assurance of radiopharmaceuticals. Report of a joint working party, *Nuclear Medicine Communications* 22 909–916 (2001).

[91] Lee GM and Midcalf B. Isolators for pharmaceutical applications. London, HMSO (1994).

[92] Regional Pharmaceutical Officers Special Interest Group. Standards for pharmaceutical services in Health Authorities, Units and Trusts in England. London, UK Radiopharmacy Group (1993).

[93] EudraLex. The rules governing medicinal products in the European Union. Vol IV. Good manufacturing practices. Medicinal products for human and veterinary use. Luxembourg, CEC (2001) http://dg3.eudra.org/F2/eudralex/vol-4/home.htm

[94] DoH. Aseptic dispensing for NHS patients. PL/CPhO(94)2, London, DoH (1994).

[95] BSI. Microbiological safety cabinets. BS 5726 Parts 1–4, London, BSI (1992).

[96] **RAMROAD** Radioactive Material (Road Transport) (Great Britain) Regulations 1996 (SI 1996 No 1350) London, HMSO.

[97] **TDGSA** Transport of Dangerous Goods (Safety Advisers) Regulations 1999 (SI 1999 No 257) London, HMSO.

[98] Sampson CB (ed). Textbook of radiopharmacy theory and practice, 2nd ed, The Netherlands, Gordon and Breach Science Publishers SA (1994).

[99] BSI. Quality management systems – requirements. BS EN ISO 9001, London, BSI (2000).

[100] Monger PN. Recent changes in UK legislation and the licensing of radiopharmacies. *Nuclear Medicine Communications* 13 411–415 (1992).

[101] **COSHH** Control of Substances Hazardous to Health (COSHH) Regulations 1999 (SI 1999 No 437) London, HMSO.

[102] BSI. Surface materials for use in radioactive areas. Guide to the selection of materials. BS 4247-2, London, BSI (1982).

[103] Radiation Protection Committee of the BIR. Patients leaving hospital after administration of radioactive substances. Working party report, *British Journal of Radiology* 72 121–125 (1999).

[104] Barrington SF, O'Doherty MJ, Kettle AG, *et al*. Radiation exposure to families of outpatients treated with radioiodine (iodine-131) for hyperthyroidism. *European Journal of Nuclear Medicine* 26 686–692 (1999).

[105] Packaging, Labelling and Carriage of Radioactive Material by Rail Regulations 1996 (SI 1996 No 2090) London, HMSO.

[106] Carriage of Dangerous Goods by Road (Driver Training) Regulations 1996 (SI 1996 No 2094) London, HMSO.

[107] Harding LK, Mostafa AB, Roden L and Williams N. Dose rates from patients having nuclear medicine investigations. *Nuclear Medicine Communications* 6 191–194 (1985).

[108] Mountford PJ and Coakley AJ. Body surface dosimetry following re-injection of ^{111}In-leucocytes. *Nuclear Medicine Communications* 10 497–501 (1989).

[109] Mountford PJ, O'Doherty MJ, Forge NI, Jeffries A and Coakley AJ. Radiation dose rates from adult patients undergoing nuclear medicine investigations. *Nuclear Medicine Communications* 12 767–777 (1991).

[110] Greaves CD and Tindale WB. Dose rate measurements from radiopharmaceuticals, implications for nuclear medicine staff and for children with radioactive parents. *Nuclear Medicine Communications* 20 179–187 (1999).

[111] Cormack J and Shearer J. Calculation of radiation exposures from patients to whom radioactive materials have been administered. *Physics in Medicine and Biology* 43 501–516 (1998).

[112] Kettle A. Iodine-131 Canterbury modelling software. Personal communication e-mail: Andrew.kettle@ekh-tr.sthames.nhs.uk (2001).

[113] Barrington SF, Kettle AG, O'Doherty MJ, *et al*. Radiation dose rates from patients receiving iodine-131 therapy for carcinoma of the thyroid. *European Journal of Nuclear Medicine* 23 123–130 (1996) (and published erratum *European Journal of Nuclear Medicine* 24 1545 (1997)).

[114] Roberts JK. Comments on the British Institute of Radiology Working Party advice for patients after radionuclide therapy. (letter) *British Journal of Radiology* 73 453–454 (2000).

[115] Waller ML. Estimating periods of non-close-contact for relatives of radioactive patients. *British Journal of Radiology* 74 100–102 (2001).

[116] Greaves CD and Tindale WB. Radioiodine therapy: care of the helpless patient and handling of the radioactive corpse. *Journal of Radiological Protection* 21 381–392 (2001).

[117] HSE. Advice of February 1989, in Radiation Protection Topic Group News Sheet No 30, York, IPEM (1989).

[118] ISO. Sealed radioactive sources. ISO 2919, Geneva, International Organization for Standardization (1999).

[119] HSE. Control of radioactive substances. Ionising Radiation Information Sheet No 8 (IRIS8) (2001) HSE web site at http://www.hse.gov.uk/pubns/irp8.pdf

[120] Radioactive Substances (Substances of Low Activity) Exemption Order 1986 (SI 1986 No 1002) London, HMSO.

[121] Merchant Shipping (Dangerous Goods and Marine Pollutants) Regulations 1997 (SI 1997 No 2367) London, HMSO.

[122] Air Navigation Order 2000 (SI 2000 No 1562) London, HMSO.

[123] Council Regulation of 8 June 1993 on shipments of radioactive substances between Member States. 93/1493/EURATOM *Off. Journal* L148 (1993).

[124] Council Directive of 15 July 1980 amending the Directives laying down the basic safety standards for the health protection of the general public and workers against the dangers of ionizing radiation. 80/836/EURATOM *Off. Journal* L246 (1980).

[125] Environment Act 1995 (chapter 25) London, HMSO.

[126] Special Waste Regulations 1996 (SI 1996 No 972) London, HMSO.

[127] Radioactive Substances (Waste Closed Sources) Exemption Order 1963 (SI 1963 No 1831) London, HMSO.

[128] Radioactive Substances (Testing Instruments) Exemption Order 1985 (SI 1985 No 1049) London, HMSO.

[129] Radioactive Substances (Prepared Uranium and Thorium Compounds) Exemption Order 1962 (SI 1962 No 2711) London, HMSO.

[130] Radioactive Substances (Basic Safety Standards) (England and Wales) Direction 2000, London, London Gazette.

[131] Radioactive Substances (Basic Safety Standards) (Scotland) Direction 2000, Edinburgh, Scottish Executive

[132] EA. Guidance on retention of records required by RSA93 certificates of registration and authorisation. Inspectors Technical Note ITN/RSA/10 (2001) (available from the EA on request).

[133] EA. Internal handbook/guidance for inspectors: liquid radioactive discharges from hospital via patients. (2000) (available from the EA on request).

[134] Driver I and Packer S. Radioactive waste discharge quantities for patients undergoing radioactive iodine therapy for thyroid carcinoma. *Nuclear Medicine Communications* 22 1129–1132 (2001).

[135] Transfrontier Shipment of Radioactive Waste Regulations 1993 (SI 1993 No 3031) London, HMSO.

[136] DoH. Planning for major incidents: the NHS guidance, chapter 9, London, DoH (2000) http://www.doh.gov.uk/epcu/epcu/rad.htm

[137] **NAIR** The NAIR handbook, Chilton, NRPB (2000) http://www.nrpb.org/radiation_incidents/nair_2000.pdf

[138] **HSG223** HSE and DoH. The regulatory requirements for medical exposure to ionising radiation: an employer's overview. Health and Safety Guidance Note 223, Sudbury, HSE Books (2001).

[139] Williams NR, Tindale WB, Lewington VJ, Nunan TO, Shields RA and Thorley PJ. Guidelines for the provision of physics support to nuclear medicine. Report of a Joint Working Group, *Nuclear Medicine Communications* 20 781–787 (1999).

[140] Ionising Radiations (Outside Workers) Regulations 1993 (SI 1993 No 2379) London, HMSO.

[141] DoH. For the Record. Health Services Circular HSC1999/053, London, DoH (1999).

[142] RCR. Guidance on the retention and destruction of NHS medical records concerned with chemotherapy and radiotherapy. Clinical oncology publication BFCO(96)3, London, RCR (1996).

[143] Health and Safety (Safety Signs and Signals) Regulations 1996 and Guidance (SI 1996 No 341) London, HMSO.

[144] BSI. Safety signs and colours. Specification for colour and design. BS 5378-1, London, BSI (1980).

[145] BSI. Specification for a basic symbol to denote the actual or potential presence of ionizing radiation. BS 3510 London, BSI (1968).

[146] BSI. Specification for colours for identification, coding and special purposes. BS 381C, London, BSI (1996).

[147] BSI. Safety signs and colours. Specification for colorimetric and photometric properties of materials. BS 5378-2, London, BSI (1980).

[148] Carriage of Dangerous Goods (Classification, Packaging and Labelling) and Use of Transportable Pressure Receptacles Regulations 1996 (SI 1996 No 2092) London, HMSO.

[149] BSI. Fire safety signs, notices and graphic symbols. Specification for fire safety signs. BS 5499-1, London, BSI (1990).

[150] BSI. Fire safety signs, notices and graphic symbols. Specification for self-luminous fire safety signs. BS 5499-2, London, BSI (1986).

[151] BSI. Fire safety signs, notices and graphic symbols. Specification for internally-illuminated fire safety signs. BS 5499-3, London, BSI (1990).

[152] **ICRP53** ICRP. Radiation dose to patients from radiopharmaceuticals. ICRP Publication 53, *Ann. ICRP* 18 Nos 1–4 (1988) and addenda 1 to 3 in ICRP Publication 62 (1991), ICRP Publication 80 (1999) and the interim report on the ICRP web page (1999).

[153] **IPSM63** Radiation protection in nuclear medicine and pathology. IPSM Report No 63, York, IPEM (1997).